# Autobiography of JOSIAH HENSON

## An Inspiration for Harriet Beecher Stowe's Uncle Tom

JOSIAH HENSON

Introduction by Robin W. Winks
*Yale University*

DOVER PUBLICATIONS, INC.
Mineola, New York

*Bibliographical Note*

This Dover edition, first published in 2003, is an unabridged republication of the work originally published by Addison-Wesley Publishing Company, Reading, Massachusetts, in 1969 under the title *An Autobiography of the Reverend Josiah Henson.*

*Library of Congress Cataloging-in-Publication Data*

Henson, Josiah, 1789–1883.
    [Autobiography of the Reverend Josiah Henson]
    Autobiography of Josiah Henson : an inspiration for Harriet Beecher Stowe's Uncle Tom / Josiah Henson ; introduction by Robin W. Winks.
        p. cm.
    Originally published: An autobiography of the Reverend Josiah Henson. Reading, Mass. : Addison-Wesley Pub. Co., 1969.
    Includes bibliographical references.
    ISBN 0-486-42863-X (pbk.)
        1. Henson, Josiah, 1789–1883. 2. Slaves—United States—Biography. 3. African Americans—Biography. 4. Fugitive slaves—United States—Biography. 5. Fugitive slaves—Canada—Biography. 6. Blacks—Canada—Biography. 7. Clergy—Canada—Biography. I. Title.

E444.H52 2003
973.7'115'092—dc21
[B]
                                                            2002041770

Manufactured in the United States of America
Dover Publications, Inc., 31 East 2nd Street, Mineola, N.Y. 11501

# CONTENTS

# INTRODUCTION

## Josiah Henson and Uncle Tom

Of the many narratives written for, and on occasion by, fugitive slaves who fled from the United States to the provinces of British North America before the Civil War, no single book has been so widely read, so frequently revised, and so influential as the autobiography of Josiah Henson. For Henson came to be identified with one of the best known figures in Nineteenth Century American literature, the venerable and self-sacrificing Uncle Tom of Harriet Beecher Stowe's most famous novel. To the popular mind then, and to many people now, Henson was undeniably Tom, the very figure from whom Mrs. Stowe borrowed large elements of plot and characterization, the figure who came to symbolize the successful fugitive, the man who permanently settled in Canada and there won fame, if not fortune, and a permanent place in the history of the abolitionist struggle.

Indeed, Henson's fame is assured, for even he came in time to believe that he was the original Uncle Tom, and his neighbors accepted this evaluation. His cabin and grave, in rural Ontario, became tourist attractions, and Dresden, ironically the center of the province's most clearly practiced color bar in the 1950's, advertised itself as the Home of Uncle Tom. At first untended, but from 1930 looked after by the Independent Order of the Daughters of the Empire and later by the Dresden Horticultural Society, the grave became the scene of Negro Masonic pilgrimages. Henson's house was opened as a museum in 1948, and the cemetery of the colony of which the house was a part was restored by the National Historic Sites Board of Canada, with plans afoot to recreate a portion of the community itself, both to instill civic pride in Negro Canadians and as a tourist attraction. The Historic Sites Board gave the considerable force of its approval to the Henson saga when it placed a plaque near the restored home in honor of the man "whose early life provided much of the material for . . . 'Uncle Tom's Cabin'."*

Henson became one of the best known of all fugitive slaves, the several editions of his narrative one of the most frequently consulted sources, his life thought to be the archetypical fugitive experience. The first version of his autobiography, published in 1849, is without guile, straight-forward, dramatic in its simplicity. But this fugitive from Kentucky, clearly intelligent and hard-working, also shared the normal desire to collect a few of the merit badges that life might offer, and when he found himself thrust into fame in a role that just might fit, he hugged his new role to himself until his death. To his credit, not until he was old and senile did Henson ever claim to be Uncle Tom, but he did nothing to stop others from making the claim for him. Those versions of his autobiography which appeared after the publication of *Uncle Tom's Cabin* in 1852 showed substantial alterations, extensions, and fabrications, and the fullest of these accounts, ghost-written for Henson by an English clergyman-editor, John Lobb, while now extremely scarce, deserves to be brought back into print not only for what it tells us about Henson and the fugitive slaves, but for the fullness of detail it provides, most of it accurate, about fugitive life in Canada, and for the almost classic opportunity it affords to study the ways in which texts might be altered to serve a cause.

For the cause of the abolitionists was served well by Henson's narrative. In many ways his saga is illustrative of the problem of the intelligent fugitive slave of the time: Henson was seldom left free to be himself, to assimilate if he wished into the mainstream of Canadian life—even of black Canadian life—for he became the focus of abolitionist attention, a tool to be used in a propaganda campaign which was not above much juggling with the facts, however proper its ultimate goals may have been. For these reasons his life, and his

---

*Toronto *Globe,* July 5, 1930, April 28, 1946; London, Ont., *Free Press,* Jan. 14, 1947; Huron *Church News,* Oct., 1959, pp. 8-9; *Museums Directory of the United States and Canada,* 2nd ed., Washington, 1965, p. 658. Efforts failed to interest the National Urban League of the United States, or the Association for the Study of Negro Life and History, in restoring the cemetery. See "Letters about 'Uncle Tom'," *The Negro History Bulletin,* 24, Dec., 1960, pp. 64-65. On Henson's Masonic connections, see Professor Fred Landon's private collection of letters, manuscripts, and clippings, at his home in London, Ontario: Alvin McCurdy to Landon, Feb. 26, 1960, and exchanges of letters between Landon and Charles Foy.

autobiographical account of it, deserve examination in some detail. And that life, and narrative, must be seen against the background of the efforts made by and on behalf of the fugitive slaves to found all-Negro colonies in Canada West, or present-day Ontario. The most significant of these attempts was one initiated in 1842 under the promising name of Dawn, and it is with Dawn that we associate Henson's Canadian sojourn.

Dawn represented one attempt to adjust to the presumed realities of a white America. No less than the European immigrants of the time, some Negroes believed in the success ethic that lay behind one of the United States's chief messages to the world: hard work, clean living, education, and an eye for the main chance would bring a man, at least a free man, even if black—and unless flawed by character or caught by bad luck—to the top. However, the Negro was flawed, in the eyes of many, by character and certainly by luck, in terms of the hard truths of a white world, and enough realized that the demise of slavery alone (which surely was coming) was not enough to give the Negro his place in the line inexorably marching toward success. Manual labor institutes, practical training, the fundamentals of a bookish education, and some understanding of how a capitalist economy actually worked were essential—or so Josiah Henson would argue later in his autobiography. A brief escape from the world was needed so that the Negro might master these tools, so that he might catch up with the white man, who had not been deprived of the necessary knowledge. A firm belief in education and the instant status it gave lay behind the many assumed titles, the Doctors, Professors, and Right Reverends who sprang so quickly from their soil. In a communal society, the Negro could train himself to use freedom, could come to follow the mores, to reflect the virtues, to accept the ethics of the dominant white society. In short, the values of the Negro community experiments were normative ones. The Negroes accepted the social environment of the North much as it was, or as they saw it to be, and they did not intend to retreat from it permanently or to reform it. Rather than turning their backs upon white society, they sought a temporary refuge in which to prepare for a full place in that society.

Dawn began in Ohio. In 1834 the Board of Trustees of the Lane Seminary in Cincinnati told students and faculty that they were not to organize anti-slavery activities, and among the Lane Rebels, as they were named, who left for the more liberal atmosphere of Oberlin College, was Hiram Wilson. In the late fall of 1836, with $25 given to him by Charles Grandison Finney, Wilson went to Upper Canada (as Ontario was then called) to see for himself how the fugitives were faring, and in the spring he returned to attend the annual meeting of the American Anti-Slavery Society as a delegate from the province. With the help of other Oberlin students, he began what he hoped would be a series of schools within the growing Negro communities, schools not restricted to Negroes, and late in 1837 he addressed the newly-formed Upper Canada Anti-Slavery Society about the merits of educating fugitives. He also borrowed heavily, and although by the fall of 1839 his work in Amherstburg, across the river from Detroit, was well-known in Northern abolitionist circles, he confessed to the Peterboro anti-slavery leader, Gerrit Smith, that he was trusting in the Lord to pay a debt of $10,000. In 1840 the American Anti-Slavery Society commended him to the "liberal patronage of every true-hearted abolitionist," and the next year Smith and others organized a Rochester-based committee to help channel funds to the several schools—ultimately fifteen in all—begun by or inspired through Wilson's work. His efforts became the Canada Mission, and since he was trusted, where itinerant Negro preachers often were not, funds, Bibles, and clothing funnelled through Wilson to the fugitive slave encampment. *

Wilson attracted the attention of a Quaker philanthropist in Skaneateles, New York, James C. Fuller, who wished to help fugitives but not to violate his principle that Americans must not interfere in Canadian matters. Schools which were controlled from the United States were not agreeable, therefore, but missions firmly rooted in Canadian soil, although run according to Wilson's princi-

*The Emancipator, Dec. 22, 1836; The Anti-Slavery Standard, July 8, 1841; Toronto Constitution, Nov. 16, 1837; American Anti-Slavery Society, Fourth Annual Report, New York, 1837, p. 19; Boston Public Library, Weston Papers, 12: Maria F. Rice to Mrs. Maria W. Chapman, Oct. 23, 1839; Historical Records Survey, Calendar of the Gerrit Smith Papers in the Syracuse University Library: General Correspondence, Albany, 1941, 2, pp. 129, 255: Wilson to Smith, Dec. 18, 1839, Ray Potter to Smith, Jan. 25, 1846; Public Archives of Canada, Ottawa [hereafter, PAC], C series, 1, 803: Wilson to Governor General Lord Sydenham, June 18, 25, 1841; PAC, G 20, 310: Rice to Metcalfe, July 3, 24, 1844; Fred Landon, "The Canadian Anti-Slavery Group," The University Magazine, 17, Dec., 1917, 542; Clayton S. Ellsworth, "Oberlin and the Anti-Slavery Movement Up to the Civil War," unpublished Ph.D. dissertation, Cornell University, 1930, pp. 47-48, 168.

ples, were acceptable. Fuller accordingly raised much of the initial money for The British-American Institute, a school for the "... Education Mental Moral and physical of the Coloured inhabitants of Canada not excluding white persons and Indians."* He sought money on a tour of England, contacted Gerrit Smith, and agreed to serve on the new school's board, and in November of 1841 the sponsors purchased two hundred acres of land near London, Canada West, for $800. Thirteen months later they opened the doors of a manual-labor school to its first twelve students. The trustees were three white men, Fuller, the Reverend John Roaf, a Congregational Minister from Toronto who was active in the anti-slavery society there,† and Frederick Stover of Norwich, Canada West, who had been associated with the British anti-slavery leader, William Wilber-force; and three Negroes, Peter Smith, George Johnson, and James C. Brown, the last having moved to Dawn from Toronto in order to help.

Around the institute grew the community, and since the whites considered that the town was in charge of the school—as, in fact, it was not—Dawn itself stood or fell on the school. The institute came to own perhaps three hundred acres of land; the Negro settlers owned another fifteen hundred, on which they raised tobacco, wheat, corn and oats. In time, the population rose to five hundred or more, and the community was served by its own saw and grist mills, a brick yard, and a rope walk. Lumbering proved modestly rewarding, and in all, the settlers increased the value of their land by over a dollar an acre within five years.

The man most responsible for Dawn's initial success was Josiah Henson, one of the few Negro leaders in Canada West who seems to

---

*Quoted in William H. and Jane H. Pease, *Black Utopia: Negro Communal Experiments in America*, Madison, Wisc., 1963, p. 64, from the Kent County Registry Office, Chatham, Ontario. The best discussion of Dawn appears in their book, pp. 63-83. Also valuable is Alexander L. Murray, "Canada and the Anglo-American Anti-Slavery Movement: A Study in International Philanthropy," unpublished Ph.D. dissertation, University of Pennsylvania, 1960, especially pp. 59-63. For Fuller's attitude on non-interference, see Historical Society of Pennsylvania, Philadelphia, Simon Gratz Autograph Collection: Fuller to William H. Seward, Dec. 31, 1837, Feb. 29, 1840; and *Calendar of the Gerrit Smith Papers*, p. 131; Fuller to Smith, Oct. 15, 1841.

†On anti-slavery activity in Canada at this time, see Robin W. Winks, " 'A Sacred Animosity': Abolitionism in Canada," in Martin B. Duberman, Ed., *The Antislavery Vanguard: New Essays on the Abolitionists*, Princeton, 1965, pp. 301-42.

have won nearly universal white approval at first, both for his own activities and, later, for being taken as Mrs. Stowe's Uncle Tom. Born near Port Tobacco, in Charles County, Maryland, on June 15, 1789, Henson passed through the hands of three owners, became a Christian in his eighteenth year, and was maimed for life when one of his master's enemies beat him with a stake, breaking his arm and, perhaps, both of his shoulder blades. At twenty-two Henson married, and during the next forty years he fathered twelve children, eight of whom survived. Recognizing that, on the whole, he was owned by a fair man, he worked hard to ingratiate himself, toiling and inducing others to toil "many an extra hour, in order to show my master what an excellent day's work had been accomplished, and to win a kind word or a benevolent deed from his callous heart."* His sense of loyalty was so strong, he personally conducted eighteen of his owner's slaves to Kentucky, passing by the Ohio shores, yet resisting the temptation to run away. He remained in Kentucky for three years, became a preacher in the Methodist Episcopal Church, and was made an unofficial overseer, trusted with considerable freedom of movement. He then returned to his owner in Maryland, preaching in Ohio while on the way, thus collecting $275, a horse, and some clothes, with which he hoped to purchase his freedom. The owner agreed to sell for $450, and by disposing of horse and clothes, Henson raised $350 and signed a note for the rest. When he returned to Kentucky, he learned that his owner now said that the sale price was $1,000, and the slave was unable to disprove this. Henson still did not flee, however, although the Ohio River was nearby.

Henson's decision to escape arose from what he regarded as moral mistreatment in New Orleans. Asked to accompany his owner's nephew south, he realized that despite denials he was to be sold, and on the journey he took up an axe to kill his sleeping companions, only to realize that as a Christian he could not. He was saved from being sold, and parted from the wife he had left in Kentucky, only

---

*The Life of Josiah Henson, formerly a Slave, Now an Inhabitant of Canada. Narrated by Himself, Boston, 1849, p. 8. This first edition is scarce: known copies are in the British Museum, the Yale University Library, the Boston Public Library, and Uncle Tom's Cabin and Museum, Dresden, Ontario. No doubt there are others, but since a reprint edition, issued by the Museum in 1965, is more readily available, page references to the edition of 1849 refer to the reprint. I cite the 1849 edition in preference to others for the pre-Canadian years since it has been embroidered less.

because his companion fell seriously ill while in Louisiana and asked Henson to take him back to his home. Henson did so, but he resolved that the decision to sell him, together with his owner's "attempt to kidnap me again, after having pocketed three-fourths of my market value, absolved me from any obligation . . . to pay him any more, or to continue in a position which exposed me to his machinations."* He decided to flee to Canada.

His escape showed foresight and considerable courage. By a ruse he drew out his son, who normally passed the night in the proprietor's house, and choosing a time when, because of the routine of the plantation, they would not be missed for three days, he crossed the Ohio River to the Indiana shore. He carried his two smallest children on his back in a large knapsack; two others walked, as did his wife. The family took a fortnight to reach Cincinnati; with the unexpected assistance of Indians, they pressed on to Sandusky, fell in with a sympathetic Scots steamer captain, and were taken to Buffalo. On October 28, 1830, about six weeks after crossing the Ohio, the Hensons threw themselves on Canadian soil, Josiah executing "sundry antics which excited the astonishment of those who were looking on."†

Josiah adjusted quickly to a life of freedom. On his second attempt he found employment. Home was an old shack, from which he expelled pigs, but in which, for the first time, his family could enjoy privacy and "some of the comforts of life, while the necessaries of food and fuel were abundant." Henson worked for both shares and wages, purchased some livestock, resumed preaching, and saw his boy Tom given two quarters' of schooling at the expense of his employer. Josiah had an excellent memory, and for some time he was able to give the impression that he could read the Bible by memorizing the passages he heard, but one day his son asked, "Why, father, can't you read?" and Josiah, a man of great and stubborn pride, confessed that he could not. The twelve-year-old lad then set out to teach him how, and in time Josiah learned "to read a little."‡ Soon after, he took employment with one Benjamin Riseley, who allowed him to call prayer meetings in his home.

---

*Ibid.*, pp. 44-45.

†*Ibid.*, p. 55.

‡*Ibid.*, pp. 59-61.

At one of these meetings a small group of Negroes decided to invest their earnings collectively in land. "It was precisely the Yankee spirit which I wished to instil into my fellow slaves, if possible," Henson later wrote.* and in the fall of 1834 he set out to find a suitable area for them. He rented cleared lots near Colchester, where he and his followers learned to raise tobacco and wheat. According to Henson, he learned that the grantee had not complied with some of the conditions for his allotment, however, and he wrote to the Lieutenant-Governor, who advised the Negroes to apply to the legislature for relief. Upon doing so they found themselves freed from rent, although now subject themselves to the usual improvement clauses. They had meant to leave the site quickly, but given this boon they remained for seven years.

Henson now was devoting most of his thought to the problems of how fugitives like himself might best adjust to Upper Canada. As he saw, "The mere delight the slave took in his freedom, rendered him, at first, contented with a lot far inferior to that which he might have attained. Then his ignorance led him to make unprofitable bargains, and he would often hire wild land on short terms, and bind himself to clear a certain number of acres; and by the time they were cleared and fitted for cultivation his lease was out, and his landlord would come in, and raise a splendid crop on the new land . . . " Too, the Negroes often raised only tobacco, tempted by the high price it brought, but this created a glut in an already depressed market, and the Negroes who had not diversified with wheat were driven to the wall. To correct this, Henson "set seriously about the business of lecturing upon the subject of crops, wages, and profits. . . . "†

While in Colchester, Henson met Hiram Wilson, and from 1836 the two worked together. When Fuller returned from England with funds to establish a manual labor institute, it was Henson and Wilson who called a convention in June, 1838, to determine how and where the money might best be spent. As Henson knew, with all the sensitivity of the self-consciously unlettered who see universal education as a panacea, Negroes increasingly were excluded from the public schools of the province, and upon his urging the delegates decided to found

*Ibid.*, p. 63.
†*Ibid.*, pp. 65-66; Boston *Recorder*, Jan. 7, 1848.

The British-American Institute. In 1842 Henson moved to Dawn. "We look to the school, and the possession of landed property by individuals, as two great means of elevation of our oppressed and degraded race . . ." he later wrote in his autobiography.* This autobiography was first published by Arthur D. Phelps in Boston early in 1849. Hoping to earn some small income for the British-American Institute, Henson spoke of his experiences to Samuel A. Eliot, a former Mayor of Boston who was well-known for his moderate anti-slavery views, and Eliot wrote *The Life of Josiah Henson, formerly a Slave, Now an Inhabitant of Canada.*† In style, pace, and proportion the account reflects the unembellished simplicity of Henson's life. Clearly, he was an unusual man, alert and intelligent. Equally clearly, he emerged as a natural leader to other Negroes, for he understood figures where they did not, and he was imaginative and independent in his approach to immediate problems. The narrative also showed that Henson was vain behind his facade of humility, proud, possessive, and prone to seek out quick approbation rather than long-range solutions. He needed to lead, and often led well, but he rather enjoyed manipulating the lives of others, if always for what he conceived to be their benefit. He seemed immensely stable, given neither to recriminations nor to a paralyzing fatalism, and in the main, he was an effective spokesman for the Negro, despite his deeply-felt need to please. If Dawn succeeded, much would be due Henson; otherwise, he was unlikely to win recognition outside a limited circle.

But three years after the publication of Henson's life, there appeared the book which was to enlarge this circle immeasurably. In 1851 a Washington weekly paper, *The National Era,* began the serial publication of a long story written by Harriet Beecher Stowe, the wife of a Professor at Bowdoin College in Maine. Originally to have

---

*Life of Josiah Henson,* p. 70; Lawson Memorial Library, University of Western Ontario, London: Henson's deed of property.

†Massachusetts Historical Society, Amos A. Lawrence Papers: Lawrence to Nathan Hale, Nov. 9, 1850, and to Samuel Morley, Nov. 30, 1852. On Eliot, nee C[laude] M. F[uess], "Samuel Atkins Eliot," *Dictionary of American Biography* [hereafter, *D.A.B.*], 6, 1931, pp. 81-82, which incorrectly dates Henson's book as 1842, and also Pease and Pease, *Black Utopia,* p. 75. Phelps was a printing agent with offices adjacent to the Boston Circulating Library. See *The Boston Directory: Containing the City Record, a General Directory of the Citizens . . . from July, 1849, to July, 1850 . . . ,* Boston, 1849, pp. 230, 336.

carried the subtitle, "The Man that Was a Thing," Mrs. Stowe's narrative, renamed "Uncle Tom's Cabin; or, Life Among the Lowly," ran in the *Era* from June 1851, until April 1852. Uncle Tom quickly built a following, and ten days before the last installment appeared, the whole was issued in two volumes, to be sold for a dollar. The novel swept the Northern states, England—where in London alone twenty different pirated editions were published within the year— and the Continent. *

In British North America as well everyone seemed to be reading about Uncle Tom. † A Montreal monthly periodical, *The Maple Leaf,* serialized the book, with an abridged conclusion, from July 1852, until the following June. The influential Toronto *Globe,* edited by an ardent abolitionist, George Brown, printed extracts and the famous fifth chapter in its entirely. The Montreal *Gazette* noted it only less favorably. Within weeks there were separate Toronto and Montreal editions based upon the Boston printing.‡ In St. Thomas, Canada West, a diorama illustrative of Mrs. Stowe's more poignant scenes was widely viewed, in Toronto strolling players dramatized the novel in the streets, and the London Mechanic's Institute Library doubled its order for copies. In Montreal *La Case de l' Oncle Tom* was an imme-

---

*Kenneth S. Lynn, Ed., *Uncle Tom's Cabin: or, Life Among the Lowly,* Cambridge, Mass., 1962, p. xxviii. The best examination of the impact of *Uncle Tom's Cabin* on England is Frank J. Klingberg, "Harriet Beecher Stowe and Social Reform in England," *American Historical Review,* 43, April, 1938, pp. 542-52, while Edith E. Lucas, *La littérature anti-esclavagiste au dix-neuvième siècle: étude sur Madame Beecher Stowe et son influence en France,* Paris, 1930, and Grace Edith MacLean, " 'Uncle Tom's Cabin' in Germany," *Americana Germanica,* n.s., 10 (1910), whole no. (New York), are adequate. The Montreal edition was taken from the first Paris printing of *La Case de l'Oncle Tom.* The sequence of publishing in England, from which the Canadian sequence may be deduced, is described in William Talbot, "Uncle Tom's Cabin: First English Editions," *The American Book Collector,* 3, June, 1933, p. 292.

†See Fred Landon, "When *Uncle Tom's Cabin* Came to Canada," *Ontario History,* 44, Jan., 1952, pp. 1-5.

‡*The Maple Leaf,* 1, July to Dec. 1852, pp. 3-13, and variously, through pp. 177-184, and 2, Jan.-June 1853; *Globe,* April 24, 27, 1852; *Gazette,* April 3, 17, 1852. Landon, "When *Uncle Tom's Cabin* Came to Canada," and other authors refer to a Halifax edition in the same year. I have examined a mint copy of this edition, held by the Yale University Library, and while the title page lists Halifax as the place of publication, I believe that Halifax, England, rather than Nova Scotia, is meant. The price is given as one shilling, but from 1858 the decimal system was used in Canada, and the Halifax merchants long before had taken up dollars and cents. The publishers, Milner and Sowerby, are unknown to the Public Archives of Nova Scotia (Miss Phyllis Blakeley to author, Oct. 7, 1966). The Yale copy is inscribed as a gift to Elizabeth Ann Langridge, and no such family name occurs in any Nova Scotian genealogies.

diate success, and Wilfrid Laurier, one day to be Canada's Prime Minister and then a boy of ten, borrowed a copy from a college friend and annoyed his landlady by burning his lamp through the night in order to finish it. Hundreds of young boys who, less than ten years later, would enter the Northern armies, devoured it in the one-volume edition. Soon incorporated into Erastus Beadle's Dime Novels, the book found an ever-expanding readership.* Only in Nova Scotia and Prince Edward Island did Mrs. Stowe receive a mixed press: in a lengthy review in *The Provincial,* a new Halifax monthly, an anonymous critic observed that *Uncle Tom's Cabin* had been discussed by everyone and that it justly condemned slavery, but he felt that its author had overdrawn her case, or that Negroes in Nova Scotia were unusually inferior. "The insufferable arrogance and uncleanly habits of Colonial negroes make it almost impossible for us to hold association with them"; "We are unwilling even to occupy the same conveyance, and disdain to sit at the same table"; "we have no hesitation in pronouncing them far inferior in morality, intelligence, and cleanliness, to the very lowest among the white population. ... " The Charlottetown *Islander* also cautioned against romancers who described exceptional cases rather than the rule.†

But the hold taken by *Uncle Tom's Cabin* on the public imagination was secure and long-lasting—certainly longer in British North America than in the United States. In 1932 a report on reading habits among Canadian secondary school students showed that Tom still was the most popular American book, and in 1952 sales in Toronto, in particular, continued briskly.‡ In its several dramatized forms "Tom" became a perennial favorite for travelling troops, and with the addition of bloodhounds to pursue Eliza across

---

*London Public Library, London, Ont., Minute Book, London Mechanics' Institute, 1851: entry for Aug. 9, 1852; Eleanor Shaw, "A History of the London Public Library," typescript, London Public Library, 1941, p. 15; Toronto *Weekly North American,* Feb. 2, 1852; St. Thomas *Weekly Dispatch,* June 21, 1853; New Glasgow, N.S., *Eastern Chronicle,* June 10, 1868; London, Ont., *Free Press,* Sept. 17, 1951; Toronto *Globe and Mail,* Dec. 2, 1952; Benjamin Sulte, "L'esclavage en Canada," *La revue Canadienne,* N.S., 8, Oct., 1911, p. 334; John I. Cooper, *Montreal, the Story of Three Hundred Years,* Montreal, 1942, p. 80.

†"Literature of Slavery," *The Provincial,* 2, Jan., 1853, pp. 3-8; *Islander,* Nov. 28, 1856.

‡Arthur A. Hauck, *Some Educational Factors affecting the Relations between Canada and the United States,* Easton, Pa., 1932, p. 22; Albert R. Hassard, " 'Uncle Tom's Cabin' Recalled," *Onward,* 41, July 18, 1931, p. 2; Toronto *Globe and Mail,* Dec. 2, 1952.

the ice floes, Tom Shows played to appreciative audiences throughout English-speaking Canada. A touring group carried Tom and related minstrelsy into New Brunswick and Nova Scotia in the 1860's, and there were minstrel and Tom shows "galore" in Halifax in the '60's and '70's.* By the 1880's rural communities might be exposed to Tommers five or six times in the decade.† Ironically, similar groups performed in Dresden, Ontario, in 1919 and 1923, a mile from Josiah Henson's grave, to segregated audiences, and into the 1920's the almost lunatic jollity, the cringing piety, and the blackface distortions of the shows continued to attract crowds in the Maritime Provinces.‡

This explosive and utterly unexpected effect of her work may have frightened Mrs. Stowe. Assuredly, the virulence of the Southern attack upon her novel, upon not only its sentiments, its plot, and its style, but also upon its allegedly factual base, disturbed her. Even friendly reviewers doubted her veracity: *The Times* of London found Tom too pure, too perfect to believe, and thought Mrs. Stowe's

---

*The first dramatization of *Uncle Tom's Cabin*, written by George L. Aiken and presented by Halifax-born George Howard in Troy, New York, in September 1852, included a scene in which Eliza crossed the ice, but did not mention Canada (*French's Standard Drama: Uncle Tom's Cabin; or, Life Among the Lowly*, New York, 1858?). Canada soon was moved to the nearside of the Ohio by Thomas Hailes Lacy in a version first performed at the Theatre Royal in Manchester, England, in February 1853 (*Lacy's Acting Edition of Plays...*, London, n.d., 12, entire), so that Eliza's "whirlleaps toward an outmost brightness" (in the words of E. E. Cummings, *Tom*, Santa Fe, 1935, p. 17) popularly reinforced the Underground Railroad myth by identifying Canada as that land of brightness. The continental French, in particular, seem to have believed that Canada was just across the Ohio from Kentucky: see J. C. Furnas, *Goodbye to Uncle Tom*, New York, 1956, p. 272.

†See Carl Wittke, *Tambo and Bones: A History of the American Minstrel Stage*, Durham, N.C., 1930, pp. 98-103, 110, 222; J. Frank Davis, "Tom Shows," *Scribner's Magazine*, 77, April, 1925, p. 350; Donald A. Smith, *At The Forks of the Grand: 20 Historical Essays on Paris, Ontario*, Paris, n.d., pp. 182-84; Phyllis R. Blakeley, *Glimpses of Halifax, 1867-1900*, Public Archives of Nova Scotia publication, no. 9, Halifax, 1949, pp. 77-78; F. Lauriston Bullard, "Uncle Tom on the Stage," *Lincoln Herald*, 48, June, 1946, p. 19; Harry Birdoff, *The World's Greatest Hit: Uncle Tom's Cabin*, New York, 1947, p. 30.

‡W. A. Hewitt, *Down the Stretch: Recollections of a Pioneer Sportsman and Journalist*, Toronto, 1958, p. 114; Toronto Public Library [hereafter, TPL], Thomas H. Scott Collection:"Behind the Footlights," Mss. autobiography, with scrapbook of broadsides and playbills; TPL, Baldwin Room: broadsides, playbills, and clippings relating to the Negro theatre in Canada; New York Library for the Performing Arts, Lincoln Center: Saint John programme, April 29, 30, May 1, 1920; Uncle Tom's Cabin Museum: playbills; Harvard College Library, Theatre Collection: playbills for LaRue's Minstrels, The Harmonears, Halifax, and Sam Sharpley's Minstrels, Quebec; Toronto *Globe*, Oct. 15, 1861; Brantford *Review*, Nov. 4, 1880.

"honest zeal" had outrun her discretion.* As the London editions mounted toward forty, as the rage for Uncle Tom swept across the Continent, his creator felt obliged to justify what she had written.† In the novel she had claimed to be a close student of the slave states, and having lived in Cincinnati at the time of the Lane revolt, she was, in fact, tolerably well-informed. But she saw that the novel could not stand alone, undefended, and she went forth to her own defense, therefore, vigorously, massively—but not forthrightly.

Accordingly, she constructed *A Key to Uncle Tom's Cabin: Presenting the Original Facts and Documents upon which the Story is Founded* ... , which was published in Boston, in 1853. The title was less than honest, for the documentation she brought together in the *Key*, while amply supporting much that she had put in her novel, had not all been in her possession at the time Uncle Tom was created; quite simply the *Key* was a *post hoc* attempt to buttress a thesis already expressed. Not unnaturally, she made the best case for herself in assembling her materials, and in an opening chapter she made clear her belief that to have injected documentation into the novel would have been to clog its narrative drive.

To collect material for her *Key*, Mrs. Stowe consulted various books while in Boston. She drew in part from Theodore Dwight Weld's horrific compilation of atrocity stories, *American Slavery as It is: Testimony of a Thousand Witnesses*, published in 1839, and she also used Eliot's *Life* of Henson, from which she quoted at some length (with slight inaccuracies), identifying him correctly as "pastor of the missionary settlement at Dawn, in Canada." She clearly did not read Henson closely, however, for she was wrong about his purchase price and about the exact itinerary of his journey from Maryland to Kentucky on his first trip. She said that Henson's chief significance lay in his Christian decision not to kill his companions while travelling to New Orleans. Once she related Henson to one of the figures in her novel, George Harris, and once she found in Henson's narrative an "instance parallel" with Tom's Christian

---

*Times*, Sept. 3, 1852.

†See Charles Dudley Warner, "The Story of Uncle Tom's Cabin," *The Atlantic Monthly*, 78, Sept., 1896, pp. 311-21, and reprinted as introduction to 1896 edition (Boston) of the novel, 1, xlii.

dedication.* Later she credited most of Uncle Tom to Weld's book, which she said she had kept in her workbasket by day and under her pillow at night.†

At no time during the early years of her success, or of Henson's small fame arising from his narrative of 1849, did Mrs. Stowe identify Henson with Uncle Tom. To the contrary, she found as many "striking parallels" to her novel in the narrative of Solomon Northrop as in Henson's. She never referred to having met Henson, and in the *Key* she cited his memoirs but not a conversation. On one occasion she said that the death scene of Uncle Tom was the first that she wrote, while living in Brunswick (in which case, no relationship to Henson was likely), but on another occasion she said that this scene was written after she had composed the death of Little Eva, and in Andover.‡ In 1878, apparently feeling that contradiction had gone too far, she said that once she had written letters for a former slave woman, who had become a servant in her own family, to a slave husband who remained in Kentucky, and that it was this "faithful slave" who was "a pattern of Uncle Tom." In the same essay she admitted that it was after her account began to appear in *The National Era* that she went to Boston to reinforce "her *repertoire* of facts" by consulting, among other books, those by Weld and Henson, particulars from which were "inwoven with the story."§ Again, the sequence is not clear, and Mrs. Stowe seemed incapable of clarifying it, but nothing said publicly by the author of *Uncle Tom* gave real substance to any contention that Josiah Henson and Uncle Tom were one and the same.

Nonetheless, they became so in the public mind, and some evidence was offered for this contention. Writing in 1911 Charles and Lyman Stowe, her son and grandson, said that she had met Henson in Boston in January of 1850, at the home of her brother, Lyman

---

*\**Key*, pp. 19, 26, 174.

†K[atherine] A[nthony], "Harriet Elizabeth Beecher Stowe," *D.A.B.*, 18, (1943), p. 117. *The Anglo-American Magazine*, 3, Aug., 1853, pp. 212-15, published in Toronto, while not liking the *Key*, felt that it provided all necessary proof that the novel was accurate.

‡See Raymond Weaver, introduction to *Limited Editions Club* issue of *Uncle Tom's Cabin*, New York, 1938, pp. vi-viii.

§Introduction to 1878 edition, as reprinted as *Old South Leaflets*, no. 82, Boston, n.d., pp. 1, 5-6; and Florine Thayer McCray, *The Life-Work of the Author of Uncle Tom's Cabin*, New York, 1889, p. 72.

Beecher.* In the 1878, or fourth, revised edition of his life, Henson asserted that he had met her in Andover, Massachusetts, and that he had told her the story of his life, and indeed in 1876 in a private letter Mrs. Stowe said that Henson had visited her there.† Upon this basis, as we shall see, Henson was able to imply and others who choose to use him for their own purposes were able to assert that he and Tom were the same man, that Tom yet lived, and that Eliza, Eva, and George were drawn from Henson's family and friends.

But none of these alleged facts will bear close scrutiny. Mrs. Stowe did not move to Andover until 1852, so if Henson visited her there, it was after she had completed all but a chapter or two of her novel. Henson was in Boston twice in 1850, but both occasions were "after the Fugitive Slave Law was passed," which was in September, so he was not in Boston in January as Charles and Lyman Stowe wrote, and in any case Mrs. Stowe was in Cincinnati in January, not reaching Boston until May.‡ The first edition of his narrative, as published in 1849, appeared early in the year, while Mrs. Stowe was still in Cincinnati, and when she began writing furiously in February of 1851, she apparently mentioned neither Henson nor his book to anyone, although she normally shared her ideas freely with her husband. Had she communed with Henson before his book was written, as he later implied, surely he or Eliot would have mentioned it in his *Life*, for he was not slow to acquire prestige by dropping names; and if they met while Mrs. Stowe was writing her book, she need not have journeyed to Boston to "re-enforce" her facts by reading his account. If Eva, Eliza, or George had any place in Henson's life,

---

*Charles Edward and Lyman Beecher Stowe, *Harriet Beecher Stowe: The Story of Her Life,* Boston, p. 144; or "How Mrs. Stowe Wrote 'Uncle Tom's Cabin'," *McClure's Magazine,* 36, April, 1911, pp. 613-14. Forrest Wilson, *Crusader in Crinoline: The Life of Harriet Beecher Stowe,* Philadelphia, 1941, pp. 249-50, and Chester E. Jorgenson, comp., *Uncle Tom's Cabin as Book and Legend,* Detroit, 1952, p. 10, accept the Stowes' statement, as does Edmund Wilson in *Patriotic Gore: Studies in the Literature of the American Civil War,* New York, 1962, pp. 31-32, but Edward Wagenknecht, *Harriet Beecher Stowe: The Known and the Unknown,* New York, 1965, stresses her inconsistency and adds that there have been rival Uncle Toms (p.157). John R. Adams, in *Harriet Beecher Stowe,* New York, 1963, pp. 56-57, expresses even greater doubts.

† On the alleged Andover meeting, see Charles Nichols, "The Origins of Uncle Tom's Cabin," *Phylon,* 19, Fall, 1958, pp. 328-34.

‡ Amos Lawrence Papers: Lawrence to Garrison, Feb. 16, 1851, on Henson; and Charles Edward Stowe, *Life of Harriet Beecher Stowe,* Boston, 1890, pp. 130-31.

surely he would have mentioned that place before 1878—at least in his 1858 edition, published well after they were household names—but he did not.* Clearly, although he later hinted otherwise, he was not the "slave husband" to whom Mrs. Stowe wrote letters on behalf of her servant, for Josiah's wife was with him in Kentucky. Equally clearly, she did not meet him, as he also suggested, while in Kentucky, for he was a slave in Daviess County, well removed from the Mason and Garrard county homes she did visit.

The books of Mrs. Stowe and Henson did morally reinforce each other, however, and she wrote an introduction to the second or 1858 edition of his book, in which he carried his story to 1852. But at this date—when association with Mrs. Stowe would bring a cachet to Henson's account—he made no mention of any meeting, nor did she in her introduction, which was bland and noncommittal. Moreover, the introduction was retained unaltered in Henson's 1878 edition, in which he claimed to have met her in Andover, but either she met Henson there after nearly all of *Uncle Tom's Cabin* was written or both unaccountably had forgotten their venue.

Under the impact of abolitionist need, Henson's desire to please led to numerous changes in successive editions of his memoirs.† Perhaps spokesmen need be neither honest nor consistent but merely convincing, and Henson was at least this, and no one had occasion to compare the various editions of his narrative. Such a comparison is revealing of his ability to weave his presence into almost any event that would provide a moral or add to his stature. He could exaggerate, transmuting the mundane into the dramatic (his broken shoulders became more crippling with each edition),‡ and he could move with the times, as he did when he excised the more obsequious passages from the original version of his life for later editions, when he struck entirely a passing reference to being arrested for debt, or

---

* The 1858 edition apparently was re-written by Samuel A. Eliot. The previous year Eliot, who had served in the House of Representatives in 1850-51, and who refused to become an abolitionist although he continued to oppose slavery, had retired to Cambridge, his investments having gone sour, to live in genteel poverty.

† On the various later editions, see the note following this essay.

‡ His manumission papers, which he ultimately regained, refer only to his having stiff arms from an injury to the elbows. See Alvin McCurdy Collection, Amherstberg, Ontario: Brice Selby, March 9, 1829, copy.

when he added a chapter in 1858 on his exploits in returning to the
South to help other fugitives to escape, a phase of his activities
unaccountably forgotten in 1849.* He incorporated a pious refusal
to participate in the Nat Turner rebellion into his local lectures,
although the rebellion actually took place after he had reached
Canada West. He claimed that he personally had written his books
although in 1849, as we have seen, he recorded that he learned to
read "a little" and one of his abolitionist supporters noted that he
could "barely write and cannot read."† In the first post-Civil War
edition of the autobiography he said he was a Captain in the Second
Essex Company of Colored Volunteers—which he was not—and that
his company captured the *Anne,* which he misspelled.

Perhaps the most important, and also the more subtle, of the
changes lay in the title of the book itself. The second account was
*Truth Stranger than Fiction: Father Henson's Story of His Own Life.*
Thus he (or more properly, Eliot for him) invoked the spirit of Lord
Byron, widely-known to be the center of one of Mrs. Stowe's
spiritual obsessions, for it was Byron who had written in 1823, that
"truth is always strange,/Stranger than fiction."‡ Throughout, he
and his editors were consistent in seeing that his life was a great
moral lesson, that original phraseology was embellished and twisted
to make a homiletic statement clearer, and that his fellow Negroes
fed upon the thought of his acceptance by Queen Victoria, Lord
John Russell, or President Rutherford B. Hayes.§ Still, Henson was

---

*See, from the 1849 (reprint) edition, pp. 8, 67 for suppressed sentences, and the 1858
edition, pp. 150-64, for an added chapter in which Henson says that he delivered one
hundred and eighteen slaves to freedom.

†On Henson's literacy, see Lawrence Papers: Lawrence to Hale, Nov. 7, 1850, in which
Lawrence notes that Henson could "barely write and cannot read," and on Nat Turner see
Jessie L. Beattie, *Black Moses, The Real Uncle Tom,* Toronto, 1957, p. 85. This unfortunate
biography confuses more than it helps, for it mixes the several editions of Henson's narrative
indiscriminately, accepts all that he says at face value, assumes that the 1849 account was
not edited (p. ix) but later wrongly names an editor (p. 172), and at several points—notably
pp. 1, 23, 36, 86, 90, 93, 107, and 110—misreads or manufactures evidence and
conversation.

‡*Don Juan,* Canto XIV, stanza 101.

§A good example of Henson's ability to enlarge his role in events is his description of his
visit with President Hayes in 1878, in which he implies that Hayes wished to see so famous a
Negro as he. In fact, Frederick Douglass, the Washington-based Negro leader, gained Henson
an audience by writing to the President's private secretary that the "aged preacher . . . is
anxious to see the face of President Hayes if but for a minute" (Rutherford B. Hayes

true to his own lights, and while, by his own admission, he managed money badly, he appears not to have abused his positions of trust for personal gain. He also resisted becoming Uncle Tom, at first, although in the end he fell to the pressures of financial need, the desire for prestige, and a fading memory.

It was not Henson who first or most persistently insisted that he was the original Uncle Tom, and since he wrote none of the lives themselves, one must find his ghost writers as culpable as he in building the legend. In public lectures long after the Civil War, Henson repeatedly was introduced as Uncle Tom, but initially he appears to have been careful not to make the claim explicit himself: "It has been spread abroad that ' "Uncle Tom" is coming,' and that is what has brought you here. Now allow me to say that my name is not Tom, and never was Tom, and that I do not want to have any other name inserted in the newspapers for me than my own. My name is Josiah Henson, always was, and always will be. I never change my colors. (Loud laughter.) I would not if I could, and could not if I would. (Renewed laughter.) Well, inquiry in the minds of some has led to a deal of inquiry on the part of others. You have read and heard some persons say that, ' "Uncle Tom" was dead, and how can he be here? It is an imposition that is being practised on

Library, Fremont, Ohio, Hayes Papers: Douglass to William King Rogers, Feb. 26, 1878), and Hayes did not think the meeting significant enough to record in his diary (see T. Harry Williams, Ed., *Hayes: The Diary of a President, 1875-1881*, New York, 1964, pp. 121-23). Other enlargements and inconsistencies appear in the various versions of Henson's ghosted works. For the 1878 edition he recalled "His Praying Mother" in a chapter not thought of before, and while in 1868 he mentioned John Scoble (misspelled Scobell) by name, a quarrel led to the English abolitionist's absence by the 1878 edition. The wording of a sign Henson placed on produce he exhibited at the London World's Fair changed slightly between the two editions, and in the latter he said he had corresponded with Lieutenant-Governor John Cockburn (meaning Colborne, further evidence that Henson spoke his account to someone else, since the two names are pronounced in approximately the same way). In 1849 he slipped his son away from his master without comment, but by 1858 he "could not refrain from an inward chuckle at the thought—how long a good night that will be!," thus giving Brian Gysin a title for his odd biography (see the end of this essay). Between 1849 and 1858 Henson quite forgot whether it was a man or woman who befriended him near Cincinnati (compare p. 48 of the former with p. 111 of the latter edition). In 1849 he said there were twenty thousand Negroes in Canada, and he gave the same figure in 1858 although elsewhere he remarked upon how many had arrived in the interim. No one of these changes, errors, or contradictions is important, and some—such as removing his master's curse, "you black son of a bitch!," and his repetitive "damned nigger," from the later editions published by the editor of the *Christian Age*—are explicable enough, but collectively they are extremely damaging.

us.' . . . Very well, I do not blame you for saying that. . . . A great many have come to me in this country and asked me if I was not dead. (Laughter.) Says I, 'Dead?' Says he, 'Yes, I heard you were dead, and read you were.' 'Well,' says I; 'I heard so too, but I never believed it yet. (Laughter.) I thought in all probability I would have found it out as soon as anybody else.' " Thus did Henson skirt the edges of truth, adding that all should realize that Mrs. Stowe was writing a novel, and concluding—with a deft change of the subject—that if the audience would refer to chapters 34 through 57 of the *Key to Uncle Tom's Cabin*, ". . . I think you will there see me."* Yet, the *Key* ran to only forty-nine chapters.

Others were less clever at avoiding the central question, or chose not to. In 1851 there appeared a London and Edinburgh edition of Henson's narrative, slightly altered, and with the first appearance of the added section devoted to aiding fugitive slaves, together with a preface by Thomas Binney, Minister of the Weigh-House Chapel in London, where Henson made one of his most effective appeals for money. This edition was an abolitionist handbook, as the 1849 version had not been, for it included an appendix on runaways in Canada, on specific fugitive slave cases, and an appeal for £2,000. The edition of 1858, printed in Boston, with Mrs. Stowe's rather flat preface replacing Binney's more impassioned one, followed. A "revised and enlarged" London edition was next, in 1877; it retained Mrs. Stowe's preface, added an introduction by George Sturge and Samuel Morley, English abolitionists, and carried a title page specifying that Henson was Uncle Tom.

The editions from 1877 were, in fact, almost entirely the work of John Lobb, the youthful managing editor of the weekly *Christian Age*. Lobb had been a religious journalist who knew how to attract an audience: when he took over the faltering *Age* in 1872, its circulation was five thousand, and in four years he raised the figure to eighty thousand. Morley and Sturge asked him to help solicit money for Henson, still in need of assistance at debt-ridden Dawn,

*Dumfries and Galloway Standard,* April 25, 1877, and first misprinted in Lobb, Ed., 1878 edition, pp. 223-24. I should like to thank the Ewart Public Library in Dumfries, Scotland, for supplying a photostat of the original report. See also D. D. Buck, *The Progression of the Race in the United States and Canada, Treating of the Great Advancement of the Colored Race,* Chicago, 1907, pp. 136, 142-49, 159, 164, 171.

and in seven months Lobb attracted £2,000.* Together with Henson, he went to Windsor Castle where they were received by Queen Victoria, who asked all of her domestic staff to come to meet the real Uncle Tom. Adding an index, drawing from Henson the promise that Lobb's would be the "only authorized edition" of his life, the editor soon had sales moving up to forty thousand. The next year they reached ninety-six thousand, whereupon Lobb made further modest revisions in the text and added extracts from Henson's addresses and an account of his audience with the Queen. In 1877 Lobb also wrote, without Henson's assistance although from his book, *The Young People's Illustrated Edition of "Uncle Tom's" Story of His Life,* which contained a preface by the Earl of Shaftesbury and "Uncle Tom's Address to the Young People of Great Britain," which Henson almost certainly did not dictate. The life was re-arranged and each chapter title, the illustrations, and even the index pointed moral lessons: "It is noble to speak the truth."†
Again, nowhere was Henson made to say specifically that he was Uncle Tom, although Lobb, outside conveniently manipulated quotation marks, did so for him. Lobb's narrative of his life sold a quarter of a million copies and became a Sunday School favorite, although Henson seems to have received very little money from the enterprise and his estate certainly received none.‡

---

* On Lobb, see his (as editor) *Talks with the Dead: Illustrated with Spirit Photographs,* London, 1906, pp. xv-xx; Register of the Royal Geographical Society, London: certificate of Election as a Fellow; and appendices to the 1877, 1878, and young people's editions of Henson's autobiography. The Journal of Queen Victoria, in the Royal Archives, Round Tower, Windsor Castle, confirms that she received Henson, his second wife, and Lobb, on March 5, 1877, and in her entry of March 4 she refers to reading the book. Henson claimed to have dined with Lord John Russell, and with the Archbishop of Canterbury, with whom he had the following unlikely conversation: " 'At what university, Sir, did thee graduate?' 'I graduated, your grace,' said I in reply, 'at the university of adversity.' 'The university of adversity,' said he, looking up with astonishment; 'where is that?' I saw his surprise, and explained . . . . 'But is it possible that you are not a scholar?' 'I am not,' said I. 'But I should never have suspected that you were not a liberally educated man . . . .' " (1858 ed., pp. 196-97). Archbishop Charles Sumner was not known as a wit, but he scarcely needed to have "adversity" explained to him. In any case, the official register, in Lambeth Palace Library, London, does not include Henson's name—although this is not conclusive evidence that the visit did not take place, of course.

† Lobb, Ed., 1878 edition, p. 176.

‡ Henson left virtually nothing to his family, and his son Peter apparently sold the little landed property that he possessed. Two aged daughters who moved to Flint, Michigan, and a grandson, Beecher Stowe Henson, later said that nothing remained save his papers, which disappeared, and a few relics, which went to a friend in Ridgetown, Ontario. See Toronto

Lobb, on the other hand, left the *Christian Age* and set himself up as a publisher. He wrote a similar life of Frederick Douglass, after Henson's death advertised the autobiography as dealing with "Legree, who maimed Josiah Henson for Life," and with "Eva, who was saved from Drowning by Josiah Henson, etc.,"* and declared that the narrative had been translated into twelve languages.† At the end of the century, Lobb turned to spiritualism; he communed with seven hundred dead over three years, including Shakespeare, Lincoln, Gladstone, Shaftesbury, and Henson, for the restless Josiah, still insinuating himself into all events, was "a frequent visitor at the seances . . . ."‡

For Mrs. Stowe, Henson would stay no more mute than he did for Lobb, and she continued to be contradictory and evasive. In 1876 the Reverend William H. Tilley, rector of the Cronyn Memorial Church in London, Ontario, sought confirmation of Henson as Tom, possibly because of a brief association of Bishop Benjamin Cronyn with Henson earlier. Mrs. Stowe's reply of May 15 was made public, but it was seldom quoted in full, and time and again her letter was cited to prove that she had admitted the relationship. In fact, she was as unclear as usual, avoiding any direct identification: "I take pleasure in indorsing with all my heart that noble man, Josiah Henson," she wrote, "to be worthy of all the aid and help which any good man may be disposed to give. It is true that a sketch of his life . . . furnished me many of the finest conceptions and incidents of 'Uncle Tom's' character, in particular the scene where he refuses to free himself by the murder of a brutal master. He once visited me in Andover and personal intercourse confirmed my high esteem I had

*Star,* June 28, 1930; *The Crisis,* 6, June, 1913, p. 65; Fred Landon Correspondence: Jean Tallach and Landon exchange, July 7, 9, 15, 1935; and Library of Congress, Carter G. Woodson Collection of Negro Papers, V: sketch of Henson by Julia [*sic*] Tallach McKinley.

*Lobb, Ed., *Talks with the Dead,* p. 118, advertisement (which was dropped from the 1907 edition of this book). Copies in the British Museum.

†Of the alleged twelve editions in translation, I have found but four, two in Swedish, and one in Dutch (all 1877). Lobb claimed there was a Welsh edition, for example, but a search by Mr. Meiner McDonald, Assistant Keeper of the Department of Printed Books, National Library of Wales, Aberystwyth, in August 1966, failed to produce one. The Bowdoin College Library does hold a copy of the rare Bergen edition of 1877, translated into Norwegian by H. C. Knutfen.

‡Lobb, Ed., *Talks with the Dead,* p. 32.

for him . . . " But she did not say when the visit took place, and as we have seen, had the visit been before she wrote most of the novel, it could not have been to Andover.* In a special editorial note to the 1881 edition of Henson's *Life,* Lobb nonetheless asserted that Mrs. Stowe had "quite settle[d] the point," quoting a barely relevant extract from *The Times.*† Plagued by further inquiries, Mrs. Stowe wrote to the editor of the Indianapolis *News* in 1882 that Uncle Tom was "not the biography of any one man."‡ She died in 1896 with the incubus of Josiah still firmly upon Tom's back.§

But of what matter is this problem of the linkage between Uncle Tom and Josiah Henson? Precisely this: as Canadians came increasingly to assign Henson's role to Tom, as the myth of the North Star, the Underground Railroad, and the Fugitives' haven "under the lion's paw"—a myth so well-explored by Larry Gara in his book, *The Liberty Line: The Legend of the Underground Railroad* (Lexington, Ky., 1961)—grew in the post-Civil War years, Canadians also came increasingly to congratulate themselves upon their lack of prejudice and to contrast themselves favorably with the immoral and once slave-ridden United States. The true contrast was favorable enough, indeed, but that the greatest, the best-known, the most pious and most Christian black fugitive of all time should have sought out Canadian soil for his resurrection bred a growing

---

* See London, Ont., *Free Press,* Aug. 20, 1932, and Windsor *Daily Record,* June 18, 1877, on the Stowe-Tilley exchange.

†Lobb, Ed., 1881 edition (as reprinted here), pp. 13-14.

‡*News,* July 27, 1882.

§Beattie, *Black Moses,* p. 206, says that Mrs. Stowe visited Henson at Dawn, while David P. Botsford, in *Amherstburg's Place in American History* (Amherstburg, 1959), pp. 14-15, asserts that she came to Amherstburg to gather information before she wrote of Uncle Tom. Both statements are nonsense, although she did visit Canada years later, in 1869, without touching upon western Ontario (Houghton Library, Harvard University, Stowe Papers: Rev. Edward Wood to Mrs. Stowe, Sept. 16, 1869). Walter Fisher, in his introduction to the 1962 reprint edition of Henson's narrative, p. v, says that Mrs. Stowe based her book "upon a fragment" of *Truth Stranger than Fiction: Father Henson's Story of His Own Life,* but this is impossible, for the edition of this title appeared in 1858, six years after *Uncle Tom's Cabin.* Ironically, the Windsor *Daily Star* (Jan. 15, 1938, July 30, 1948) insisted that the real Eliza had lived in the old Elliott home, which had been owned by Upper Canada's largest slaver in the Eighteenth Century. See also R. C. Smedley, *History of the Underground Railroad in Chester and the Neighboring Counties of Pennsylvania,* Lancaster, Pa., 1883, p. 32, and Clare Taylor, "Notes on American Negro Reformers in Victorian Britain," British Association for American Studies *Bulletin,* N.S., no. 2, March 1961, pp. 40-51.

Canadian self-satisfaction with racial conditions above the forty-ninth parallel. If Uncle Tom came to Canada, could conditions need improving? With every passing year since the late 1860's a stream of self-congratulatory Canadian newspaper accounts, editorials, and memoirs appears in April or September, on the anniversaries of the outbreak of the Civil War or of the passage of the Fugitive Slave Act, in which Henson has been cited as ample and sole evidence to prove that Canadians shared none of the American racial virus, that in this one area, at least, the pressures of continentalism had been resisted successfully.* That many Negroes agreed with Martin Delany in saying that Mrs. Stowe knew nothing about black men;† that Henson himself allegedly wrote that "in Canada, black children are despised";‡ that many Canadian Negroes had concluded that Henson was self-serving and sly;§ even that to Negroes "Uncle Tom" was becoming a pejorative term—all was ignored in the recurrent annual flush of pleasure over the presence of "the real Uncle Tom's grave" on Canadian soil.

Yet, while Henson was self-aggrandizing, having seen quickly enough that a popular identification with the decade's most

---

*For examples of the various forms the annual eulogies take, see the following, representative of dozens more: Montreal *Family Herald and Weekly Star*, Sept. 19, 1928; Toronto *Globe*, Jan. 19, 1935; Montreal *Star*, June 9, 1937; Detroit *Times*, May 1, 1938; Tannis Lee, "Uncle Tom's Cabin," *Imperial Oil Company Review*, 13, April, 1952, pp. 4-6; Hamilton *Review*, July 18, 1952; *The Canadian Woodman*, Oct., 1952, p. 2; *The Sentinel*, Dec., 1957, pp. 6-7; Winifred Kincade, *The Torch: Ontario Monuments to Great Names*, Regina, 1962, pp. 153-57.

†*Frederick Douglass' Paper*, April 1, 1853, quoted in Howard H. Bell, "Negro Nationalism in the 1850s," *Journal of Negro Education*, 35, Winter, 1966, p. 101.

‡Lobb, *Young People's Illustrated Edition*, pp. 12-16.

§Some of Henson's contemporaries doubted that he was Mrs. Stowe's Uncle Tom, although none appears to have been heard. Most scholarly works on the Negro, local histories of Ontario, and general accounts of abolitionism also accept the identification, but four scholars have questioned the association: In 1946 J. Winton Coleman, Jr., in "Mrs. Stowe, Kentucky, and Uncle Tom's Cabin," *Lincoln Herald*, 48, June, p. 6, presented a better case for Lewis Clarke, who escaped in 1841 and who did talk with Mrs. Stowe; in 1937 Fred Landon challenged the association, Montreal *Star*, June 22, and in 1947 he somewhat harshly noted that Henson "made little practical contribution to the welfare of his people," *Canadian Historical Review*, 28, Dec., p. 440. In 1958 William H. and Jane H. Pease, in "Uncle Tom and Clayton: Fact, Fiction, and Mystery," *Ontario History*, 50, Spring, pp. 62, 68, found him "shrewdly devious" and a "Mystery." In 1907 William Harrison, in "Uncle Tom's Prototype," *Canadian Magazine*, 28, April, pp. 530-36, tried to substitute a fictitious Lemuel Page for Henson. But in 1964 Alex Haley still thought Henson to be the "majority candidate" for the role ("In 'Uncle Tom' are Our Guilt and Hope," *The New York Times Magazine*, March 1, p. 23).

rapidly-selling book could do him no harm, whatever little he gained financially he apparently did give to the community he died serving. The rest of his story we know from his own account, and although he added color to it and allowed Lobb to embroider events, the basic outline is quite accurate. Henson did pioneer a saw mill for Dawn, one which helped the community as well as himself, and he did exhibit his wares at the great London Exhibition, to the advantage of his colony, since he dramatically drew attention to the plight as well as to the resourcefulness of the fugitives in Canada West. He was deeply involved in litigation over his management at Dawn, and he broke sharply with members of the British and Foreign Anti-Slavery Society, developments at which he only hints in his narrative.

But for the most part the historian must conclude that Henson's motives were appropriate both to the needs of Dawn and to his own needs and that his opponents were mistaken. He also found himself in serious trouble, as he notes, for recruiting Negro Canadians to serve in the Northern armies during the Civil War, but charges that he kept their bounty money for himself seem to have been false. His trip to England and Scotland during the summer of 1876 was undertaken largely to raise funds to clear a mortgage he had been forced to accept in order to fight a law suit against him, and while the money he thus raised was for his personal use, one may argue—as he did—that the law suit itself arose from his efforts to help keep Dawn and its successor settlements active. He clearly was fractious, devious, and by the time he had worn the mantle of fame for some years, also paternalistic toward his less fortunate brethren. He lost valuable friends among the American abolitionist community before the war by not paying his debts, forcing them to cancel loans as a gift to the movement for which he was taken to be a spokesman, and he lost other friends among the Negro community by taking over functions of leadership which were not his to take.* As his once warm supporter turned cool, Amos A. Lawrence, wrote to John Scoble, some of Henson's ability lay in being able to cajole people into doing what they knew to be financially unwise.† Edmund

---

*On these controversies, consult Pease and Pease, *Black Utopia,* pp. 76-83, 176-77.

† Henson borrowed $2,800 from J. Ingersoll Bowditch, Samuel Eliot, and Amos Lawrence (Rhodes House Library, Oxford University, Anti-Slavery Papers C 19/21: Lawrence to Scoble, March 30, 1851), a sum which Scoble finally liquidated for $1,500 (Lawrence Papers: Lawrence to Roaf, Dec. 22, 1852, June 30, 1853), by which time all three of the creditors had turned against Dawn (*ibid.*: Lawrence to Scoble, May 7, 1853).

Quincy, who served several times as editor of *The Liberator* during William Lloyd Garrison's absence, concluded that Henson "was a time-serving sycophant."* But Henson's force continued to be an appealing one, and the money he earned on lecture tours continued to find its way into the diminished Negro community over which he served increasingly as patriarch. He was scorned by some but, it would appear, loved by more, and if he served himself, he also served others.

In the year before his death Henson lectured in the Park Street Baptist Church in Hamilton, Ontario; he was ninety-three and past caring, and for the first time he categorically, without the protective use of third-person and subjunctive phrases, assured his listeners that he was Uncle Tom, exhibiting a picture Queen Victoria had given to him, rambling on for two and a half hours, until led from the platform.† He had embraced the legend himself. In May of 1883, when he died, fifty wagons followed his hearse to the graveside, a Negro band from nearby Chatham played, nine Negro preachers prayed, and Josiah's body was frozen in ice.

In fairness to Henson, one must realize that the controversy that grew about him was not, in fact, over Henson so much as over that for which he stood. Those who disliked *Uncle Tom's Cabin*, either because it was thought to be anti-Southern or, later, because of the servile Negro it depicted, cast much of their dislike toward Henson, while those who embraced the novel and its figures embraced him too. And among abolitionists, Henson could not hope to win universal approval, for the movement itself was split into warring camps. Henson attended a state convention of anti-slavery delegates in New Bedford, Massachusetts, in 1858, and there he strongly opposed the immediatist, violent approach of a portion of those

*Truman Nelson, Ed., *Documents of Upheaval: Selections from William Lloyd Garrison's* The Liberator, 1831-1865, New York, 1966, p. 239. Henson also lost the support of Mary Estlin and Maria Weston Chapman, partially because of his controversy with Scoble over the administration of the Dawn School, and partially because in 1851 he solicited funds on the basis of testimonials one of which, at least, was false (Weston Papers: John Bishop Estlin to Miss E. Wigham, May 3, and Fanny N. Tribe to Mary A. Estlin, June 12, 1851, and Mrs. Emma Michell to Maria W. Chapman, Aug. 30, 1852). The Rhodes House Anti-Slavery papers, as well as the Lawrence, Weston, and Samuel Gay Papers—the last at Columbia University—contain many letters about the feud between Henson and Scoble. On these developments, see Robin W. Winks, *The Negro in Canada*, New Haven (forthcoming).

†Hamilton *Times*, Jan. 13, 1882. On Victoria's picture, see the New York Public Library's Schomburg Collection, abolition materials, item 137: Henson Ms. [on visit to England], 1876.

present. When Charles L. Remond, a Garrisonian activist, recom-
mended that a committee be appointed to prepare an address to the
slaves in the Southern states suggesting that they resort to armed
insurrection, Henson was on his feet with a powerful speech which
was instrumental to the defeat of the motion. "As he didn't want to
see three or four thousand men hung before this time," Henson
remarked, "he should oppose any such action, head, neck and
shoulders," now; the idea of armed insurrection was "ridiculous."*
So it was, too, and Henson's influence undoubtedly was in the right
direction, but there were those, such as Remond, who thought him
cowardly. Ultimately Henson was to suffer the greatest irony of all:
precisely through his successful self-identification with Uncle Tom,
and because of his own moderate views on matters of race, he would
become synonymous for many with the paths of moderation and
even accommodation to the white community which the mid-
Twentieth Century's black power advocate now rejects.

The problems that Henson's life and his much-altered autobiography raise are important ones. Indeed, because of the many changes
in his narrative, the events with which Henson may appropriately be
associated—the arrival of the fugitive slaves, the rise and decline of
the Negro community movement in Canada, and the role in the
abolitionist movement of those fugitives who elected to remain
permanently resident in Canada—are more than ordinarily unclear. In
*Tales of Unrest* Joseph Conrad wrote that "The sustained invention
of a really telling lie demands a talent which I do not possess," and
Henson might well have said the same, for his story was substantially
true, accurate enough to be accepted by many but not accurate
enough to trust completely, especially where matters of nuance arise.
Perhaps most of the problems that Henson's *Life* leaves for us are no
more important than the question of how badly injured, and in
precisely what way, he was. But as the quintessential Canadian
Negro, the successful fugitive, Henson's account remains important
to the broader story of how the abolition of slavery itself took place.

Here, then, is an unusual and important book, reprinted for the
first time since it appeared in Canada in 1881. This edition is selected
over the several others because it is the fullest, containing as it does
all of the material added between 1851 and 1879 together with

---

*Herbert Aptheker, *A Documentary History of the Negro People in the United States,* New
York, 1951, pp. 406-08, drawing upon *The Liberator* for August 13, 1858.

Lobb's own conclusion. Copies of all editions are scarce, and but two copies of the Ontario edition have been traced: to the University of Western Ontario, in London, and to the Widener Library at Harvard University. The author wishes to thank the latter for making available the copy from which the present edition has been prepared. For the first time since Henson's death, a book which has been much in demand by scholars and libraries, a book which is a singular landmark within abolitionist literature, is back in print. I should also like to thank those who read an intermediate draft of this essay, in whole or in part, and gave me the benefits of their criticisms: Professor and Mrs. William H. Pease of the University of Maine, Professor Edward Wagenknecht of Boston University, Professor C. Vann Woodward of Yale University, and Mr. Joseph S. Van Why, Curator of the Stowe-Day Foundation in Hartford, Connecticut. None, of course, is responsible for any errors that remain or for my interpretations.

A Note on the Printing History of Henson's Autobiography

The first *Life of Josiah Henson, formerly a Slave, Now an Inhabitant of Canada. Narrated by Himself,* as ghost-written by Samuel A. Eliot, appeared in Boston in 1849. It has been reprinted once, with different pagination, by The Observer Press of Dresden, Ontario, for Uncle Tom's Cabin and Museum in Dresden. This edition, which appeared in 1965, includes a brief Foreword and the text of the plaque that demarks Henson's house. The 1849 edition appeared in London and Edinburgh in 1851 as *The Life of Josiah Henson, formerly a Slave: As Narrated by Himself.* The second edition, substantially revised, was retitled *Truth Stranger than Fiction: Father Henson's Story of His Own Life,* and was published in Boston in 1858 and in London in 1859. As noted in the text, all further revisions were in the hands of John Lobb, who usually listed himself on the title-pages as the editor. The third edition, "revised and enlarged," was Lobb's *"Uncle Tom's Story of His Life": An Autobiography of the Rev. Josiah Henson (Mrs. Harriet Beecher Stowe's "Uncle Tom"), From 1789 to 1876,* published in London in 1877. In the same year Lobb's *The Young People's Illustrated Edition of "Uncle Tom's" Story of His Life (From 1789 to 1877)* appeared, also in London, to be followed in 1878 with Lobb's London edition of *An Autobiography of the Rev. Josiah Henson (Mrs. Harriet Beecher Stowe's "Uncle Tom"): From 1789 to 1877*, with added material of a minor nature. In 1879 Lobb published, with the Henson portion of the text changed no further, *"Truth Stranger than Fiction": An Autobiography of the Rev. Josiah Henson (Mrs. Harriet Beecher Stowe's "Uncle Tom"), From 1789 to 1879*, on this occasion in Boston, and with a new preface by Mrs. Stowe, notes by Wendell Phillips and John Greenleaf Whittier, and an appendix by Gilbert Haven.

The fullest version of the Henson narrative to appear during his lifetime was the one which is reprinted here. This, Lobb's *An Autobiography of the Rev. Josiah Henson ("Uncle Tom") From 1789 to 1881*, was the first edition to be published in Canada, appearing in London, Ontario in 1881. It contained the Stowe, Phillips, Whittier, and Haven additions, but with the 1878 rather than the 1879 introduction, and a Conclusion written by Lobb, although not so designated. This version was the "revised and enlarged" edition. Some slight additions were made to the final edition, Lobb's *The Autobiography of the Rev. Josiah Henson ('Uncle Tom') From 1789 to 1883*, London, 1890, to include Henson's death, but some of the added matter was cut, so that the Ontario volume remains the fullest. There is also a disputed edition, normally ascribed to Halifax, Nova Scotia, in 1852, of the original Henson narrative of 1849, but (see the last footnote on p. xiv) I am convinced that this edition was published in England and that it, therefore, is merely a pirated edition of the London and Edinburgh printing of 1851. Of these original English-language editions, all save those of 1852, 1879, and 1881 are in the British Museum; the provenance of the others is discussed in the relevant footnotes, as is the question of editions in translation (see p. xxv). All but the 1849 edition have a picture of Henson as a frontispiece. The young people's edition includes a tipped-in tintype, usually missing (but present in the British Museum's copy), of Lobb and Henson—the only available picture of the former—and introduces an appendix on Henson's visit to the King Edward Industrial School and Girls' Refuge in 1877 that does not appear elsewhere.

In addition to the 1965 reprinting of the edition of 1849, there has been a reprint edition of the version of 1858, without Mrs. Stowe's preface, and with an introduction by Walter Fisher: *Father Henson's*

*Story of His Own Life,* New York, 1962. A fragment of the 1858 narrative has been reprinted in Harvey Wish, ed., *Slavery in the South: First-Hand Accounts of the Ante-Bellum American Southland . . . ,* New York, 1964, pp. 23-36. The youthful Henson appears on the cover of the 1962 reprinting, while the elderly Henson is depicted in all other editions. The latter picture is also available singly from the Museum in Dresden.

Although the first edition of Henson's memoir bears the imprint of Arthur D. Phelps, the original publishers were to have been Charles C. Little and James Brown, booksellers in Cambridge and Watertown respectively (*Boston Directory 1849,* p. 190). This is shown by the original manuscript copy of the narrative as taken down by Samuel Eliot. The manuscript, now in the Boston Public Library, was given by Miss Mary L. Bullard of Manchester-by-the-Sea in 1897, and it clearly states that Little and Brown were to publish the manuscript for the author, and that Eliot had written it.

I have made a line-by-line comparison between the manuscript and the first edition and find no changes of importance. There are numerous quite minor alterations—added commas, corrected spellings, the insertion of Roman numerals for the chapters of the Bible, and the substitution of *and* for &—and the original contains italicized words and insertions which have been regularized in the printed copy. The one omission of substance occurs at the end, where the final line of the manuscript was not printed; there are also changes of nuance by the substitution of other words on pages 17, 23, and 32 of the manuscript, and a garbled Biblical quotation is corrected. The manuscript apparently was read back to Henson when Eliot completed it.

## A Note on Henson's Biographers

Josiah Henson has been unfortunate in his biographers. The only acceptable statement on Henson is B[enjamin] B[rawley], "Josiah Henson," *D.A.B.,* 8, pp. 564-65, together with an obituary in the New York *Daily Tribune* for May 6, 1883. In addition to Jessie L. Beattie's *Black Moses* (see the footnote on p. xxi) there is Brion Gysin's *To Master—A Long Good Night: The Story of Uncle Tom, A*

*Historical Narrative,* New York, 1946, which is fictionalized and hostile. Gysin denounced Henson as "an appeaser" (New York *Times,* Feb. 2, 1947) even before "Uncle Tom" was a widely used synonymn for a racial Quisling. W. B. Hartgrove, "The Story of Josiah Henson," *Journal of Negro History,* 3, January, 1918, pp. 1-21, is an utterly useless article taken directly from the 1858 edition of the autobiography, which Hartgrove frequently misreads. Margaret K. Zieman, "The Story Behind the Real Uncle Tom," in Canada's *Macleans Magazine,* 67, June, 1954, pp. 20-21, 42-44, 46, helped renew the Canadian hagiography. Aileen Ward, "In Memory of Uncle Tom," *Dalhousie Review,* 20, October, 1940, pp. 335-338, is quite without merit. Annie E. Duncan, "Josiah Henson," *The Negro History Bulletin,* 4, April, 1941, pp. 146-47, 163-64, is for children, while Lois M. Jones, "Josiah Henson's Lumbering Operations in Canada," *ibid.,* p. 157, is by a child. Elizabeth Ross Haynes, *Unsung Heroes,* New York, 1921, pp. 191-206; H. A. Tanser, "Josiah Henson, the Moses of His People," *Journal of Negro Education,* 12, Fall, 1943, pp. 630-32; and Jean Tallach, "The Story of Rev. Josiah Henson," Kent Historical Society, *Papers & Records,* 7, 1951, pp. 43-52, uncritically accept all that Henson wrote. Herbert Hill, in "Uncle Tom: An Enduring American Myth," *The Crisis,* 72, May, 1965, pp. 289-95, 325, also accepts Henson's own word but defends him as a Negro folk hero. *The American Bookseller,* 10, October, 1880, 257, unqualifiedly identified Henson with Mrs. Stowe's Tom, and recent books continue to do so. See, for example, Milton Meltzer, ed., *In Their Own Words: A History of the American Negro,* New York, 1964, p. 84, and William Chapple, *The Story of Uncle Tom,* Dresden, n.d., which draws heavily upon Henson's 1858 edition. A bit more guardedly, *The Encyclopedia Americana,* New York, 1963, 14, 109, concludes that Henson was "the basis for the character" of Tom. Richard Bardolph, *The Negro Vanguard,* Vintage ed., New York, 1961, accepts Henson's "chance meeting" with Mrs. Stowe but rightly concludes that "his peculiar place in history rests on the success with which he exploited his identification with Mrs. Stowe's hero" (p. 59). A brief, circumspect, summary of Henson's contributions appears in William Breyfogle, *Make Free: The Story of the Underground Railroad,* Philadelphia, 1958, pp. 184-89.

*New Haven, Connecticut*                                   R. W. W.
*September, 1967*

AN

# AUTOBIOGRAPHY

OF THE

# REV. JOSIAH HENSON

("Uncle Tom")

*From* 1789 *to* 1881

WITH A PREFACE BY MRS. HARRIET BEECHER STOWE

AND

Introductory Notes by George Sturge, S. Morley, Esq., M.P.,
Wendell Phillips, and John G. Whittier

EDITED BY

JOHN LOBB, F.R.G.S.

———————

REVISED AND ENLARGED

———————

LONDON, ONTARIO:
SCHUYLER, SMITH & CO.
1881

*(Only Authorized Edition, and Copyright)*

# PREFACE

The numerous friends of the author of this work will need no greater recommendation than his name to make it welcome. Among all the singular and interesting records to which the institution of American slavery has given rise, we know of none more striking, more characteristic and instructive, than that of Josiah Henson.

Born a slave—a slave in effect in a heathen land—and under a heathen master, he grew up without Christian light or knowledge, and like the Gentiles spoken of by St. Paul, "without the law did by nature the things that are written in the law." One sermon, one offer of salvation by Christ, was sufficient for him, as for the Ethiopian eunuch, to make him at once a believer from the heart and a preacher of Jesus.

To the great Christian doctrine of forgiveness of enemies and the returning of good for evil, he was by God's grace made a faithful witness, under circumstances that try men's souls and make us all who read it say, "Lead us not into such temptation." We earnestly commend this portion of his narrative to those who, under much smaller temptations, think themselves entitled to render evil for evil.

The African race appear as yet to have been companions only of the sufferings of Christ. In the melancholy scene of His death—while Europe in the person of the Roman delivered Him unto death, and Asia in the person of the Jew clamoured for His execution—Africa was represented in the person of Simon the Cyrenean, who came patiently bearing after Him the load of the cross; and ever since then poor Africa has been toiling on, bearing the weary cross of contempt and oppression after Jesus. But they who suffer with Him shall also reign; and when the unwritten annals of slavery shall appear in the judgment, many Simons who have gone meekly bearing their cross after Jesus to unknown graves, shall rise to thrones and crowns!

Verily a day shall come when He shall appear for those His hidden ones, and then "many that are last shall be first, and the first shall be last."

HARRIET BEECHER STOWE

*Andover, Mass.*

# INTRODUCTORY NOTES

By George Sturge, S. Morley, Esq., M.P.,

Wendell Phillips, and John G. Whittier


On Rev. J. Henson's visit to England, Samuel Morley, Esq., M.P., and George Sturge, kindly undertook to be the treasurers of the fund to liquidate the claims of his mortgages. In response to our request for a few words introductory to "Uncle Tom's Life," we have the following from George Sturge. "My knowledge of Josiah Henson dates from his visit to this country twenty-five years ago, when my late brother Thomas Sturge, with other friends of the negro race, helped to establish 'The Dawn Institute for the Education of Coloured People in Canada.' I regard Josiah Henson in many respects as a remarkable man. When I contemplate his unselfish efforts (at great risk to himself) to rescue his brethren in slavery, after he had obtained his own liberty, and his labours as a free man to educate and enlighten them, I consider that there are few men now living who have done so much for the negro race. When it is remembered, too, that he was a slave for forty-two years, his life affords an encouraging *example* of what may be done, even by one who has laboured under the greatest disadvantages, who is earnestly desirous to benefit his race. His Christian simplicity, and the absence of all bitter feeling towards those who have oppressed him, will have commended him to all who have made his acquaintance. The life of 'Uncle Tom,' now extended in its records to the present date, will be found by its readers to possess deep interest, and will doubtless be favourably received. On submitting these observations to Samuel Morley, his remark was, 'I thoroughly agree with them.' "

*Sydenham*

Dear Sir,—I am glad to hear that Father Henson's "Life" is to be again offered to the public. It is one of the most valuable and suggestive of the stories written by fugitive slaves. The simplicity of the narrative, its pathos, and the close, minute view it gives of the inner working of the slave system, make it a most effective argument.

While we are thankful such appeals are no longer necessary to break the actual chain, their value is rather increased than lessened, to every thoughtful man, by the present state of affairs. All the light the nation can get touching the mood and nature of the white South is sorely needed to-day. Every line and every fact that weakens the North to its danger is invaluable.

Besides, as materials for history, these biographies are of great value. Frederika Bremer said, "the fate of the negro is the romance of your history."

Gather up, then, all these fragments, that nothing be lost.—Yours cordially,

WENDELL PHILLIPS

I take pleasure in commending this new edition of the Auto- biography of Josiah Hensen to all who can sympathise with unmerited suffering borne with Christian patience, and who can honour hero- ism, fortitude, and self-denying philanthropy. No one, I am per- suaded, can read his remarkable story without feeling respect for his sagacity, prudence, energy, and business capacity, and reverence for his integrity and Christian character, manifested under extraordinary and difficult circumstances.

The early life of the author, as a slave, gives a fearful inside view of that detestable system which John Wesley justly pronounced "the vilest beneath the sun"; and proves that in the terrible pictures of "Uncle Tom's Cabin" there is "nothing extenuate or aught set down in malice."

Apart from the general interest of the narrative, the purchaser of it will have the satisfaction of contributing to a praiseworthy enterprise of Christian charity. Its venerable author, now in his ninetieth year, is seeking to erect a meeting-house in the township where he resides, for the benefit of the people of his race in that vicinity, and the profits of this edition will be devoted to that object.

JOHN G. WHITTIER

*Danvers*

## EDITORIAL NOTE

Having heard that some persons have expressed doubts as to the identity of the Rev. Josiah Henson with the "Uncle Tom" of Mrs. Stowe's book, chiefly because Mrs. Stowe *kills* her hero, we deem it only just to all parties to give the following explanation and corroboration. We candidly confess that, when one has read the pathetic and powerful description of "Uncle Tom's" end by Mrs. Stowe — a chapter which has brought tears into the eyes of thousands, and which has impressed many a heart with the beauty and glory of true religion—it is not easy to think of him as still alive, and therefore we can quite understand and even appreciate the scepticism which is alleged to exist in some minds. But reflecting persons will allow that, the great aim of Mrs. Stowe being to show the horrors of slavery to the uttermost, and many unhappy slaves having been murdered by cruel and brutal masters—some under circumstances even more horrible than those surrounding the murder of her "Uncle Tom"—Mrs. Stowe was quite justified in using the novelist's privilege even to the "bitter end," to give her story all the effect possible. In a literary, artistic point of view, the story would have been incomplete without it, and faithfulness to her design and to the mournful facts of slave life demanded it. But, nevertheless, the truth remains unaltered and unalterable; and that the life of the Rev. Josiah Henson suggested to Mrs. Stowe the conception of her "immortal hero," can be most satisfactorily established, as will appear from the following condensed statement. When Mr. Henson had been eight years a free man in Canada, he published the story of his forty-two years' slave life in the States. This was in 1849. The book attracted the attention of Mrs. Stowe, whose mind was then (providentially, it is evident) much exercised upon the subject of slavery, as an American Institution, and more especially in its relation to Christian churches and Christianity. Mrs. Stowe believed, with the great and good John Wesley, that slavery is "the sum of all human villainy," and she intensely longed to produce a book which, by its dramatic power, would show the wickedness and horrors of the slave-trade, and thus promote its overthrow. And no one can doubt that her "Uncle Tom" mightily contributed to this grand result. Accordingly, at Mrs. Stowe's request, Mr. Henson visited her, and gave further particulars of his own life, and satisfactorily corroborated the incidents and events recorded in his book. George Harris (husband of Eliza), who is still living, also visited Mrs. Stowe the same year, and supplied her with information from his own experience; and thus from their *joint history*, taken from their own lips, and from Mr. Henson's book, Mrs. Stowe derived the *chief* material for her "Uncle Tom's Cabin," which appeared in the year 1850. Reference to the work which Mrs. Stowe subsequently produced—viz., "A Key to Uncle Tom's Cabin;" presenting the original Facts and Documents upon which the Story is founded; together with corroborative Statements verifying the truth of the work—will show that the above conclusion is fully justified. On page 34 of the "Key" Mrs. Stowe writes:—"Let the reader peruse the account which George Harris gives of the sale of his mother and her children, and then read the following account given by the venerable Josiah Henson," &c. Doubtless Mrs. Stowe availed herself of information from other sources, but that Mr. Henson furnished the idea of her "Uncle Tom" is clear from page 52 of the "Key." "A last instance, *parallel* with that of Uncle Tom, is to be found in the published memoirs of the venerable Josiah Henson, now a clergyman in Canada," &c., &c. We asked Mr. Henson a few questions concerning some of the characters introduced by Mrs. Stowe, and received the following particulars, which, we doubt not, will interest our readers. "Aunt Chloe was my first wife, whose real name was Charlotte. She was famed as a good cook. Her beautiful singing of spiritual songs first won my heart. She was a true Christian, and died a very happy death." "The incident of young George Shelby taking horse to overtake Haley the trader really occurred. The young man was George Riley." "Three Quakers, Dr. Stanton, Senator Bird, and Levi Coffin, and their wives, showed me much sympathy, and helped me. Senator Bird sheltered me when escaping from slavery." "I knew

George and Eliza Harris and their little son Harry quite well." "Mrs. Stowe's description of Topsy is quite correct: her real name was Dinah." "Eva, (Susan), daughter of Mr. St.Clare (the true name), I really did rescue from drowning. The accident took place at the mouth of Blackford's Creek, River Ohio." "Casey I knew well. Her name was Polly, she was cook at Litton's." "While I was at Litton's (Mrs. Stowe's Legree) young George Riley (Mrs. Stowe's George Shelby) really did visit me." Further corroboration might be adduced, but we feel assured our readers will be satisfied that the renowned "Uncle Tom" was none other than the Rev. Josiah Henson, whom thousands in this country have seen and heard with pleasure, and we trust with profit also. On Mr. Henson's first visit to this country, twenty-five years ago, he enjoyed the confidence and esteem of many of the foremost men both in the Church and the State. Some of those distinguished persons still live, and have shown by their sympathy and support, in this his last visit, that their confidence and esteem have not waxed less by the lapse of years; though, of course, circumstances are changed, seeing that in that time American negro slavery has ceased to exist. The culmination of Mr. Henson's visit was the magnificent farewell-meeting in Mr. Spurgeon's world-known tabernacle, with the *truly illustrious* Earl of Shaftesbury in the chair. Those who were present will, perhaps, never forget the enthusiasm of that meeting, and we are sure a delightful remembrance of it will abide in Mr. Henson's mind to his dying day. The *Times, Daily News,* and other London papers contained notices of the meeting. The *Times* of February 2nd favoured us with a review of "Uncle Tom's Story of his Life," for which we are deeply grateful, and which we hope will quite settle the point that it was Mr. Henson's autobiography that first suggested to Mrs. Stowe the idea of her hero. The Leading Journal (the *Times*) thus commences its notice of our book:—

"Among the crowd of competitors who from all parts of the earth thronged to show their wares at the Exhibition of 1851 was a single negro exhibitor. All he had to display were four black walnut boards, but they were of the finest grain and texture, were beautifully French polished, and in the end were awarded a medal. It bore the inscription, 'This is the produce of the industry of a fugitive slave from the United States, whose residence is Dawn, Canada.' In the autobiography of that fugitive slave, first published at Boston a couple of years before, republished in this country in the very year of the Exhibition, and of which the latest recast is now before us in its thirtieth thousand, after a career of six weeks, lay the germ of that remarkable work of fiction, the circulation of which has been exceeded by that of no book save the Bible, and which our author may be forgiven for believing was 'the wedge that finally rent asunder' the gigantic fabric of American slavery 'with a fearful crash.' Yet such, in spite of the nursery protest that 'Uncle Tom' was killed in the book, and that Father Henson, therefore, can be no more than his ghost, is an undoubted fact, as a glance at the chapter on her hero in Mrs. Stowe's 'Key to Uncle Tom's Cabin' must convince any reader."

On behalf of Mr. Henson and those friends who so kindly co-operated with ourselves, we have to express warmest thanks to a generous and sympathising Christian public for the noble contribution of £2,000. By this splendid generosity the difficulties which oppressed and harassed Mr. Henson in his work in Canada have been removed, and some provision made for the comfort of himself and wife in their declining days. To ourselves it has been a work of Christian love, and we have had more than our reward in the success of our efforts, and in intercourse with so many Christian friends of whom we shall ever entertain grateful and affectionate recollections.

JOHN LOBB

*January,* 1881

# MRS. H. BEECHER STOWE'S "UNCLE TOM"

## CHAPTER I

### MY BIRTH AND CHILDHOOD

Earliest Memories—Born in Maryland—My Father's Fight with an Overseer—One Hundred
Stripes and His Ear Cut Off—Throws Away His Banjo and Becomes Morose—Sold South

The story of my life, which I am about to record, is one full of
striking incident. Keener pangs, deeper joys, more singular vicissitudes, few have been led in God's providence to experience. As I
look back on it through the vista of more than eighty years, and
scene after scene rises before me, an ever fresh wonder fills my mind.
I delight to recall it. I dwell on it as did the Jews on the marvellous
history of their rescue from the bondage of Egypt. Time has touched
with its mellowing fingers its sterner features. The sufferings of the
past are now like a dream, and the enduring lessons left behind, make
me to praise God that my soul has been tempered by Him in so fiery
a furnace and under such heavy blows.

I was born June 15th, 1789, in Charles county, Maryland, on a
farm belonging to Mr. Francis Newman, about a mile from Port
Tobacco. My mother was a slave of Dr. Josiah McPherson, but hired
to Mr. Newman, to whom my father belonged. The only incident I
can remember which occurred while my mother continued on Mr.
Newman's farm, was the appearance one day of my father with his
head bloody and his back lacerated. He was beside himself with
mingled rage and suffering. The overseer had brutally assaulted my

mother, when my father sprang upon him like a tiger. In a moment
the overseer was down, and, mastered by rage, my father would have
killed him but for the entreaties of my mother, and the overseer's
own promise that nothing should ever be said of the matter. The
promise was kept—like most promises of the cowardly and debased—
as long as the danger lasted.

The laws of slave states provide means and opportunities for
revenge so ample, that miscreants like him never fail to improve
them. "A nigger has struck a white man;" that is enough to set a
whole county on fire; no question is asked about the provocation.
The authorities were soon in pursuit of my father. The penalty was
one hundred lashes on the bare back, and to have the right ear nailed
to the whipping-post, and then severed from the body. For a time
my father kept out of the way, hiding in the woods, and at night
venturing into some cabin in search of food. But at length the strict
watch set baffled all his efforts. His supplies cut off, he was fairly
starved out, and compelled by hunger to come back and give himself
up.

The day for the execution of the penalty was appointed. The
negroes from the neighboring plantations were summoned to witness
the scene. A powerful blacksmith named Hewes laid on the stripes.
Fifty were given, during which the cries of my father might be heard
a mile, and then a pause ensued. True, he had struck a white man,
but as valuable property he must not be damaged. Judicious men felt
his pulse. Oh! he could stand the whole. Again and again the thong
fell on his lacerated back. His cries grew fainter and fainter, till a
feeble groan was the only response to the final blows. His head was
then thrust against the post, and his right ear fastened to it with a
tack; a swift pass of a knife, and the bleeding member was left
sticking to the place. Then came a hurra from the degraded crowd,
and the exclamation, "That's what he's got for striking a white
man."

In the estimation of the illiterate, besotted poor whites who
constituted the witnesses of such scenes in Charles county, Maryland,
the man who did not feel rage enough at hearing of "a nigger"
striking a white, to be ready to burn him alive, was only fit to be
lynched out of the neighbourhood.

Previous to this affair, my father, from all I can learn, had been a good-humoured and light-hearted man, the ringleader in all fun at corn-huskings and Christmas buffoonery. His banjo was the life of the farm, and all night long at a merry-making would he play on it while the other negroes danced. But from this hour he became utterly changed. Sullen, morose, and dogged, nothing could be done with him. The milk of human kindness in his heart was turned to gall. He brooded over his wrongs. No fear or threats of being sold to the far south—the greatest of all terrors to the Maryland slave—would render him tractable. So off he was sent to Alabama. What was his after-fate neither my mother nor I have ever learned; the great day will reveal all. This was the first chapter in my history.

# CHAPTER II

## MY FIRST GREAT TRIAL

Origin of My Name—A Kind Master—He is Drowned—My Mother's Prayer—A Slave Auction—Torn from My Mother—Severe Sickness—A Cruel Master—Sold Again and Restored to My Mother

After the sale of my father by Newman, Dr. McPherson would no longer hire out my mother to him. She returned, accordingly, to his estate. He was far kinder to his slaves than the planters generally were, never suffering them to be struck by any one. He was a man of good, kind impulses, liberal, jovial, hearty. No degree of arbitrary power could ever lead him to cruelty. As the first negro child ever born to him, I was his especial pet. He gave me his own Christian name, Josiah, and with that he also gave me my last name, Henson, after an uncle of his, who was an officer in the revolutionary war. A bright spot in my childhood was my residence with him—bright, but, alas! fleeting. Events were rapidly maturing which were to change the whole aspect of my life. The kind doctor was not exempt from that failing which too often besets easy, social natures in a dissipated community. He could not restrain his convivial propensities. Although he maintained a high reputation for goodness of heart and an almost saint-like benevolence, the habit of intemperance steadily gained ground, and finally occasioned his death. Two negroes on the plantation found him one morning lying dead in the middle of a narrow stream, not a foot in depth. He had been away the night previous at a social party, and when returning home had fallen from his horse, probably, and being too intoxicated to stagger through the stream, fell and was drowned. "There's the place where massa got drownded at;" how well I remember having it pointed out to me in those very words.

For two or three years my mother and her young family of six children had resided on the doctor's estate, and we had been in the main very happy. She was a good mother to us, a woman of deep piety, anxious above all things to touch our hearts with a sense of religion. How or where she acquired her knowledge of God, or her acquaintance with the Lord's Prayer, which she so frequently taught us to repeat, I am unable to say. I remember seeing her often on her knees, and hearing her pray by repeating constant ejaculations, and short phrases which were within my infant comprehension, and have remained in my memory to this hour.

Our term of happy union as one family was now, alas! at an end. The doctor's death was a great calamity to us, for the estate and the slaves were to be sold and the proceeds divided among the heirs. The first sad announcement that the sale was to be; the knowledge that all ties of the past were to be sundered; the frantic terror at the idea of being sent "down south;" the almost certainty that one member of a family will be torn from another; the anxious scanning of purchasers' faces; the agony at parting, often for ever, with husband, wife, child—these must be seen and felt to be fully understood. Young as I was then, the iron entered into my soul. The remembrance of the breaking up of McPherson's estate is photographed in its minutest features in my mind. The crowd collected round the stand, the huddling group of negroes, the examination of muscle, teeth, the exhibition of agility, the look of the auctioneer, the agony of my mother—I can shut my eyes and see them all.

My brothers and sisters were bid off first, and one by one, while my mother, paralysed by grief, held me by the hand. Her turn came, and she was bought by Isaac Riley, of Montgomery county. Then I was offered to the assembled purchasers. My mother, half-distracted with the thought of parting for ever from all her children, pushed through the crowd, while the bidding for me was going on, to the spot where Riley was standing. She fell at his feet, and clung to his knees, entreating him in tones that a mother only could command, to buy her *baby* as well as herself, and spare to her one, at least, of her little ones. Will it, can it be believed that this man, thus appealed to, was capable not merely of turning a deaf ear to her supplication, but of disengaging himself from her with such violent blows and kicks, as to reduce her to the necessity of creeping out of his reach, and mingling the groan of bodily suffering with the sob of a breaking heart? As she crawled away from the brutal man, I heard her sob out, "Oh, Lord Jesus, how long, how long shall I suffer this way?" I must have been then between five and six years old.

I was bought by a stranger named Robb, and truly a robber he was to me. He took me to his home, about forty miles distant, and put me into his negro quarters with about forty others, of all ages, colours, and conditions, all strangers to me. Of course nobody cared for me. The slaves were brutalised by this degradation, and had no sympathy for me. I soon fell sick, and lay for some days almost dead on the ground. Sometimes a slave would give me a piece of corn-bread, or a bit of herring. Finally I became so feeble that I could not move. This, however, was fortunate for me; for in the course of a few weeks, Robb met Riley, who had bought my mother, and offered to sell me to him cheap. Riley said he was afraid "the little nigger would die;" but he agreed, finally, to pay a small sum for me in horse-shoeing if I lived, and nothing if I died. Robb was a tavern-keeper, and owned a line of stages with the horses, and lived near Montgomery Court House; Riley carried on blacksmithing about five miles from that place. This clenched the bargain, and I was soon sent to my mother. A blessed change it was. I had been lying on a lot of rags, thrown on a dirt floor. All day long I had been left alone, crying for water, crying for mother; the slaves, who left at daylight, when they returned cared nothing for me. Now, I was once more with my best friend on earth, and under her care; destitute as she was of the proper means of nursing me, I recovered my health, and grew to be an uncommonly vigorous boy and man.

I faithfully served Riley for many years. He was coarse and vulgar in his habits, and unprincipled and cruel in his general deportment. His slaves had little opportunity for relaxation from wearying labour, were supplied with the scantiest means of sustaining their toil by necessary food, and had no security for personal rights. When such a master is a tyrant, the slaves often become cringing, treacherous, false, and thieving. Riley and his slaves were no exception to the general rule, but might be cited as apt illustrations of the nature of the relation.

# CHAPTER III

## MY BOYHOOD AND YOUTH

Early Employment—Slave-Life—Food, Lodging, Clothing—Amusements—Gleams of Sunshine—My Knight-Errantry—Become an Overseer and General Superintendent

My earliest employments were, to carry buckets of water to the men at work, and to hold a horse-plough, used for weeding between the rows of corn. As I grew older and taller, I was entrusted with the care of master's saddle-horse. Then a hoe was put into my hands, and I was soon required to do the day's work of a man; and it was not long before I could do it, at least as well as my associates in misery.

A description of the everyday life of a slave on a southern plantation illustrates the character and habits of the slave and the slaveholder, created and perpetuated by their relative position. The principal food of those upon my master's plantation consisted of corn-meal, and salt herrings; to which was added in summer a little buttermilk, and the few vegetables which each might raise for himself and his family, on the little piece of ground which was assigned to him for the purpose, called a truck-patch.

In ordinary times we had two regular meals in a day: breakfast at twelve o'clock, after labouring from daylight, and supper when the work of the remainder of the day was over. In harvest season we had three. Our dress was of tow-cloth; for the children, nothing but a shirt; for the older ones a pair of pantaloons or a gown in addition, according to the sex. Besides these, in the winter a round jacket or overcoat, a wool-hat once in two or three years, for the males, and a pair of coarse shoes once a year.

We lodged in log huts, and on the bare ground. Wooden floors were an unknown luxury. In a single room were huddled, like cattle, ten or a dozen persons, men, women, and children. All ideas of refinement and decency were, of course, out of the question. We had neither bedsteads, nor furniture of any description. Our beds were collections of straw and old rags, thrown down in the corners and boxed in with boards; a single blanket the only covering. Our favourite way of sleeping, however, was on a plank, our heads raised on an old jacket and our feet toasting before the smouldering fire. The wind whistled and the rain and snow blew in through the cracks, and the damp earth soaked in the moisture till the floor was miry as a pig-sty. Such were our houses. In these wretched hovels were we penned at night, and fed by day: here were the children born and the sick—neglected.

Notwithstanding this system of management I grew to be a robust and vigorous lad. At fifteen years of age there were few who could compete with me in work or sport. I was as lively as a young buck, and running over with animal spirits. I could run faster, wrestle better, and jump higher than anybody about me, and at an evening shakedown in our own or a neighbor's kitchen, my feet became absolutely invisible from the rate at which they moved. All this caused my master and my fellow-slaves to look upon me as a wonderfully smart fellow, and prophecy the great things I should do when I became a man. My vanity became vastly inflamed, and I fully coincided in their opinion. Julius Caesar never aspired and plotted for the imperial crown more ambitiously than did I to out-hoe, out-reap, out-husk, out-dance, out-strip every competitor; and from all I can learn he never enjoyed his triumph half as much. One word of commendation from the petty despot who ruled over us would set me up for a month.

God be praised, that, however hedged in by circumstances, the joyful exuberance of youth will bound at times over them all. Ours is a light-hearted race. The sternest and most covetous master cannot frighten or whip the fun out of us; certainly old Riley never did out of me. In those days I had many a merry time, and would have had, had I lived with nothing but moccasins and rattlesnakes in Okafenoke swamp. Slavery did its best to make me wretched, but, along with memories of miry cabins, frosted feet, weary toil under the blazing sun, curses and blows, there flock in others, of jolly Christmas times, dances before old massa's door for the first drink of egg-nog, extra meat at holiday times, midnight-visits to apple-orchards, broiling stray chickens, and first-rate tricks to dodge work. The God who makes the lambs gambol, the kittens play, the birds sing, and the fish leap, gave me a light, merry, and joyous heart. True it was, that the fun and freedom of Christmas, at which time my master relaxed his front, was generally followed up by a portentous back-action, under which he drove and cursed worse than ever; still the fun and freedom were fixed facts; we had had them and he could not help it.

Besides these pleasant memories I have others of a deeper and richer kind. I early learned to employ my spirit of adventure for the benefit of my fellow-sufferers. The condition of the male slave is bad enough; but that of the female, often compelled to perform severe labour, sick or well, unpitied and unaided, is one that arouses the spirit of sympathy in every heart not dead to all feeling. The miseries which I saw many of the women suffer, often oppressed me with a load of sorrow. No *white* knight, rescuing a white fair lady from cruel oppression, ever felt the throbbing of a chivalrous heart more intensely than I, a *black* knight, did, when running down a chicken to hide it in an out-of-the-way place till dark, that I might be able then to carry it to some poor overworked black fair one, to whom it was at once food, luxury, and medicine. No Scotch borderer, levying black mail or sweeping off a drove of cattle, ever felt more assured of the justice of his act than I of mine, when I was driving a pig or a sheep a mile or two into the woods, to slaughter for the good of those whom Riley was starving. I felt good, moral, heroic.

Was this wrong? I can only say in reply, that, at this distance of time, my conscience does not reproach me for it. Then I esteemed it among the best of my deeds. It was my training in the luxury of doing good, in the divinity of a sympathetic heart, in the righteousness of indignation against the cruel and oppressive. There and then was my soul made conscious of all the chivalry of which my circumstances and condition in life admitted. I love the sentiment in its splendid environment of castles, and tilts, and gallantry; but having fallen on other times, I loved it also in the homely guise of Sambo as Paladin, Dinah as an oppressed maiden, and old Riley as grim oppressor.

By means of the influence thus acquired, the great amount of work I performed upon the farm, and by the detection of the knavery of the overseer, who plundered his employer for more selfish ends, was caught in the act and dismissed, I was promoted to be superintendent of the farm-work, and managed to raise more than double the crops, with more cheerful and willing labour, then was ever seen on the estate before.

I was now, practically, overseer. My pride and ambition had made me master of every kind of farmwork. But, like all ambition, its reward was increase of burdens. The crops of wheat, oats, barley, potatoes, corn, tobacco, all had to be cared for by me. I was often compelled to start at midnight with the waggon for the distant market, to drive on through mud and rain till morning, sell the produce, reach home hungry and tired, and nine times out of ten, reap my sole reward in curses for not getting higher prices. My master was a fearful blasphemer. Clearly as he saw my profitableness to him, he was too much of a brute to reward me with kindness or even decent treatment. Previous to my attaining this important station, however, an incident occurred which produced so powerful an influence on my intellectual development, my character, condition, my religious culture, and in short, on my whole nature, body and soul, that it deserves especial notice and commemoration. This, however, requires another chapter.

# CHAPTER IV

## MY CONVERSION

My Praying Mother —A Good Man —Hear A Sermon for the First Time —Its Effect Upon
Me —Prayer and Communion —Its First Fruits

I remember being torn from a dear and affectionate mother; I saw
her tears and heard her groans; I remember all the particulars. From a
little boy up I have remembered my mother; I remember what the
prayers of my dear mother were: I have heard her pray for me; for
she was a good Christian woman before I was born; and I thank God
that I was born of a good Christian mother, a mother whose prayers
fell on my ear. Of all earthly blessings there is none can approach to
a good mother. I remember her entreaties; I remember her prayers to
God for me. Blessed is the child, the son or daughter, that has the
prayers of a mother. I remember well the feeling that those prayers
wrought upon my heart, though I was but a boy.

My heart exults with gratitude when I mention the name of a good
man who first taught me the blessedness of religion. His name was
John McKenny. He lived at Georgetown, a few miles only from
Riley's plantation; his business was that of a baker, and his character
was that of an upright, benevolent Christian. He was noted especially
for his detestation of slavery, and his resolute avoidance of the
employment of slave-labour in his business. He would not even hire a
slave, the price of whose toil must be paid to his master, but
contented himself with the work of his own hands, and with such
free labour as he could procure. His reputation was high, not only for
this almost singular abstinence from what no one about him thought
wrong, but for his general probity and excellence. This man
occasionally served as a minister of the Gospel, and preached in a
neighbourhood where preachers were somewhat rare at that period.
One Sunday when he was to officiate in this way, at a place three or

*23*

four miles distant, my mother urged me to ask master's permission to go and hear him. I had so often been beaten for making such a request that I refused to make it. My mother came to me and said: "Now, my son, I want you to go and ask master to let you go down and hear Mr. McKenny preach." I said to my mother: "I do not want to go; I am afraid he will beat me." She said: "Go and ask him." I turned round, like many other boys, and said I would not go. She was standing against a rail; she dropped her head down and shed a tear. I stood and looked at her and was touched at her sorrow. I said: "I will go, mother." She said: "That is right." I went up to the house, and just before I got to the door, master saw my shadow. He turned round and asked what I wanted. I said: "I want to ask you if I can go to the meeting." "Where?" "Down at Newport Mill." "Who is going to preach?" "Mr. McKenny." "What do you want to hear him preach for?" Here I was in a difficulty; I did not know what I wanted to go for, and I told him so. "What good will it do for you?" Here I was at another point. "Who put that into your head?" There was another thing; I did not want to get my poor old mother into trouble. But she had always told me to tell the truth. So I answered: "My mother." "Ah," said he, "I thought it was your mother. I suppose she wants to have you spoilt. When will you come back?" "As soon as meeting is over." Well, I went to the meeting, I heard the preacher, but I could not see him. They would not let niggers go into the meeting. I went all round the house; I could hear him, and at last I got in front of the door. I saw him with his hands raised, looking up to heaven, and he said, with emphasis: "Jesus Christ, the Son of God, tasted death for every man; for the high, for the low, for the rich, for the poor, the bond, the free, the negro in his chains, the man in gold and diamonds." His heart was filled with the love of Christ, and by the power of the Spirit of God he preached a universal salvation through Jesus Christ. I stood and heard it. It touched my heart, and I cried out: "I wonder if Jesus Christ died for me." And then I wondered what could have induced Him to die for me. I was then eighteen years old, I had never heard a sermon, nor any conversation whatever, upon religious topics, except what I had heard from my mother, on the responsibility of all to a Supreme Being. This was Heb. ii. 9, the first text of the Bible to which I had ever listened, knowing it to be such. I have never forgotten it, and scarely a day has passed since, in which I have not recalled it, and the sermon that was preached from it.

The divine character of Jesus Christ, His tender love for mankind, His forgiving spirit, His compassion for the outcast and despised, His cruel crucifixion and glorious ascension, were all depicted, and some of the points were dwelt on with great power; great, at least, to me, who then heard of these things for the first time in my life. Again and again did the preacher reiterate the words *"for every man."* These glad tidings, this salvation, were not for the benefit of a select few only. They were for the slave as well as the master, the poor as well as the rich, for the persecuted, the distressed, the heavy-laden, the captive; even for me among the rest, a poor, despised, abused creature, deemed by others fit for nothing but unrequited toil—but mental and bodily degradation. Oh, the blessedness and sweetness of feeling that I was loved! I would have died that moment with joy, and I kept repeating to myself, "The compassionate Saviour about whom I have heard 'loves me,' 'He looks down in compassion from heaven on me,' 'He died to save my soul,' and 'He'll welcome me to the skies.' " I was transported with delicious joy. I seemed to see a glorious being, in a cloud of splendour, smiling down from on high. In sharp contrast with the experience I had felt of the contempt and brutality of my earthly master, I basked, as it were, in the benign smiles of this Heavenly Being. I thought, "He'll be my dear refuge—He'll wipe away all tears from my eyes." "Now I can bear all things; nothing will seem hard after this." I felt sure that if "Massa Riley" only knew Him, he would not live such a coarse, wicked, cruel life. Swallowed up in the beauty of the divine love, I "loved my enemies, and prayed for them that did despitefully use and entreat me."

Revolving the things which I had heard in my mind as I went home, I became so excited that I turned aside from the road into the woods, and prayed to God for light and for aid with an earnestness, which, however unenlightened, was at least sincere and heartfelt; and which the subsequent course of my life has led me to imagine was acceptable to Him who heareth prayer. At all events, I date my conversion, and my awakening to a new life—a consciousness of power and a destiny superior to anything I had before conceived of—from this day, so memorable to me. I used every means and opportunity of inquiry into religious matters; and so deep was my conviction of their superior importance to everything else, so clear my perception of my own faults, and so undoubting my observation of the darkness and sin that surrounded me, that I could not help talking much on these subjects with those about me; and it was not long before I began to pray with them, exhort them, and impart to the poor slaves those little glimmerings of light from another world, which had reached my own eye. In a few years I became quite an esteemed preacher among them, and I believe that, through the grace of God, I was useful to many.

I must return, however, for the present, to the course of my life in secular affairs, the facts of which it is my principal object to relate.

# CHAPTER V

## MAIMED FOR LIFE

Taking Care of My Drunken Master—His Fight with an Overseer—Rescue Him—Am Terribly Beaten by the Overseer—My Master Seeks Redress at Law, but Fails—Sufferings Then and Since—Retain My Post as Superintendent

The difference between the manner in which it was designed that all men should regard one another as children of the same Father, and the manner in which men of different colour actually treated each other, is well exemplified by an incident that happened to me within a year or two from this period; that is, when I was nineteen or twenty years old. My master's habits were such as were common enough among the dissipated planters of the neighborhood; and one of their frequent practices was to assemble on Saturday or Sunday, which were their holidays, and gamble, run horses, or fight game-cocks, discuss politics, and drink whisky and brandy-and-water all day long. Perfectly aware that they would not be able to find their own way home at night, each one ordered his body-servant to come after him and help him home. I was chosen for this confidential duty by my master; and many were the times I have held him on his horse, when he could not hold himself in the saddle, and walked by his side in darkness and mud from the tavern to his house. Quarrels and brawls of the most violent description were frequent consequences of these meetings; and whenever they became especially dangerous, and glasses were thrown, dirks drawn, and pistols fired, it was the duty of the slaves to rush in, and each one drag his master from the fight, and carry him home. To tell the truth, this was a part of my business for which I felt no reluctance. I was young, remarkably athletic and self-relying, and in such affrays I carried it with a high hand, and would elbow my way among the whites,—whom it would have been almost death for me to strike,—seize my master and drag him out, mount him on his horse, or crowd him into his buggy, with the ease with which I would handle a bag of corn. I knew that I was doing for him what he could not do for himself, showing my superiority to others, and acquiring their respect in some degree, at the same time.

On one of these occasions my master got into a quarrel with his brother's overseer, Bryce Litton. All present sided with Litton against him, and soon there was a general row. I was sitting, at the time, out on the front steps of the tavern, and hearing the scuffle, rushed in to look after my charge. My master, a stout man and a terrible bruiser, could generally hold his own in an ordinary general fight, and clear a handsome space around him; but now he was cornered, and a dozen were striking at him with fists, crockery, chairs, and anything that came handy. The moment he saw me, he hallooed, "That's it Sie! pitch in! show me fair play." It was a rough business, and I went in roughly, shoving, tripping, and doing my best for the rescue. With infinite trouble, and many a bruise on my head and shoulders, I at length got him out of the room. He was crazy with drink and rage, and struggled hard with me to get back and renew the fight. But I managed to force him into his waggon, jump in, and drive off.

By ill-luck, in the height of the scuffle, Bryce Litton got a severe fall. Whether the whisky he had drunk, or a chance-shove from me, was the cause, I am unable to say. He, however, attributed it to me, and treasured up his vengeance for the first favourable opportunity. The opportunity soon came.

About a week afterwards, I was sent by my master to a place a few miles distant, on horseback with some letters. I took a short cut through a lane, separated by gates from the high road, and bounded by a fence on each side. This lane passed through a part of the farm owned by my master's brother, and his overseer was in the adjoining field, with three negroes, when I went by. On my return, half an hour afterwards, the overseer was sitting on the fence, but I could see nothing of the black fellows. I rode on, utterly unsuspicious of any trouble; but as I approached, he jumped off the fence, and at the same moment two of the negroes sprang up from under the bushes where they had been concealed, and stood with him immediately in front of me, while the third sprang over the fence just behind me. I was thus enclosed between what I could no longer doubt were hostile forces. The overseer seized my horse's bridle and ordered me to alight, in the usual elegant phraseology addressed by such men to slaves. I asked what I was to alight for. "To take the worst flogging you ever had in your life, you black scoundrel." He added many oaths that I will not repeat. "But what am I to be flogged for, Mr. L.?" I asked. "Not a word," said he, "but 'light at once, and take off your jacket." I saw there was nothing else to be done, and slipped off the horse on the opposite side from him. "Now take off your shirt," cried he; and as I demurred at this he lifted a stick he had in his hand to strike me, but so suddenly and violently that he frightened the horse, which broke away from him and ran home. I was thus left without means of escape to sustain the attacks of four men as well as I might. In avoiding Mr. L.'s blow, I had accidentally got into a corner of the fence where I could not be approached except in front. The overseer called upon the negroes to seize me; but they, knowing something of my physical power, were slow to obey. At length they did their best, and as they brought themselves within my reach I knocked them down successively; and I gave one of them, who tried to trip up my feet, when he was down, a kick with my heavy shoe, which knocked out several teeth, and sent him howling away.

Meanwhile Bryce Litton beat my head with a stick, not heavy enough to knock me down, but it drew blood freely. He shouted all the while, "Won't you give up! won't you give up!" adding oath after oath. Exasperated at my defence, he suddenly seized a heavy fence-rail and rushed at me with rage. The ponderous blow fell; I lifted my arm to ward it off, the bone cracked like a pipe-stem, and I fell headlong to the ground. Repeated blows then rained on my back till both shoulder-blades were broken, and the blood gushed copiously from my mouth. In vain the negroes interposed. "Didn't you see the nigger strike me?" Of course they must say "Yes," although the lying coward had avoided close quarters, and fought with his stick alone. At length, his vengeance satisfied, he desisted, telling me "to remember what it was to strike a white man."

Meanwhile an alarm had been raised at the house by the return of the horse without his rider, and my master started off with a small party to learn what the trouble was. When he first saw me he swore with rage. "You've been fighting, you mean nigger!" I told him Bryce Litton had been beating me, because he said I shoved him the other night at the tavern, when they had a fuss. Seeing how much I was injured, he became still more fearfully mad; and after having me carried home, mounted his horse and rode over to Montgomery Court House to enter a complaint. Little good came of it. Litton swore that when he spoke to me in the lane I "sassed" him, jumped off my horse, attacked him, and would have killed him but for the help of his negroes. Of course no negro's testimony was admitted against a white man, and he was acquitted. My master was obliged to pay all the costs of court; and although he had the satisfaction of calling Litton a liar and scoundrel, and giving him a tremendous bruising, still even this partial compensation was rendered less gratifying by what followed, which was a suit for damages and a heavy fine.

My sufferings after his cruel treatment were intense. Besides my broken arm and the wounds on my head, I could feel and hear the pieces of my shoulder-blades grate against each other with every breath. No physician or surgeon was called to dress my wounds, and I never knew one to be called on Riley's estate on any occasion whatever. "A nigger will get well anyway," was a fixed principle of faith, and facts seemed to justify it. The robust, physical health produced by a life of outdoor labour, made our wounds heal with as little inflammation as they do in the case of cattle. I was attended by my master's sister, Miss Patty, as we called her, the Esculapius of the plantation. She was a powerful, big-boned woman, who flinched at no responsibility, from wrenching out teeth to setting bones. I have seen her go into the house and get a rifle to shoot a furious ox that the negroes were in vain trying to butcher. She splintered my arm and bound up my back as well as she knew how. Alas! it was but cobbler's work. From that day to this I have been unable to raise my hands as high as my head. It was five months before I could work at all, and the first time I tried to plough, a hard knock of the coulter against a stone shattered my shoulder-blades again, and gave me even greater agony than at first. And so I have gone through life maimed and mutilated. Practice in time enabled me to perform many of the farm labours with considerable efficiency; but the free, vigorous play of the muscles of my arm was gone for ever.

I retained my situation as overseer, together with the especial favor of my master, who was pleased with saving the expense of a large salary for a white superintendent, and with the superior crops I was able to raise for him. I will not deny that I used his property more freely than he would have done himself, in supplying his people with better food; but if I cheated him in this way, in small matters, it was unequivocally for his own benefit in more important ones; and I accounted, with the strictest honesty, for every dollar I received in the sale of the property entrusted to me. Gradually the disposal of everything raised on the farm,—the wheat, oats, hay, fruit, butter, and whatever else there might be,—was confided to me, as it was quite evident that I could and did sell for better prices than any one else he could employ, and he was quite incompetent to attend to the business himself. For many years I was his factotum, and supplied him with all his means for all his purposes, whether they were good or bad. I had no reason to think highly of his moral character; but it was my duty to be faithful to him in the position in which he placed me; and I can boldly declare, before God and man, that I was so. I forgave him the causeless blows and injuries he had inflicted on me in my childhood and youth, and was proud of the favour he now showed me, and of the character and reputation I had earned by strenuous and persevering efforts.

# CHAPTER VI

## A RESPONSIBLE JOURNEY

My Marriage—Marriage of My Master—His Ruin—Comes to Me for Aid—A Great Enterprise
Undertaken—Long and Successful Journey—Incidents by the Way—Struggle Between
Inclination and Duty—Duty Triumphant

When I was about twenty-two years of age, I married a very efficient, and, for a slave, a very well-taught girl, belonging to a neighbouring family reputed to be pious and kind. I first met her at the religious meetings which I attended. She has borne me twelve children, seven of whom still survive and promise to be the comfort of my declining years.

For a considerable period, my occupations were to superintend the farming operations, and to sell the produce in the neighbouring markets of Washington and Georgetown. Many respectable people, yet living there, may possibly have some recollection of "Siah," or "Sie," (as they used to call me,) as their market-man; but if they have forgotten me, I remember them with an honest satisfaction.

At length my master, at the age of forty-five, married a young woman of eighteen, who had some little property, and more thrift. Her economy was remarkable, and she added no comfort to the establishment. She had a younger brother, Francis, to whom Riley was appointed guardian, and who used to complain of the meanness of the provision made for the household; he would often come to me, with tears in his eyes, to tell me he could not get enough to eat. I made him my friend for life, by sympathising with him and satisfying his appetite, by sharing with him the food I took care to provide for my own family. He is still living, and, I understand, one of the wealthiest men in Washington city.

*32*

After a time, however, continual dissipation was more than a match for domestic saving. My master fell into difficulty, and from difficulty into a lawsuit with a brother-in-law, who charged him with dishonesty in the management of property confided to him in trust. The lawsuit was protracted enough to cause his ruin of itself.

Harsh and tyrannical as my master had been, I really pitied him in his present distress. At times he was dreadfully dejected, at others, crazy with drink and rage. Day after day would he ride over to Montgomery Court House about his business, and every day his affairs grew more desperate. He would come into my cabin to tell me how things were going, but spent the time chiefly in lamenting his misfortunes and cursing his brother-in-law. I tried to comfort him as best I could. He had confidence in my fidelity and judgment, and partly through pride, partly through that divine spirit of love I had learned to worship in Jesus, I entered with interest into all his perplexities. The poor, drinking, furious, shiftless, moaning creature was utterly incapable of managing his affairs.

One night in the month of January, long after I had fallen asleep, he came into my cabin and waked me up. I thought it strange, but for a time he said nothing, and sat moodily warming himself at the fire. Then he began to groan and wring his hands. "Sick, massa?" said I. He made no reply, but kept on moaning. "Can't I help you in any way, massa?" I spoke tenderly, for my heart was full of compassion at his wretched appearance. At last, collecting himself, he cried, "Oh, Sie! I'm ruined, ruined, ruined!" "How so, massa?" "They've got judgment against me, and in less than two weeks every nigger I've got will be put up and sold." Then he burst into a storm of curses at his brother-in-law. I sat silent, powerless to utter a word. Pity for him and terror at the anticipation of my own family's future fate filled my heart. "And now, Sie," he continued, "there's only one way I can save anything. You can do it; won't you, won't you?" In his distress he rose and actually threw his arms around me. Misery had levelled all distinctions. "If I can do it, massa, I will. What is it?" Without replying he went on, "Won't you, won't you? I raised you Sie; I made you overseer; I know I have abused you, Sie, but I didn't mean it." Still he avoided telling me what he wanted. "Promise me you'll do it, boy." He seemed resolutely bent on having my promise first, well knowing from past experience, that what I agreed to do I spared no pains to accomplish. Solicited in this way, with urgency and tears, by the man whom I had so zealously served for over thirty years, and who now seemed absolutely dependent upon his slave; impelled, too, by the fear which he skilfully awakened, that the sheriff would seize every one who belonged to him, and that all would be separated, or perhaps sold to go to Georgia, or Louisiana—an object of perpetual dread to the slave of the more northern States—I consented, and promised faithfully to do all I could to save him from the fate impending over him.

At last the proposition came. "I want you to run away, Sie, to my brother Amos in Kentucky, and take all the servants with you." I could not have been more startled had he asked me to go to the moon. "Kentucky, massa? Kentucky? I don't know the way." "Oh, it's easy enough for a smart fellow like you to find it; I'll give you a pass and tell you just what to do." Perceiving that I hesitated, he endeavoured to frighten me by again referring to the terrors of being sold and taken to Georgia.

For two or three hours he continued to urge the undertaking, appealing to my pride, my sympathies, and my fears, and at last, appalling as it seemed, I told him I would do my best. There were eighteen negroes, besides my wife, two children, and myself to transport nearly a thousand miles, through a country about which I knew nothing, and in mid-winter, for it was the month of February, 1825. My master proposed to follow me in a few months, and establish himself in Kentucky,

My mind once made up, I set earnestly about the needful preparations. They were few and easily made. A one-horse waggon, well-stocked with oats, meal, and bacon, for our own and the horse's support, was soon made ready. My pride was aroused in view of the importance of my responsiblity, and heart and soul I became identified with my master's project of running off his negroes. The second night after the scheme was formed, we were under way. Fortunately for the success of the undertaking, these people had long been under my direction and were devotedly attached to me in return for the many alleviations I had afforded to their miserable condition, the comforts I had procured them, and the consideration I had always manifested for them. Under these circumstances, no difficulty arose from want of submission to my authority. The dread of being separated, and sold away down south, should they remain on the old estate, united them as one man, and kept them patient and alert.

We started from home about eleven o'clock at night, and till the following noon made no permanent halt. The men trudged on foot, the children were put into the waggon, and now and then my wife rode for a while. On we went through Alexandria, Culpepper, Fauquier, Harper's Ferry, Cumberland, over the mountains on the National Turnpike to Wheeling. In all the taverns along the road there were regular places for the droves of negroes who were continually passing through the country under the care of overseers. In these we lodged, and our lodging constituted our only expense, for our food we carried with us. To all who asked questions I showed my master's pass, authorising me to conduct his negroes to Kentucky, and often was the encomium of "smart nigger" bestowed on me, to my immense gratification.

At the place where we stopped for the night, we often met negro-drivers with their droves, who were almost uniformly kept chained to prevent them from running away. The inquiry was often propounded to me by the drivers, "Whose niggers are those?" On being informed, the next inquiry usually was, "Where are they going?" "To Kentucky." "Who drives them?" "Well, I have charge of them," was my reply. "What a smart nigger!" was the usual exclamation, with an oath. "Will your master sell you? Come in and stop with us." In this way I was often invited to pass the evening with them in the bar-room; their negroes, in the meantime, lying chained in the pen, while mine were scattered around at liberty.

Arriving at Wheeling, in pursuance of the plan laid down by my master, I sold the horse and waggon, and purchased a large boat, called in that region, a yawl. Our mode of locomotion was now decidedly more agreeable than tramping along day after day at the rate we had kept up ever since leaving home. Very little labour at the oars was necessary. The tide floated us steadily along, and we had ample leisure to sleep and recruit our strength.

A New and unexpected trouble now assailed me. On passing along the Ohio shore, we were repeatedly told by persons conversing with us that we were no longer slaves but free men, if we chose to be so. At Cincinnati, especially, crowds of coloured people gathered round us, and insisted on our remaining with them. They told us we were fools to think of going on and surrendering ourselves up to a new owner; that now we could be our own masters, and put ourselves out of all reach of pursuit. I saw that the people under me were getting much excited. Divided counsels and signs of insubordination began to manifest themselves. I began, too, to feel my own resolution giving way. Freedom had ever been an object of my ambition, though no other means of obtaining it had occurred to me but purchasing myself. I had never dreamed of running away. I had a sentiment of honour on the subject. The duties of the slave to his master as appointed over him in the Lord, I had ever heard urged by ministers and religious men. Entrancing as the ideas were, that the coast was clear for a run for freedom, that I might liberate my companions, might carry off my wife and children, and some day own a house and land, and be no longer despised and abused, still my notions of right were against it. I had promised my master to take his property to Kentucky, and deposit it with his brother Amos. Pride, too, came in to confirm me. I had undertaken a great thing; my vanity had been flattered all along the road by hearing myself praised; I thought it would be a feather in my cap to carry it through thoroughly, and had often painted the scene in my imagination of the final surrender of my charge to Master Amos, and the immense admiration and respect with which he would regard me.

Under the influence of these impressions, and seeing that the allurements of the crowd were producing a manifest effect, I sternly assumed the captain, and ordered the boat to be pushed off into the stream. A shower of curses followed me from the shore; but the negroes under me, accustomed to obey, and, alas! too degraded and ignorant of the advantages of liberty to know what they were forfeiting, offered no resistance to my command.

Often since that day has my soul been pierced with bitter anguish, at the thought of having been thus instrumental in consigning to the infernal bondage of slavery, so many of my fellow-beings. I have wrestled in prayer with God for forgiveness. Having experienced myself the sweetness of liberty, and knowing too well the after-misery of a number of these slaves, my infatuation has often seemed to me to have been the unpardonable sin. But I console myself with the thought that I acted according to my best light, though the light that was in me was darkness. Those were my days of ignorance. I knew not then the glory of free manhood, or that the title-deed of the slave-owner is robbery and outrage.

What advantages I may have personally lost by thus throwing away an opportunity of obtaining freedom! But the perception of my own strength of character, the feeling of integrity, the sentiment of high honour, I thus gained by obedience to what I believed right, are advantages which I prize. He that is faithful over a little, will be faithful over much. Before God I tried to do my best, and the error of judgment lies at the door of the degrading system under which I had been nurtured.

# CHAPTER VII

## A NEW HOME

Become a Methodist Preacher—My Poor Companions Sold—My Agony—Sent for Again—
Interview with a Kind Methodist Preacher—Visit Free Soil and Begin My Struggle for
Freedom

I arrived at Davis county, Kentucky, about the middle of April,
1825, and delivered myself and my companions to my owner's
brother, Mr. Amos Riley, who had a large plantation with from
eighty to one hundred negroes. His house was situated about five
miles south of the Ohio River, and fifteen miles above the Yellow
Banks, on Big Blackfords Creek. There I remained three years, and
was employed meantime on the farm, of which I had the general
management, in consequence of the recommendation for ability and
honesty which I brought with me from Maryland. The situation was,
in many respects, more comfortable than the one I had left. The
farm was larger and more fertile, and there was a greater abundance
of food, which is, of course, one of the principal sources of the
comfort of a slave, debarred as he is from so many enjoyments which
other men can obtain. Sufficiency of food is an important item in
any man's account of life; it is tenfold more so in that of the slave,
whose appetite is always stimulated by his arduous labour, and
whose mind is little occupied by thought on subjects of deeper
interest. My post of superintendent gave me some advantages, of
which I did not fail to avail myself, particularly with regard to those
religious privileges, which, since I first heard of Christ and Christianity, had greatly occupied my mind. In Kentucky, the opportunities
of attending the preaching of whites, as well as of blacks, were more
numerous; and partly by attending them, and the camp-meetings
which occurred from time to time, and partly from studying
carefully my own heart, and observing the developments of character

*38*

around me, in all the stations of life which I could watch, I became better acquainted with those religious feelings which are deeply implanted in the breast of every human being, and learned by practice how best to arouse them, and keep them excited, how to stir up the callous and indifferent, and, in general, to produce some good religious impressions on the ignorant and thoughtless community by which I was surrounded.

No great amount of theological knowledge is requisite for the purpose. If it had been, it is manifest enough that preaching never could have been my vocation; but I am persuaded that, speaking from the fulness of a heart deeply impressed with its own sinfulness and imperfection, and with the mercy of God, in Christ Jesus, my humble ministrations have not been entirely useless to those who have had less opportunity than myself to reflect upon these all-important subjects. It is certain that I could not refrain from the endeavour to do what I saw others doing in this field; and I laboured at once to improve myself and those about me in the cultivation of the harvests which ripen only in eternity. I cannot but derive some satisfaction, too, from the proofs I have had that my services have been acceptable to those to whom they have been rendered. In the course of three years, from 1825 to 1828, I availed myself of all the opportunities of improvement which occurred, and was admitted as a preacher by a Quarterly Conference of the Methodist Episcopal Church.

In the spring of the year 1828, news arrived from my master that he was unable to induce his wife to accompany him to Kentucky, and that he must therefore remain where he was. He sent out an agent to sell all his slaves, except me and my family, and to carry back the proceeds to him. And now another of those heartrending scenes was to be witnessed, which had impressed itself so deeply on my childish soul. Husbands and wives, parents and children, were to be separated for ever. Affections, which are as strong in the African as in the European, were to be cruelly disregarded; and the iron selfishness generated by the hateful "institution," was to be exhibited in its most odious and naked deformity. I was exempted from a personal share in the dreadful calamity; but I could not see without the deepest grief, the agony of my associates. It was like that my own mother had once manifested, when I was separated from her for a time. I could not refrain from feeling the bitterest hatred of the system, and of those who sustained it. What else, indeed, could be the feeling of a slave, liable at every moment of his life to these frightful and unnecessary calamities, which might be caused by the caprice, or the supposed necessities of the slaveholders, and inflicted upon him without sympathy or redress, under the sanction of the laws which upheld the institution?

As I surveyed this scene, and listened to the groans and outcries of my afflicted companions, my eyes were opened, and I lamented that I had prevented them from availing themselves of the opportunity for acquiring freedom which offered itself at Cincinnati. I had only thought of being faithful to my master's interests, and nothing of the welfare of the slaves. Oh! what would I not have given to have had the chance offered once more! But now, through me, were they doomed to wear out life miserably in the hot and pestilential climate of the far south. Death would have been welcome to me in my agony. From that hour I saw through, hated, and cursed the whole system of slavery. One absorbing purpose occupied my soul—to gain freedom, self-assertion, and deliverance from the cruel caprices and fortunes of dissolute tyrants. Once to get away, with my wife and children, to some spot where I could feel that they were indeed *mine*—where no grasping master could stand between me and them, as arbiter of their destiny—was a heaven yearned after with insatiable longing. For it I stood ready to pray, toil, dissemble, plot like a fox, and fight like a tiger. All the noble instincts of my soul, and all the ferocious passions of my animal nature, were aroused and quickened into vigorous action.

The object of my old master Riley in directing that I and my family should be exempted from the sale, was a desire on his part to get me back to Maryland, and employ me in his own service. His best farms had been taken away from him, and but a few tracts of poor land remained, which he cultivated with hired labour after I took his slaves, and month by month he grew poorer and more desperate. He had written to his brother Amos to give me a pass and let me travel back; but this his brother was reluctant to do, as I saved him the expense of an overseer, and he moreover was aware that no legal steps could be taken to force him to comply. I knew of all this, but dared not seem anxious to return, for fear of exciting suspicion.

In the course of the summer of 1828, a Methodist preacher, a most excellent white man, visited our neighbourhood, and I became acquainted with him. He was soon interested in me, and visited me frequently, and one day talked to me in a confidential manner about my position. He said, "You ought to be free. You have too much capacity to be confined to the limited and comparatively useless sphere of a slave, and though it must not be known that I have spoken to you on this subject, yet, if you will obtain Mr. Amos's consent to go to see your old master in Maryland, I will try and put you in a way by which I think you may succeed in buying yourself." He said this to me more than once; and as it was in harmony with all my aspirations and wishes, was flattering to my self-esteem, and gratified my impatience to bring matters to a direct issue, I now resolved to make the attempt to get the necessary leave. The autumn work was over, I was no longer needed in the fields, and a better chance would never offer itself. Still I dreaded to make the proposal. So much hung on it, such fond hopes were bound up with it, that I trembled for the result.

I opened the subject one Sunday morning while shaving Mr. Amos, and adroitly managed, by bringing the shaving brush close to his mouth whenever he was disposed to interrupt me, to "get a good say" first. Of course, I made no allusion to my plan of buying myself, but urged my request on the sole ground of a desire to see my old master. To my surprise, he made little objection. I had been faithful to him, and gained, in his rude way of showing it, his regard. Long before spring I would be back again. He even told me I had earned such a privilege.

The certificate he gave me, allowed me to pass and repass between Kentucky and Maryland as servant of Amos Riley. Furnished with this, and with a letter of recommendation from my Methodist friend to a brother preacher in Cincinnati, I started about the middle of September, 1828, for the east.

A new era in my history now opened upon me. A letter I carried with me to a kind-hearted man in Cincinnati, procured me a number of invaluable friends, who entered heart and soul into my plans. They procured me an opportunity to preach in two or three of the pulpits of the city, and I made my appeal with that eloquence which spontaneously breaks forth from a breast all alive and fanned into a glow by an inspiring project. Contact with those who were free themselves, and a proud sense of exultation in taking my destiny into my own hands, gave me the sacred "gift of tongues." I was pleading an issue of life and death, of heaven and hell, and such as heard me felt this in their hearts. In three or four days I left the city with no less a sum than one hundred and sixty dollars in my pockets, and with a soul jubilant with thanksgiving, and high in hope, directed my steps towards Chillicothe, to attend the session of the Ohio Conference of the Methodist Episcopal Church. My kind friend accompanied me, and, by his influence and exertions, still further success attended me.

By his advice, I then purchased a decent suit of clothes and an excellent horse, and travelled from town to town, preaching as I went. Everywhere I met with kindness. The contrast between the respect with which I was treated and the ordinary abuse of plantation life, gratified me in the extreme, as it must any one who has within him one spark of personal dignity as a man. The sweet enjoyment of sympathy, moreover, and the hearty "God speed you, brother!" which accompanied every dollar I received, were to my long-starved heart a celestial repast, and angels' food. Liberty was a glorious hope in my mind; not as an escape from toil, for I rejoiced in toil when my heart was in it, but as the avenue to a sense of self-respect, to ennobling occupation, and to association with superior minds. Still, dear as was the thought of liberty, I still clung to my determination to gain it in one way only—by purchase. The cup of my affliction was not yet full enough to lead me to disregard all terms with my master.

# CHAPTER VIII

## RETURN TO MARYLAND

Reception from My Old Master—A Slave Again—Appeal to an Old Friend—Buy My Freedom—Cheated and Betrayed—Back to Kentucky, and a Slave Again

Before I left Ohio and set my face towards Montgomery county, I was master of two hundred and seventy-five dollars, besides my horse and clothes. Proud of my success, I enjoyed the thought of showing myself once more in the place where I had been known simply as "Riley's head-nigger;" and it was with no little satisfaction that about Christmas I rode up to the old house.

My master gave me a boisterous reception, and expressed great delight at seeing me. "What have you been doing, Sie? you've turned into a regular black gentleman." My horse and dress sorely puzzled him, and I soon saw they irritated him. The clothes I wore were certainly better than his. Very soon the workings of that tyrannical hate with which the coarse and brutal, who have no inherent superiority, ever regard the least sign of equality in their dependents, were visible in his manner. His face seemed to say, "I'll take the gentleman out of you pretty soon." I gave him an account of my preaching which was consistent with the truth, and explained my appearance, but did not betray to him my principal purpose. He soon asked to see my pass, and when he found it authorised me to return to Kentucky, handed it to his wife, and desired her to put it into his desk. The manoeuvre was cool and startling. I heard the old prison-gate clang, and the bolt shoot into the socket once more. But I said nothing and resolved to manoeuvre also.

After putting my horse in the stable I retired to the kitchen, where my master told me I was to sleep for the night. Oh, how different from my accommodations in the free States, for the last three months, was that crowded room, with its earth floor, its filth and stench! I looked around me with a sensation of disgust. The negroes present were strangers to me. I found my mother had died during my absence, and every tie which had ever connected me with the place was broken. Full of gloomy reflections at my loneliness, and the poverty-stricken aspect of the whole farm, I sat down, and while my companions were snoring in unconsciousness, I kept awake, thinking how I could escape from this accursed spot. I knew of but one friend to whom I could appeal—"Master Frank," the brother of Riley's wife, before mentioned, who was now of age, and had established himself in business in Washington. I thought he would take an interest in me, for I had done much to lighten his sorrows when he was an abused and harshly-treated boy in the house. To him I resolved to go, and as soon as I thought it time to start, I saddled my horse and rode up to the house. It was early in the morning, and my master had already gone to the tavern on his usual business, when Mrs. Riley came out to look at my horse and equipments. "Where are you going, 'Siah?" was the natural question. I replied, "I am going to Washington, mistress, to see Mr. Frank, and I must take my pass with me, if you please." "Oh, everybody knows you here; you won't need your pass." "But I can't go to Washington without it. I may be met by some surly stranger, who will stop me and plague me, if he can't do anything worse." "Well, I'll get it for you," she answered; and glad I was to see her return with it in her hand, and to have her give it to me, while she little imagined its importance to my plan.

My reception by Master Frank was all I expected, as kind and hearty as possible. He was delighted at my appearance, and I immediately told him all my plans and hopes. He entered cordially into them, and expressed a strong sympathy for me. I found that he thoroughly detested Riley, whom he charged with having defrauded him of a large proportion of his property which he had held as guardian, though, as he was not at warfare with him, he readily agreed to negotiate for my freedom, and bring him to the most favourable terms. Accordingly, in a few days he rode over to the house, and had a long conversation with him on the subject of my emancipation. He disclosed to him the facts that I had got some money and *my pass,* and urged that I was a smart fellow, who was bent upon getting his freedom, and had served the family faithfully for many years; that I had really paid for myself a hundred times over, in the increased amount of produce I had raised by my skill and influence; and that if he did not take care, and accept a fair offer when I made it to him, he would find some day that I had the means to do without his help, and that he would see neither me nor my money; that with my horse and my pass I was pretty independent of him already, and he had better make up his mind to do what was really inevitable, and do it with a good grace. By such arguments as these, Mr. Frank not only induced him to think of the thing, but before long brought him to an actual bargain, by which he agreed to give me my manumission-papers for four hundred and fifty dollars, of which three hundred and fifty dollars were to be in cash, and the remainder in my note. My money and my horse enabled me to pay the cash at once, and thus my great hope seemed in a fair way of being realised.

Some time was spent in the negotiation of this affair, and it was not until the 9th of March, 1829, that I received my manumission-papers in due form of law. I prepared to start at once on my return to Kentucky; and on the 10th, as I was getting ready, in the morning, for my journey, my master accosted me in the most friendly manner, and entered into conversation with me about my plans. He asked me what I was going to do with my certificate of freedom; whether I was going to show it, if questioned on the road. I told him, "Yes." "You'll be a fool if you do," he rejoined. "Some slave-trader will get hold of it, and tear it up, and you'll be thrown into prison, sold for your jail-fees, and be in his possession before any of your friends can help you. Don't show it at all. Your pass is enough. Let me enclose your papers for you under cover to my brother. Nobody will dare to break a seal, for that is a state-prison matter; and when you arrive in Kentucky you will have it with you all safe and sound."

For this friendly advice, as I thought it, I felt extremely grateful. Secure in my happiness, I cherished no suspicion of others. I accordingly permitted him to enclose my precious papers in an envelope composed of several wrappers, and after he had sealed it with three seals, and directed it to his brother in Davies county, Kentucky, he gave it to me, and I carefully stowed it in my carpet-bag. Leaving immediately for Wheeling, to which place I was obliged to travel on foot, I there took boat, and in due time reached my destination. I was arrested repeatedly on the way; but by insisting always on being carried before a magistrate, I succeeded in escaping all serious impediments by means of my pass, which was quite regular, and could not be set aside by any responsible authority.

The boat which took me down from Louisville, landed me about dark, and my walk of five miles brought me to the plantation at bedtime. I went directly to my own cabin, and found my wife and little ones well. Of ourse, we had enough to communicate to each other. I soon found that I had something to learn as well as to tell. Letters had reached the "great house,"—as the master's was always called,—long before I arrived, telling them what I had been doing. The children of the family had eagerly communicated the good news to my wife—how I had been preaching, and raising money, and making a bargain for my freedom. It was not long before Charlotte began to question me, with much excitement, how I had raised the money. She evidently thought I had stolen it. Her opinion of my powers as a preacher was not exalted enough to permit her to believe I had gained it as I really did. I contrived, however, to quiet her fears on this score. "But how are you going to raise enough to pay the remainder of the thousand dollars?" "What thousand dollars?" "The thousand dollars you are to give for your freedom." Oh, how those words smote me! At once I suspected treachery. Again and again I questioned her as to what she had heard. She persisted in repeating the same story as the substance of my master's letters. Master Amos said I had paid three hundred and fifty dollars down, and when I had made up six hundred and fifty more I was to have my free papers. I now began to perceive the trick that had been played upon me, and to see the management by which Riley had contrived that the only evidence of my freedom should be kept from every eye but that of his brother Amos, who was requested to retain it until I had made up the balance I was reported to have agreed to pay. Indignation is a faint word to express my deep sense of such villainy. I was alternately beside myself with rage, and paralysed with despair. My dream of bliss was over. What could I do to set myself right? The only witness to the truth, Master Frank, was a thousand miles away. I could neither write to him, nor get any one else to write. Every man about me who could write was a slaveholder. I dared not go before a magistrate with my papers, for fear I should be seized and sold down the river before anything could be done. I felt that every white man's hand was against me. "My God! my God! why hast Thou forsaken me?" was my bitter cry. One thing only seemed clear. My papers must never be surrendered to Master Amos. I told my wife I had not seen them since I left Louisville. They might be in my bag, or they might be lost. At all events I did not wish to look myself. If she found them there, and hid them away, out of my knowledge, it would be the best disposition to make of them.

The next morning, at the blowing of the horn, I went out to find Master Amos. I found him sitting on a stile, and as I drew near enough for him to recognise me, he shouted out a hearty welcome in his usual style. "Why, halloa, Sie! is that you? Got back, eh! I'm glad to see you! why, you're a regular black gentleman!" And he surveyed my dress with an appreciative grin. "Well, Boy, How's your master? Isaac says you want to be free. Want to be free, eh! I think your master treats you pretty hard, though. Six hundred and fifty dollars don't come so easy in old Kentuck. How does he ever expect you to raise all that? It's too much, boy, it's too much." In the conversation that followed I found my wife was right. Riley had no idea of letting me off, and supposed I could never raise the six hundred and fifty dollars if his brother obtained possession of me.

Master Amos soon asked me if I had not a paper for him. I told him I had had one, but the last I saw of it was at Louisville, and now it was not in my bag, and I did not know what had become of it. He sent me back to the landing to see if it had been dropped on the way. Of course I did not find it. He made, however, little stir about it, for he had intentions of his own to keep me working for him, and regarded the whole as a trick of his brother's to get money out of me. All he said about the loss was, "Well, boy, bad luck happens to everybody, sometimes."

All this was very smooth and pleasant to a man who was in a frenzy of grief at the base and apparently irremediable trick that had been played upon him. I had supposed that I should soon be free to start out and gain the hundred dollars which would discharge my

obligation to my master. But I perceived that I was to begin again
with my old labours. It was useless to give expression to my feelings,
and I went about my work with as quiet a mind as I could, resolved
to trust in God, and never despair.

# CHAPTER IX

## TAKEN SOUTH, AWAY FROM WIFE AND CHILDREN

Start for New Orleans—Study Navigation on the Mississippi—The Captain Struck Blind—
Find Some of My Old Companions—The Lower Depths

Things went on in this way about a year. From time to time Master
Amos joked me about the six hundred and fifty dollars, and said his
brother kept writing to know why I did not send something. It was
"diamond cut diamond" with the two brothers. Mr. Amos had no
desire to play into the hands of Mr. Isaac. He was glad enough to
secure my services to take care of his stock and his people.

One day my master suddenly informed me that his son Amos, a
young man about twenty-one years of age, was going down the river
to New Orleans, with a flat-boat loaded with produce from the farm,
and that I was to go with him. He was to start the next day, and I
was to accompany him and help him dispose of his cargo to the best
advantage.

This intimation was enough. Though it was not distinctly stated,
yet I well knew what was intended, and my heart sunk within me at
the prospect of this fatal blight to all my long-cherished hopes. There
was no alternative but death itself; still I thought that there was hope
as long as there was life, and I would not despair even yet. The
expectation of my fate, however, produced the degree of misery
nearest to that of despair, and it is in vain for me to attempt to
describe the wretchedness I experienced as I made ready to go on
board the flat-boat. I had little preparation to make, to be sure; but
there was one thing that seemed to me important. I asked my wife to
sew my manumission-paper securely in a piece of cloth, and to sew
that again round my person. I thought that its possession might be
the means of saving me yet, and I would not neglect anything that

49

offered the smallest chance of escape from the frightful servitude
with which I was threatened.

The immediate cause of this movement on the part of Master Amos
I never fully understood. It grew out of a frequent exchange of
letters, which had been kept up between him and his brother in
Maryland. Whether as a compromise between their rival claims it was
agreed to sell me and divide the proceeds, or that Master Amos, in
fear of my running away, had resolved to turn me into riches without
wings, for his own profit, I never knew. The fact of his intention,
however, was clear enough; and God knows it was a fearful blow.

My wife and children accompanied me to the landing, where I bade
them an adieu which might be for life, and then stepped into the
boat, manned by three white men, who had been hired for the trip.
Mr. Amos and myself were the only other persons on board. The
load consisted of beef-cattle, pigs, poultry, corn, whisky, and other
articles which were to be sold as we dropped down the river,
wherever they could be disposed of to the greatest advantage. It was
a common trading-voyage to New Orleans, the interest of which
consisted not in the incidents that occurred, not in storms,
shipwreck, or external disaster of any sort; but in the storm of
passions contending within me, and the imminent risk of the
shipwreck of my soul, which was impending over me nearly the
whole period of the voyage. One circumstance, only, I will mention,
illustrating, as other events in my life have often done, the counsel of
the Saviour, "He that will be chief among you, let him be your
servant."

We were all bound to take our turn at the helm, sometimes under
direction of the captain, and sometimes on our own responsibility, as
he could not be always awake. In the daytime there was less
difficulty than at night, when it required some one who knew how to
avoid sandbars and snags in the river; the captain was the only person
on board who had this knowledge. But whether by day or by night,
as I was the only negro in the boat, I was compelled to stand at least
three turns at the helm to any other person's one; so that, from being
much with the captain, and frequently thrown upon my own
exertions, I learned the art of steering and managing the boat far
better than the rest. I watched the manoeuvres necessary to shoot by
a "sawyer," to land on a bank, avoid a snag, or a steamboat, in the

rapid current of the Mississippi, till I could do it as well as the captain. After a while, he was attacked by a disease of the eyes; they became very much inflamed and swollen. He was soon rendered totally blind, and unable to perform his share of duty. I was the person who could best take his place, and I was in fact master of the boat from that time till our arrival at New Orleans.

After the captain became blind, we were obliged to lie by at night, as none of the rest of us had been down the river before; and it was necessary to keep watch all night, to prevent depredations by the negroes on shore, who used frequently to attack such boats as ours, for the sake of the provisions on board.

On our way down the river we stopped at Vicksburg, and I got permission to visit a plantation a few miles from the town, where some of my old companions whom I had brought from Kentucky were living. It was the saddest visit I ever made. Four years in an unhealthy climate and under a hard master had done the ordinary work of twenty. Their cheeks were literally caved in with starvation and disease. They described their daily life, which was to toil half-naked in malarious marshes, under a burning, maddening sun, exposed to poison of mosquitoes and black gnats, and they said they looked forward to death as their only deliverance. Some of them fairly cried at seeing me there, and at the thought of the fate which they felt awaited me. Their worst fears of being sold down South had been more than realised. I went away sick at heart, and to this day the remembrance of that wretched group haunts me.

# CHAPTER X

## A TERRIBLE TEMPTATION

Sigh for Death—A Murder in My Heart—The Axe Raised—Conscience Speaks and I Am Saved—God be Praised!

All outward nature seemed to feed my gloomy thoughts. I know not what most men see in voyaging down the Mississippi. If gay and hopeful, probably much of beauty and interest. If eager merchants, probably a golden river, freighted with the wealth of nations. I saw nothing but portents of woe and despair. Wretched slave-pens; a smell of stagnant waters; half-putrid carcases of horses or oxen floating along, covered with turkey-buzzards and swarms of green flies,—these are the images with which memory crowds my mind. My faith in God utterly gave way. I could no longer pray or trust. I thought He had abandoned me and cast me off for ever. I looked not to Him for help. I saw only the foul miasmas, the emaciated frames of my negro companions; and in them saw the sure, swift, loving intervention of the one unfailing friend of the wretched,—death! Yes; death and the grave! "There the wicked cease from troubling, and the weary are at rest. There the prisoners rest together; they hear not the voice of the oppressor." Two years of this would kill me. I dwelt on the thought with melancholy yet sweet satisfaction. Two years! and then I should be free. Free! ever my cherished hope, though not as I had thought it would come.

As I paced backwards and forwards on the deck, during my watch, I revolved in my mind many a painful and passionate thought. After all that I had done for Isaac and Amos Riley, after all the regard they had professed for me, such a return as this for my services, such as evidence of their utter disregard of my claims upon them, and the

*52*

intense selfishness with which they were ready to sacrifice me, at any moment, to their supposed interest, turned my blood to gall, and changed me from a lively, and, I will say, a pleasant-tempered fellow, into a savage, morose, dangerous slave. I was going not at all as a lamb to the slaughter; but I felt myself becoming more ferocious every day; and as we approached the place where this iniquity was to be consummated, I became more and more agitated with an almost uncontrollable fury. I said to myself, "If this is to be my lot, I cannot survive it long. I am not so young as those whose wretched condition I have but just seen, and if it has brought them to such a condition, it will soon kill me. I am to be taken to a place and a condition where my life is to be shortened, as well as made more wretched. Why should I not prevent this wrong if I can, by shortening the lives of those who intend to accomplish such injustice? I can do the last easily enough. They have no suspicion of me, and they are at this moment under my control, and in my power. There are many ways in which I can dispatch them and escape; and I feel that I should be justified in availing myself of the first good opportunity." These thoughts did not flit across my mind's eye and then disappear, but they fashioned themselves into shapes which grew larger and seemed firmer every time they presented themselves; at length my mind was made up to convert the phantom-shadows into a positive reality.

I resolved to kill my four companions, take what money there was in the boat, scuttle the craft, and escape to the north. It was a poor plan, maybe, and would very likely have failed; but it was as well contrived, under the circumstances, as the plans of murderers usually are. Blinded by passion, and stung to madness as I was, I could not see any difficulty about it. One dark, rainy night, within a few days' sail of New Orleans, my hour seemed to have come. I was alone on the deck, Master Amos and the hands were all asleep below, and I crept down noiselessly, got hold of an axe, entered the cabin, and looking by the aid of the dim light there for my victims, my eyes fell upon Master Amos, who was nearest to me, my hand slid along the axe-handle, I raised it to strike the fatal blow,—when suddenly the thought came to me, "What! commit *murder!* and you a Christian?" I had not called it murder before, but self-defence, to prevent others from murdering me. I thought it was justifiable, and even praiseworthy. All at once the truth burst upon me that it was a crime. I was going to kill a young man who had done nothing to injure me, but was only obeying the commands of his father. I was about to lose the fruit of all my efforts at self-improvement, the character I had acquired, and the peace of mind that had never deserted me. All this came upon me with a distinctness which almost made me think I heard it whispered in my ear; and I believe I even turned my head to listen. I shrunk back, laid down the axe, and thanked God, as I have done every day since, that I did not commit that murder.

My feelings were still agitated, but they were changed. I was filled with shame and remorse for the design I had entertained, and fearing that my companions would detect it in my face, or that a careless word would betray my guilty thoughts, I remained on deck all night, instead of rousing one of the men to relieve the watch, and nothing brought composure to my mind but the solemn resolution I then made, to resign myself to the will of God, and take with thankfulness, if I could, but with submission, at all events, whatever He might decide should be my lot. I reflected that if my life were reduced to a brief term, I should have less to suffer; that it was better to die with a Christian's hope, and a quiet conscience, than to live with the incessant recollection of a crime that would destroy the value of life, and under the weight of a secret that would crush out the satisfaction that might be expected from freedom and every other blessing.

It was long before I recovered my self-control and serenity. Yet I believe that no one but those to whom I have told the story myself, ever suspected me of having entertained such thoughts for a moment.

# CHAPTER XI

## PROVIDENTIAL DELIVERANCE

Offered for Sale—Examined by Purchasers—Plead with My Young Master in Vain—Man's Extremity, God's Opportunity—Good for Evil—Return North—My Increased Value—Resolve to Be a Slave No Longer

In a few days after this trying crisis in my life, we arrived at New Orleans. The little that remained of our cargo was soon sold, the men were discharged, and nothing was left but to dispose of me, and break up the boat, and then Master Amos intended to take passage on a steamboat, and go home. There was no longer any disguise about the disposition which was to be made of me. Master Amos acknowledged that such were his instructions, and he set about fulfilling them. Several planters came to the boat to look at me; I was sent on some hasty errand that they might see how I could run; my points were canvassed as those of a horse would have been; and, doubtless, some account of my various faculties entered into the discussion of the bargain, that my value as a domestic animal might be enhanced. Master Amos had talked, with apparent kindness, about getting me a good master who would employ me as a coachman, or as a house-servant; but as time passed on I could discern no particular effort of the kind.

In our intervals of leisure I tried every possible means to move his heart. With tears and groans I besought him not to sell me away from my wife and children. I dwelt on my past services to his father, and called to his remembrance a thousand things I had done for him personally. I told him about the wretched condition of the slaves I had seen near Vicksburg. Sometimes he would shed tears himself, and say he was sorry for me. But still I saw his purpose was unchanged. He now kept out of my way as much as possible, and

55

forestalled every effort I made to talk with him. His conscience evidently troubled him. He knew he was doing a cruel and wicked thing, and wanted to escape from thinking about it. I followed him up hard, for I was supplicating for my life. I fell down and clung to his knees in entreaties. Sometimes when too closely pressed, he would curse and strike me. May God forgive him! And yet it was not all his fault; he was made so by the accursed relation of slave-master and slave. I was property,—not a man, not a father, not a husband. And the laws of property and self-interest, not of humanity and love, bore sway.

At length everything was wound up but this single affair. I was to be sold the next day, and Master Amos was to set off on his return in a steamboat at six o'clock in the afternoon. I could not sleep that night; its hours seemed interminably long, though it was one of the shortest of the year. The slow way in which we had come down had brought us to the long days and heats of June; and everybody knows what the climate of New Orleans is at that period of the year.

And now occurred one of those sudden, marked interpositions of Providence, by which in a moment, the whole current of a human being's life is changed; one of those slight and, at first, unappreciated contingencies, by which the faith that man's extremity is God's opportunity is kept alive. Little did I think, when just before daylight Master Amos called me and told me he felt sick, how much my future was bound up in those few words. His stomach was disordered, and I advised him to lie down again, thinking it would soon pass off. Before long he felt worse, and it was soon evident that the river-fever was upon him. He became rapidly ill, and by eight o'clock in the morning was utterly prostrate. The tables were now turned. I was no longer property, no longer a brute-beast to be bought and sold, but his only friend in the midst of strangers. Oh, how different was his tone from what it had been the day before! He was now the supplicant, a poor, terrified object, afraid of death, and writhing with pain; there lay the late arbiter of my destiny. How he besought me to forgive him! "Stick to me, Sie! Stick to me, Sie! Don't leave me, don't leave me. I'm sorry I was going to sell you." Sometimes he would say he had only been joking, and never intended to part with me. Yes, the tables were utterly turned. He entreated me to dispatch matters, sell the flat-boat in which we had been living, and get him and his trunk, containing the proceeds of the trip, on board the steamer as quickly as possible. I attended to all his requests, and by twelve o'clock that day, he was in one of the cabins of the steamer appropriated to sick passengers.

O, my God! how my heart sang jubilees of praise to Thee, as the steamboat swung loose from the levee and breasted the mighty tide of the Mississippi! Away from this land of bondage and death! Away from misery and despair! Once more exulting hope possessed me, and I thought, if I do not now find my way to freedom, may God never give me a chance again!

Before we had proceeded many hours on our voyage, my young master appeared to be better. The change of air in a measure revived him; and well it was for him that such was the case. Short as his illness had been, the fever had raged like a fire, and he was already near death. I watched and nursed him like a mother; for all remembrance of personal wrong was obliterated at the sight of his peril. His eyes followed me in entreaty wherever I went. His strength was so entirely gone, that he could neither speak nor move a limb, and could only indicate his wish for a teaspoonful of gruel, or something to moisten his throat, by a feeble motion of his lips. I nursed him carefully and constantly. Nothing else could have saved his life. It hung by a thread for a long time. We were twelve days in reaching home, for the water was low at that season, particularly in the Ohio River; and when we arrived at our landing, he was still unable to speak, and could only be moved on a litter. Something of this sort was fixed up at the landing, on which he could be carried to the house, which was five miles off; and I got a party of the slaves belonging to the estate to form relays for the purpose. As we approached the house, the surprise at seeing me back again, and the perplexity to imagine what I was bringing along, with such a party, were extreme; but the discovery was soon made which explained the strange appearance; and the grief of father and mother, brothers and sisters, made itself seen and heard. Loud and long were the lamentations over poor Amos; and when the family came a little to themselves, great were the commendations bestowed upon me for my care of him and of the property.

Although we reached home by the 10th of July, it was not until the middle of August that Master Amos was well enough to leave his chamber. To do him justice, he manifested strong gratitude towards me. Almost his first words after recovering his strength sufficiently to talk, were in commendation of my conduct. "If I had sold him I should have died." On the rest of the family no permanent impression seemed to have been made. The first few words of praise were all I ever received. I was set at my old work. My merits, whatever they were, instead of exciting sympathy or any feeling of attachment to me, seemed only to enhance my market-value in their eyes. I saw that my master's only thought was to render me profitable to himself. From him I had nothing to hope, and I turned my thoughts to myself and my own energies.

Before long I felt assured another attempt would be made to dispose of me. Providence seemed to have interfered once to defeat the scheme, but I could not expect such extraordinary circumstances to be repeated; and I was bound to do everything in my power to secure myself and my family from the wicked conspiracy of Amos Riley against my life, as well as against my natural rights, and those which I had acquired, even under the barbarous laws of slavery, by the money I had paid for myself. If Isaac had only been honest enough to adhere to his bargain, I would have adhered to mine, and paid him all I had promised. But his attempt to kidnap me again, after having pocketed three-fourths of my market value, in my opinion, absolved me from all obligation to pay him any more, or to continue in a position which exposed me to his machinations.

# CHAPTER XII

## ESCAPE FROM BONDAGE

Solitary Musings—Preparations for Flight—A Long Good Night to Master—A Dark Night on the River—Night Journeys in Indiana—On the Brink of Starvation—A Kind Woman—A New Style of Drinking Cup—Reach Cincinnati

During the bright and hopeful days I spent in Ohio, while away on my preaching tour, I had heard much of the course pursued by fugitives from slavery, and became acquainted with a number of benevolent men engaged in helping them on their way. Canada was often spoken of as the only sure refuge from pursuit, and that blessed land was now the desire of my longing heart. Infinite toils and perils lay between me and that haven of promise, enough to daunt the stoutest heart; but the fire behind me was too hot and fierce to let me pause to consider them. I knew the North Star—blessed be God for setting it in the heavens! Like the Star of Bethlehem, it announced where my salvation lay. Could I follow it through forest, and stream, and field, it would guide my feet in the way of hope. I thought of it as my God-given guide to the land of promise far away beneath its light. I knew that it had led thousands of my poor, hunted brethren to freedom and blessedness. I felt energy enough in my own breast to contend with privation and danger; and had I been a free, untrammelled man, knowing no tie of father or husband, and concerned for my own safety only, I would have felt all difficulties light in view of the hope that was set before me. But, alas! I had a wife and four dear children; how should I provide for them? Abandon them I could not; no! not even for the blessed boon of freedom. They, too, must go. They, too, must share with me the life of liberty.

It was not without long thought upon the subject that I devised a plan of escape. But at last I matured it. My mind fully made up, I communicated the intention to my wife. She was overwhelmed with terror. With a woman's instinct she clung to hearth and home. She knew nothing of the wide world beyond, and her imagination peopled it with unseen horrors. She said, "We shall die in the wilderness, we shall be hunted down with bloodhounds; we shall be brought back and whipped to death." With tears and supplications she besought me to remain at home, contented. In vain I explained to her our liability to be torn asunder at any moment; the horrors of the slavery I had lately seen; the happiness we should enjoy together in a land of freedom, safe from all pursuing harm. She had not suffered the bitterness of my lot, nor felt the same longing for deliverance. She was a poor, timid, unreasoning slave-woman.

I argued the matter with her at various times, till I was satisfied the argument alone would not prevail. I then told her deliberately, that though it would be a cruel trial for me to part with her, I would nevertheless do it, and take all the children with me except the youngest, rather than remain at home, only to be forcibly torn from her, and sent down to linger out a wretched existence in the dens I had lately visited. Again she wept and entreated, but I was sternly resolute. The whole night long she fruitlessly urged me to relent; exhausted and maddened, I left her, in the morning, to go to my work for the day. Before I had gone far, I heard her voice calling me, and waiting till I came up, she said, at last, she would go with me. Blessed relief! my tears of joy flowed faster than had hers of grief.

Our cabin, at this time, was near the landing. The plantation itself extended the whole five miles from the house to the river. There were several distinct farms, all of which I was overseeing, and therefore I was riding about from one to another every day. Our oldest boy was at the house with Master Amos; the rest of the children were with my wife.

The chief practical difficulty that had weighed upon my mind, was connected with the youngest two of the children. They were of three and two years respectively, and of course would have to be carried. Both stout and healthy, they were a heavy burden, and my wife had declared that I should break down under it before I had got five miles from home. Sometime previously I had directed her to make me a large knapsack of tow-cloth, large enough to hold them both, and arranged with strong straps to go round my shoulders. This done, I had practised carrying them night after night, both to test my own strength and accustom them to submit to it. To them it was fine fun, and to my great joy I found I could manage them successfully. My wife's consent was given on Thursday morning, and I resolved to start on the night of the following Saturday. Sunday was a holiday; on Monday and Tuesday I was to be away on farms distant from the house; thus several days would elapse before I should be missed, and by that time I should have got a good start.

At length the eventful night arrived. All things were ready, with the single exception that I had not yet obtained my master's permission for little Tom to visit his mother. About sundown I went up to the great house to report my work, and after talking for a time, started off, as usual, for home; when, suddenly appearing to recollect something I had forgotten, I turned carelessly back, and said, "Oh, Master Amos, I most forgot. Tom's mother wants to know if you won't let him come down a few days; she wants to mend his clothes and fix him up a little." "Yes, boy, yes; he can go." "Thankee, Master Amos; good night, good night. The Lord bless you!" In spite of myself I threw a good deal of emphasis into my farewell. I could not refrain from an inward chuckle at the thought—how long a good night that will be! The coast was all clear now, and, as I trudged along home, I took an affectionate look at the well-known objects on my way. Strange to say, sorrow mingled with my joy; but no man can live long anywhere without feeling some attachment to the soil on which he labours.

It was about the middle of September, and by nine o'clock all was ready. It was a dark, moonless night, when we got into the little skiff, in which I had induced a fellow-slave to set us across the river. It was an anxious moment. We sat still as death. In the middle of the stream the good fellow said to me, "It will be the end of me if this is ever found out; but you won't be brought back alive, Sie, will you?" "Not if I can help it," I replied; and I thought of the pistols and knife I had bought some time before of a poor white. "And if they're too many for you, and you get seized, you'll never tell my part in this business?" "Not if I'm shot through like a sieve." "That's all," said he, "and God help you." Heaven reward him. He, too, has since followed in my steps; and many a time in a land of freedom have we talked over that dark night on the river.

In due time we landed on the Indiana shore. A hearty, grateful farewell was spoken, such as none but companions in danger can utter, and I heard the oars of the skiff propelling him home. There I stood in the darkness, my dear ones with me, and the dim unknown future before us. But there was little time for reflection. Before daylight should come on, we must put as many miles behind us as possible, and be safely hidden in the woods. We had no friends to look to for assistance, for the population in that section of the country was then bitterly hostile to the fugitive. If discovered, we should be seized and lodged in jail. In God was our only hope. Fervently did I pray to Him as we trudged on cautiously and stealthily, as fast as the darkness and the feebleness of my wife and boys would allow. To her, indeed, I was compelled to talk sternly; she trembled like a leaf, and even then implored me to return.

For a fortnight we pressed steadily on, keeping to the road during the night, hiding whenever a chance vehicle or horseman was heard, and during the day burying ourselves in the woods. Our provisions were rapidly giving out. Two days before reaching Cincinnati they were utterly exhausted. All night long the children cried with hunger, and my poor wife loaded me with reproaches for bringing them into such misery. It was a bitter thing to hear them cry, and God knows I needed encouragement myself. My limbs were weary, and my back and shoulders raw with the burden I carried. A fearful dread of detection ever pursued me, and I would start out of my sleep in terror, my heart beating against my ribs, expecting to find the dogs and slave-hunters after me. Had I been alone, I would have borne starvation, even to exhaustion, before I would have ventured in sight of a house in quest of food. But now something must be done; it was necessary to run the risk of exposure by daylight upon the road.

The only way to proceed was to adopt a bold course. Accordingly, I left our hiding-place, took to the road, and turned towards the south, to lull any suspicion that might be aroused were I to be seen going the other way. Before long I came to a house. A furious dog rushed out at me, and his master following to quiet him, I asked if he would sell me a little bread and meat. He was a surly fellow. "No, I have nothing for niggers!" At the next, I succeeded no better, at first. The man of the house met me in the same style; but his wife, hearing our conversation, said to her husband, "How can you treat any human being so? If a dog was hungry I would give him something to eat." She then added, "We have children, and who knows but they may some day need the help of a friend." The man laughed and told her that if she took care of niggers, he wouldn't. She asked me to come in, loaded a plate with venison and bread, and, when I laid it into my handkerchief, and put a quarter of a dollar on the table, she quietly took it up and put it in my handkerchief, with an additional quantity of venison. I felt the hot tears roll down my cheeks as she said, "God bless you;" and I hurried away to bless my starving wife and little ones.

A little while after eating the venison, which was quite salt, the children became very thirsty, and groaned and sighed so that I went off stealthily, breaking the bushes to keep my path, to find water. I found a little rill, and drank a large draught. Then I tried to carry some in my hat; but, alas! it leaked. Finally, I took off both shoes, which luckily had no holes in them, rinsed them out, filled them with water, and carried it to my family. They drank it with great delight. I have since then sat at splendidly-furnished tables in Canada, the United States, and England; but never did I see any human beings relish anything more than my poor famishing little ones did that refreshing draught out of their father's shoes. That night we made a long run, and two days afterwards we reached Cincinnati.

# CHAPTER XIII

## JOURNEY TO CANADA

I now felt comparatively at home. Before entering the town I hid my wife and children in the woods, and then walked on alone in search of my friends. They welcomed me warmly, and just after dusk my wife and children were brought in, and we found ourselves hospitably cheered and refreshed. Two weeks of exposure to incessant fatigue, anxiety, rain, and chill, made it indescribably sweet to enjoy once more the comfort of rest and shelter.

I have sometimes heard harsh and bitter words spoken of those devoted men who were banded together to succour and bid God speed to the hunted fugitive; men who, through pity for the suffering, voluntarily exposed themselves to hatred, fines, and imprisonment. If there be a God who will have mercy on the merciful, great will be their reward. In the great day when men shall stand in judgment before the Divine Master, crowds of the outcast and forsaken of earth, will gather around them, and in joyful tones bear witness, "We were hungry and ye gave us meat, thirsty and ye gave us drink, naked and ye clothed us, sick and ye visited us." And He Who has declared that, "inasmuch as ye have done it unto the least of these My brethren, ye have done it unto Me," will accept the attestation, and hail them with His welcome, "Come ye blessed of My Father." Their glory shall yet be proclaimed from the house-tops, and may that "peace of God which the world can neither give nor take away" dwell richly in their hearts!

Among such as those—good Samaritans, of whom the Lord would says, "Go ye and do likewise,"—our lot was now cast. Carefully they provided for our welfare until our strength was recruited, and then they set us thirty miles on our way by waggon.

We followed the same course as before—travelling by night and resting by day—till we arrived at the Scioto, where we had been told we should strike the military road of General Hull, made in the last war with Great Britain, and might then safely travel by day. We found the road, accordingly, by the large sycamore and elms which marked its beginning, and entered upon it with fresh spirits early in the day. Nobody had told us that it was cut through the wilderness, and I had neglected to provide any food, thinking we should soon come to some habitation, where we could be supplied. But we travelled on all day without seeing one, and lay down at night, hungry and weary enough. The wolves were howling around us, and though too cowardly to approach, their noise terrified my poor wife and children. Nothing remained to us in the morning but a little piece of dried beef, too little, indeed, to satisfy our cravings, but enough to afflict us with intolerable thirst. I divided most of this amongst us, and then we started for a second day's tramp in the wilderness. A painful day it was to us. The road was rough, the underbrush tore our clothes and exhausted our strength; trees that had been blown down, blocked the way; we were faint with hunger, and no prospect of relief opened up before us. We spoke little, but steadily struggled along; I with my babes on my back, my wife aiding the two other children to climb over the fallen trunks and force themselves through the briers. Suddenly, as I was plodding along a little ahead of my wife and the boys, I heard them call me, and turning round saw my wife prostrate on the ground. "Mother's dying," cried Tom; and when I reached her, it seemed really so. From sheer exhaustion she had fallen in surmounting a log. Distracted with anxiety, I feared she was gone. For some minutes no sign of life was manifest; but after a time she opened her eyes, and finally recovering enough to take a few mouthfuls of the beef, her strength returned, and we once more went bravely on our way. I cheered the sad group with hopes I was far from sharing myself. For the first time I was nearly ready to abandon myself to despair.

Starvation in the wilderness was the doom that stared me and mine
in the face. But again, "man's extremity was God's opportunity."

We had not gone far, and I suppose it was about three o'clock in
the afternoon, when we discerned some persons approaching us at no
great distance. We were instantly on the alert, as we could hardly
expect them to be friends. The advance of a few paces showed me
they were Indians, with packs on their shoulders; and they were so
near that if they were hostile it would be useless to try to escape. So
I walked along coldly, till we came close upon them. They were bent
down with their burdens, and had not raised their eyes till now; and
when they did so, and saw me coming towards them, they looked at
me in a frightened sort of a way for a moment, and then, setting up a
peculiar howl, turned round, and ran as fast as they could. There
were three or four of them, and what they were afraid of I could not
imagine. There was no doubt they were frightened, and we heard
their wild and prolonged howl, as they ran, for a mile or more. My
wife was alarmed, too, and thought they were merely running back
to collect more of a party, and then would come and murder us; and
she wanted to turn back. I told her they were numerous enough to
do that, if they wanted to, without help; and that as for turning
back, I had had quite too much of the road behind us, and that it
would be a ridiculous thing that both parties should run away. If
they were disposed to run, I would follow. We did follow, and the
noise soon ceased. As we advanced, we could discover Indians
peeping at us from behind the trees, and dodging out of sight if they
thought we were looking at them. Presently we came upon their
wigwams, and saw a fine-looking, stately Indian, with his arms
folded, waiting for us to approach. He was, apparently, the chief; and
saluting us civilly, he soon discovered we were human beings, and
spoke to his young men, who were scattered about, and made them
come in and give up their foolish fears. And now curiosity seemed to
prevail. Each one wanted to touch the children, who were as shy as
partridges with their long life in the woods; and as they shrunk away,
and uttered a little cry of alarm, the Indian would jump back too, as
if he thought they would bite him. However, a little while sufficed to
make them understand whither we were going, and what we needed;
and then they supplied our wants, fed us bountifully, and gave us a
comfortable wigwam for our night's rest. The next day we resumed

our march, having ascertained from the Indians that we were only about twenty-five miles from the lake. They sent some of their young men to point out the place where we were to turn off, and parted from us with as much kindness as possible.

In passing over the part of Ohio near the lake, where such an extensive plain is found, we came to a spot overflowed by a stream, across which the road passed. I forded it first, with the help of a sounding-pole, and then taking the children on my back, first the two little ones, and then the others, one at a time, and, lastly, my wife, I succeeded in getting them safely across. At this time the skin was worn from my back to an extent almost equal to the size of the knapsack.

One more night was passed in the woods, and in the course of the next forenoon, we came out upon the wide, treeless plain which lies south and west of Sandusky city. The houses of the village were in plain sight. About a mile from the lake I hid my wife and children in the bushes, and pushed forward. I was attracted by a house on the left, between which and a small coasting vessel, a number of men were passing and repassing with great activity. Promptly deciding to approach them, I drew near, and scarcely had I come within hailing distance, when the captain of the schooner cried out, "Hollo there, man! you want to work?" "Yes sir!" shouted I. "Come along, come along; I'll give you a shilling an hour. Must get off with this wind." As I came near, he said, "Oh, you can't work; you're crippled." "Can't I?" said I; and in a minute I had hold of a bag of corn, and followed the gang in emptying it into the hold. I took my place in the line of labourers next to a coloured man, and soon got into conversation with him. "How far is it to Canada?" He gave me a peculiar look, and in a minute I saw he knew all. "Want to go to Canada? Come along with us, then. Our captain's a fine fellow. We're going to Buffalo." "Buffalo; how far is that from Canada?" "Don't you know, man? Just across the river." I now opened my mind frankly to him, and told him about my wife and children. "I'll speak to the captain," said he. He did so, and in a moment the captain took me aside, and said, "The Doctor says you want to go to Buffalo with your family." "Yes, sir." "Well, why not go with me!" was his frank reply. "Doctor says you've got a family." "Yes, sir." "Where do you stop?" "About a mile back." "How long have you been here?" "No time," I answered, after a moment's hesitation. "Come, my good fellow, tell us all about it. You're running away, ain't you?" I saw he was a friend, and opened my heart to him. "How long will it take you to get ready?" "Be here in half an hour, sir." "Well, go along and get them." Off I started; but before I had run fifty feet, he called me back. "Stop," said he; "you go on getting the grain in. When we get off, I'll lay to over opposite that island, and send a boat back. There's a lot of regular nigger-catchers in the town below, and they might suspect you if you brought your party out of the bush by daylight." I worked away with a will. Soon the two or three hundred bushels of corn were aboard, the hatches fastened down, the anchor raised, and the sails hoisted.

I watched the vessel with intense interest as she left her moorings. Away she went before the free breeze. Already she seemed beyond the spot at which the captain agreed to lay to, and still she flew along. My heart sank within me; so near deliverance, and again to have my hopes blasted, again to be cast on my own resources! I felt that they had been making sport of my misery. The sun had sunk to rest, and the purple and gold of the west were fading away into grey. Suddenly, however, as I gazed with a weary heart, the vessel swung round into the wind, the sails flapped, and she stood motionless. A moment more, and a boat was lowered from her stern, and with a steady stroke made for the point at which I stood. I felt that my hour of release had come. On she came, and in ten minutes she rode up handsomely on to the beach.

My black friend and two sailors jumped out, and we started off at once for my wife and children. To my horror, they were gone from the place where I left them. Overpowered with fear, I supposed they had been found and carried off. There was no time to lose, and the men told me I would have to go alone. Just at the point of despair, however, I stumbled on one of the children. My wife, it seemed, alarmed at my long absence, had given up all for lost, and supposed I had fallen into the hands of the enemy. When she heard my voice, mingled with those of the others, she thought my captors were leading me back to make me discover my family, and in the extremity of her terror she had tried to hide herself. I had hard work to satisfy her. Our long habits of concealment and anxiety had rendered her suspicious of every one; and her agitation was so great that for a time she was incapable of understanding what I said, and went on in a sort of paroxysm of distress and fear. This, however, was soon over, and the kindness of my companions did much to facilitate the matter.

And now we were off for the boat. It required little time to embark our baggage—one convenience, at least, of having nothing. The men bent their backs with a will, and headed steadily for a light hung from the vessel's mast. I was praising God in my soul. Three hearty cheers welcomed us as we reached the schooner, and never till my dying day shall I forget the shout of the captain—he was a Scotchman—"Coom up on deck, and clop your wings and craw like a rooster; you're a free nigger as sure as you're a live mon." Round went the vessel, the wind plunged into her sails as though innoculated with the common feeling—the water seethed and hissed past her sides. Man and nature, and, more than all, I felt the God of man and nature, who breathes love into the heart and maketh the winds His ministers, were with us. My happiness that night rose at times to positive pain. Unnerved by so sudden a change from destitution and danger to such kindness and blessed security, I wept like a child.

The next evening we reached Buffalo, but it was too late to cross the river that night. "You see those trees," said the noble-hearted captain, next morning, pointing to a group in the distance; "they grow on free soil, and as soon as your feet touch that, you're a *mon*. I want to see you go and be a freeman. I'm poor myself, and have nothing to give you; I only sail the boat for wages; but I'll see you across. Here, Green," said he to a ferryman, "What will you take this man and his family over for—he's got no money?" "Three shillings." He then took a dollar out of his pocket and gave it to me. Never shall I forget the spirit in which he spoke. He put his hand on my head and said, "Be a good fellow, won't you?" I felt streams of emotion running down in electric courses from head to foot. "Yes," said I; "I'll use my freedom well; I'll give my soul to God." He stood waving his hat as we pushed off for the opposite shore. God bless him! God bless him eternally! Amen!

It was the 28th of October, 1830, in the morning, when my feet first touched the Canada shore. I threw myself on the ground, rolled in the sand, seized handfuls of it and kissed them, and danced around, till, in the eyes of several who were present, I passed for a madman. "He's some crazy fellow," said a Colonel Warren, who happened to be there. "Oh, no, master! don't you know? I'm free!" He burst into a shout of laughter. "Well, I never knew freedom make a man roll in the sand in such a fashion." Still I could not control myself. I hugged and kissed my wife and children, and, until the first exuberant burst of feeling was over, went on as before.

# CHAPTER XIV

## NEW SCENES AND A NEW HOME

A Poor Man in a Strange Land—Begin to Acquire Property—Resume Preaching—Boys Go to School—What Gave Me a Desire to Learn to Read—A Day of Prayer in the Woods

There was not much time to be lost, though, in frolic even, at this extraordinary moment. I was a stranger in a strange land, and had to look about me at once for refuge and resource. I found a lodging for the night, and the next morning set about exploring the interior for the means of support. I knew nothing about the country or the people, but kept my eyes and ears open, and made such inquiries as opportunity afforded. I heard, in the course of the day, of a Mr. Hibbard, who lived some six or seven miles off. He was a rich man, as riches were counted there, had a large farm, and several small tenements on it, which he was in the habit of letting to his labourers. To him I went immediately, though the character given him by his neighbours was not, by any means, unexceptionably good. But I thought he was not, probably, any worse than those I had been accustomed to serve, and that I could get along with him, if honest and faithful work would satisfy him. In the afternoon I found him, and soon struck a bargain with him for employment. I asked him if there was any house where he would let me live. He said, "Yes," and led the way to an old two-story sort of shanty, into the lower story of which the pigs had broken, and had apparently made it their resting-place for some time. Still, it was a house, and I forthwith expelled the pigs, and set about cleaning it for the occupancy of a better sort of tenants. With the aid of a hoe and shovel, hot water and a mop, I got the floor into a tolerable condition by midnight, and only then did I rest from my labour. The next day I brought the

71

rest of the Hensons, the only furniture I had, to *my house*, and though there was nothing there but bare walls and floors, we were all in a state of great delight, and my wife laughed and acknowledged that it was better than a log cabin with an earth-floor. I begged some straw of Mr. Hibbard, and confining it by logs in the corners of the room, I made beds of it three feet thick, upon which we reposed luxuriously after our long fatigues.

Another trial awaited me which I had not anticipated. In consequence of the great exposures we had been through, my wife and all the children fell sick; and it was not without extreme peril that they escaped with their lives.

My employer soon found that my labour was of more value to him than that of those he was accustomed to hire; and as I consequently gained his favour, and his wife took quite a fancy to mine, we soon procured some of the comforts of life, while the necessaries of life, food and fuel, were abundant. I remained with Mr. Hibbard three years, sometimes working on shares, and sometimes for wages; and I managed in that time to procure some pigs, a cow, and a horse. Thus my condition gradually improved, and I felt that my toils and sacrifices for freedom had not been in vain. Nor were my labours for the improvement of myself and others, in more important things than food and clothing, without effect. It so happened that one of my Maryland friends arrived in this neighbourhood, and hearing of my being here, inquired if I ever preached now, and spread the reputation I had acquired elsewhere for my gifts in the pulpit. I had said nothing myself, and had not intended to say anything of my having ever officiated in that way. I went to meeting with others, when I had an opportunity, and enjoyed the quiet of the Sabbath when there was no assembly. I could not refuse to labour in this field, however, when afterwards desired to do so; and I was from this time frequently called upon, not by blacks alone, but by all classes in my vicinity—the comparatively educated, as well as the lamentably ignorant—to speak to them on their duty, responsibility, and immortality, on their obligations to themselves, their Saviour, and their Maker.

I am aware it must seem strange to many that a man so ignorant, unable to read, and having heard so little as I had of religion, natural or revealed, should be able to preach acceptably to persons who had enjoyed greater advantages than myself. I can explain it only by reference to our Saviour's comparison of the kingdom of heaven to a plant which may spring from a seed no bigger than a mustard-seed, and may yet reach such a size, that the birds of the air may take shelter therein. Religion is not so much knowledge as wisdom; and observation upon what passes without, and reflection upon what passes within a man's heart, will give him a larger growth in grace than is imagined by the devoted adherents of creeds, or the confident followers of Christ, who call Him "Lord, Lord," but do not the things which He says.

Mr. Hibbard was good enough to give my eldest boy, Tom, two quarters' schooling, to which the schoolmaster added more, of his own kindness, so that my boy learned to read fluently and well. It was a great advantage, not only to him, but to me; for I used to get him to read much to me in the Bible, especially on Sunday mornings, when I was going to preach; and I could easily commit to memory a few verses, or a chapter, from hearing him read it over.

One beautiful summer Sabbath I rose early, and called him to come and read to me. "Where shall I read, father". "Anywhere, my son," I answered, for I knew not how to direct him. He opened upon Psalm ciii., "Bless the Lord, O my soul: and all that is within me, bless His holy name;" and as he read this beautiful outpouring of gratitude, which I now first heard, my heart melted within me. I recalled, with all the rapidity of which thought is capable, the whole current of my life; and, as I remembered the dangers and afflictions from which the Lord had delivered me, and compared my present condition with what it had been, not only my heart but my eyes overflowed, and I could neither check nor conceal the emotion which overpowered me. The words, "Bless the Lord, O my soul," with which the Psalm begins and ends, were all I needed, or could use, to express the fulness of my thankful heart. When he had finished, Tom turned to me and asked, "Father, who was David?" He had observed my excitement, and added, "He writes pretty, don't he?" and then repeated his question. It was a question I was utterly unable to answer. I had never heard of David, but could not bear to acknowledge my ignorance to my own child. So I answered, evasively, "He was a man of God, my son." "I suppose so," said he, "but I want to know something more about him. Where did he live?

What did he do?" As he went on questioning me, I saw it was in vain to attempt to escape, and so I told him frankly I did not know. "Why, father," said he, "can't you read?" This was a worse question than the other, and, if I had any pride in me at the moment, it took it all out of me pretty quick. It was a direct question, and must have a direct answer; so I told him at once I could not. "Why not?" said he. "Because I never had an opportunity to learn, nor anybody to teach me." "Well, you can learn now, father." "No, my son, I am too old, and have not time enough. I must work all day, or you would not have enough to eat." "Then you might do it at night." "But still there is nobody to teach me. I can't afford to pay anybody for it, and, of course, no one can do it for nothing." "Why, father, *I'll teach you*. I can do it, I know. And then you'll know so much more that you will be able to talk better, and preach better." The little fellow was so earnest, there was no resisting him; but it is hard to describe the conflicting feelings within me at such a proposition from such a quarter. I was delighted with the conviction that my children would have advantages I had never enjoyed; but it was no slight mortification to think of being instructed by my young son. Yet ambition, and a true desire to learn, for the good it would do my own mind, conquered the shame, and I agreed to try. But I did not reach this state of mind instantly.

I was greatly moved by the conversation I had with Tom, so much so, that I could not undertake to preach that day. The congregation were disappointed, and I passed the Sunday in solitary reflection in the woods. I was too much engrossed with the multitude of my thoughts to return home to dinner, and spent the whole day in secret meditation and prayer, trying to compose myself, and ascertain my true position. It was not difficult to see that my predicament was one of profound ignorance, and that I ought to use every opportunity of enlightening it. I began to take lessons of Tom, therefore, immediately, and followed it up every evening, by the light of a pine knot, or some hickory bark, which was the only light I could afford. Weeks passed, and my progress was so slow that poor Tom was almost discouraged, and used to drop asleep sometimes, and whine a little over my dulness, and talk to me very much as a schoolmaster talks to a stupid boy, till I began to be afraid that my age, nearly fifty, my want of practice in looking at such little scratches, the daily fatigue, and the dim light, would be effectual preventives of my ever acquiring the art of reading. But Tom's perseverance and mine conquered at last, and in the course of the winter I did really learn to read a little.

It was, and has been ever since, a great comfort to me to have made this acquisition; though it has made me comprehend better the terrible abyss of ignorance into which I had been plunged all my previous life. It made me also feel more deeply and bitterly the oppression under which I had toiled and groaned, the crushing and cruel nature of which I had not appreciated, till I found out, in some slight degree, from what I had been debarred. At the same time it made me more anxious than before, to do something for the rescue and the elevation of those who were suffering the same evils I had endured, and who did not know how degraded and ignorant they really were.

# CHAPTER XV

## LIFE IN CANADA

Condition of the Blacks in Canada—A Tour of Exploration—Appeal to the Legislature—Improvements

After about three years had passed, I improved my condition again by taking service with a gentleman by the name of Riseley, whose residence was only a few miles distant. He was a man of more elevation of mind than Mr. Hibbard, and of superior abilities. At his place I began to reflect, more and more, upon the circumstances of the blacks, who were already somewhat numerous in this region. I was not the only one who had escaped from the States, and had settled on the first spot in Canada which they had reached. Several hundreds of coloured persons were in the neighbourhood, and, in the first joy of their deliverance, they were living in a way, which, I could see, led to little or no progress in improvement. They were content to have the proceeds of their labour at their own command, and had not the ambition for, or the perception of what was within their easy reach, if they did but know it. They were generally working for hire upon the lands of others, and had not yet dreamed of becoming independent proprietors themselves. It soon became my great object to awaken them to a sense of the advantages which were within their grasp; and Mr. Riseley, seeing clearly the justness of my views, and willing to co-operate with me in the attempt to make them generally known among the blacks, permitted me to call meetings at his house of those who were known to be amongst the most intelligent and successful of our class. At these meetings we considered and discussed the subject, till we were all of one mind; and it was agreed, among the ten or twelve of us who assembled at them, that we would invest our earnings in land, and undertake the task—which, though no light one certainly, would yet soon reward us for our effort—of settling upon wild lands, which we could call our own, and where every tree which we felled, and every bushel of corn we raised, would be for ourselves; in other words, where we could secure all the profits of our own labour.

The advantages of such a course of procedure have been exemplified for two hundred years and more, by the people who have thereby acquired an indestructible character for energy, enterprise, and self-reliance. It was precisely this energetic spirit which I wished to instil into my fellow-slaves, if possible; and I was not deterred from the task by the perception of the immense contrast in all their habits and character generated by long ages of freedom and servitude, activity and sloth, independence and subjection. My associates agreed with me, and we resolved to select some spot among the many offered to our choice, where we could colonize, and raise our own crops, eat our own bread, and be, in short, our own masters. I was deputed to explore the country, and find a place to which I would be willing to migrate myself; and they all said they would go with me, whenever such a one should be found. I set out accordingly in the autumn of 1834, and travelled on foot all over the extensive region between Lakes Ontario, Erie, and Huron. When I came to the territory east of Lake St. Clair and Detroit River, I was strongly impressed with its fertility and its superiority, for all our purposes, to any other spot I had seen. I determined this should be the place; and so reported, on my return, to my future companions. They were wisely cautious, however, and sent me off again in the summer, that I might see it at the opposite seasons of the year, and be better able to judge of its advantages. I found no reason to change my opinion, but upon going farther towards the head of Lake Erie, I discovered an extensive tract of government-land, which, for some years, had been granted to a Mr. McCormick upon certain conditions, and which he had rented out to settlers upon such terms as he could obtain. This land being already cleared, offered some advantages for the immediate raising of crops, which were not to be overlooked by persons whose resources were so limited as ours. We determined to go there first, for a time, and with the proceeds of what we could earn there, to make our purchases in Dawn afterwards. This plan was followed, and some dozen or more of us settled upon those lands the following spring, and accumulated something by the crops of wheat and tobacco we were able to raise.

I discovered, before long, that McCormick had not complied with the conditions of his grant, and was not, therefore, entitled to the rent he exacted from the settlers. I was advised by Sir John Cockburn, to whom I applied on the subject, to appeal to the legislature for relief. We did so; and though McCormick was able, by the aid of his friends, to defeat us for one year, yet we succeeded the next, upon a second appeal, and were freed from all rent thereafter, so long as we remained. Still, this was not our own land. The government, though it demanded no rent, might set up the land for sale at any time, and then we should, probably, be driven off by wealthier purchasers, with the entire loss of all our improvements, and with no retreat provided. It was manifest that it was altogether better for us to purchase before competition was invited; and we kept this fully in mind during the time we stayed there. We remained in this position six or seven years; and all this while the coloured population was increasing rapidly around us, and spreading very fast into the interior settlements and the large towns. The immigration from the United States was incessant, and some, I am willing to admit, were brought hither with my knowledge and connivance; and I will now proceed to give a short account of the plans and operations I had arranged for the liberation of some of my brethren, which I hope may prove interesting to the reader.

# CHAPTER XVI

## CONDUCTING SLAVES TO CANADA

Sympathy for the Slaves—James Lightfoot—My First Mission to the South—A Kentucky Company of Fugitives—Safe at Home

The degraded and hopeless condition of a slave can never be properly felt by him while he remains in such a position. After I had tasted the blessings of freedom, my mind reverted to those whom I knew were groaning in captivity, and I at once proceeded to take measures to free as many as I could. I thought that, by using exertion, numbers might make their escape as I did, if they had some practical advice on how to proceed.

I was once attending a very large meeting at Fort Erie, at which a great many coloured people were present. In the course of my preaching, I tried to impress upon them the importance of the obligations they were under; first, to God, for their deliverance; and then, secondly, to their fellow-men, to do all that was in their power to bring others out of bondage. In the congregation was a man named James Lightfoot, who was of a very active temperament, and had obtained his freedom by fleeing to Canada, but had never thought of his family and friends whom he had left behind, until the time he heard me speaking, although he himself had been free for some five years. However, that day the cause was brought home to his heart. When the service was concluded, he begged to have an interview with me, to which I gladly acceded, and an arrangement was made for further conversation on the same subject one week from that time. He then informed me where he came from, also to whom he belonged, and that he had left behind a dear father and mother, three sisters and four brothers; and that they lived on the

Ohio River, not far from the city of Maysville. He said that he never saw his duty towards them to be so clear and unmistakable as he did at that time, and professed himself ready to co-operate in any measures that might be devised for their release. During the short period of his freedom he had accumulated some little property, the whole of which, he stated, he would cheerfully devote to carrying out those measures; for he had no rest, night nor day, since the meeting above mentioned.

I was not able at that time to propose what was best to be done, and thus we parted; but in a few days he came to see me again on the same errand. Seeing the agony of his heart in behalf of his kindred, I consented to commence the painful and dangerous task of endeavouring to free those whom he so much loved. I left my own family in the hands of no other save God, and commenced the journey alone, on foot, and travelled thus about four hundred miles. But the Lord furnished me with strength sufficient for the undertaking. I passed through the States of New York, Pennsylvania, and Ohio—free States, so called—crossed the Ohio River into Kentucky, and ultimately found his friends in the place he had described.

I was an entire stranger to them, but I took with me a small token of their brother who was gone, which they at once recognised; and this was to let them know that he had gone to Canada, the land of freedom, and had now sent a friend to assist them in making their escape. This created no little excitement. But his parents had become so far advanced in years that they could not undertake the fatigue; his sisters had a number of children, and they could not travel; his four brothers and a nephew were young men, and sufficiently able for the journey, but the thought of leaving their father and mother, and sisters, was too painful; and they also considered it unsafe to make the attempt then, for fear that the excitement and grief of their friends might betray them; so they declined going at that time, but promised that they would go in a year if I would return for them.

To this I assented, and then went between forty and fifty miles into the interior of Kentucky, having heard that there was a large party ready to attempt their escape if they had a leader to direct their movements. I travelled by night, resting by day, and at length reached Bourbon county, the place where I expected to find these people. After a delay of about a week, spent in discussing plans, making arrangements, and other matters, I found that there were about thirty collected from different States, who were disposed to make the attempt. At length, on a Saturday night, we started. The agony of parting can be better conceived than described; as, in their case, husbands were leaving their wives, mothers their children, and children their parents. This, at first sight, will appear strange, and even incredible; but when we take into consideration the fact, that at any time they were liable to be separated, by being sold to what are termed "nigger traders," and the probability that such an event would take place, it will, I think, cease to excite any surprise.

We succeeded in crossing the Ohio River in safety, and arrived in Cincinnati the third night after our departure. Here we procured assistance; and, after stopping a short time to rest, we started for Richmond, Indiana. This is a town which had been settled by Quakers, and there we found friends indeed, who at once helped us on our way, without loss of time; and after a difficult journey of two weeks, through the wilderness, we reached Toledo, Ohio, a town on the south-western shore of Lake Erie, and there we took passage for Canada, which we reached in safety. I then went home to my family, taking with me a part of this large party, the rest finding their friends scattered in other towns, perfectly satisfied with my conduct in the matter, in being permitted to be the instrument of freeing such a number of my fellow-creatures.

# CHAPTER XVII

## SECOND JOURNEY ON THE UNDERGROUND RAILROAD

A Shower of Stars—Kentuckians—A Stratagem—A Providence—Conducted across the Miami River by a Cow—Arrival at Cincinnati—One of the Party Taken Ill—We Leave Him to Die—Meet a "Friend"—A Poor White Man—A Strange Impression—Once More in Canada

I remained at home, working on my farm, until the next autumn, about the time I had promised to assist in the restoring to liberty the friends of James Lightfoot, the individual who had excited my sympathy at the meeting at Fort Erie. In pursuance of this promise, I again started on my long journey into Kentucky.

On my way, that strange occurrence happened, called the great meteoric shower. The heavens seemed broken up into streaks of light and falling stars. I reached Lancaster, Ohio, at three o'clock in the morning, found the village aroused, the bells ringing, and the people exclaiming, "The day of judgment is come!" I thought it was probably so; but felt that I was in the right business, and walked on through the village, leaving the terrified people behind. The stars continued to fall till the light of the sun appeared.

On arriving at Portsmouth, in the State of Ohio, I had a very narrow escape from being detected. The place was frequented by a number of Kentuckians, who were quite ready to suspect a coloured man, if they saw anything unusual about him. I reached Portsmouth in the morning, and waited until two in the afternoon for the steamboat, so that I might not arrive in Maysville till after dark. While in the town I was obliged to resort to a stratagem, in order to avoid being questioned by the Kentuckians I saw in the place. To this end I procured some dried leaves, put them into a cloth and bound it all round my face, reaching nearly to my eyes, and pretended to be so seriously affected in my head and teeth as not to be able to speak. I then hung around the village till the time for the evening boat, so as to arrive at Maysville in the night. I was accosted by several during my short stay in Portsmouth, who appeared very anxious to get some particulars from me as to who I was, where I was going, and to whom I belonged. To all their numerous inquiries I merely shook my head, mumbled out indistinct answers, and acted so that they could not get anything out of me; and, by this artifice, I succeeded in avoiding any unpleasant consequences. I got on board the boat and reached Maysville, Kentucky, in the evening, about a fortnight from the time I had left Canada.

On landing, a wonderful providence happened to me. The second person I met in the street was Jefferson Lightfoot, brother of the James Lightfoot previously mentioned, and one of the party who had promised to escape if I would assist them. He stated that they were still determined to make the attempt, decided to put it into execution the following Saturday night, and preparations for the journey were at once commenced. The reason why Saturday night was chosen on this and the previous occasion was, that from not having to labour the next day, and being allowed to visit their families, they would not be missed until the time came for their usual appearance in the field, at which period they would be some eighty or a hundred miles away. During the interval I had to keep myself concealed by day, and used to meet them by night to make the necessary arrangements.

From fear of being detected, they started off without bidding their father or mother farewell, and then, in order to prevent the bloodhounds from following on our trail, we seized a skiff, a little below the city, and made our way down the river. It was not the shortest way, but it was the surest.

It was sixty-five miles from Maysville to Cincinnati, and we thought we could reach that city before daylight, and then take the stage for Sandusky. Our boat sprung a leak before we had got half way, and we narrowly escaped being drowned; providentially, however, we got to the shore before the boat sunk. We then took another boat, but this detention prevented us from arriving at Cincinnati in time for the stage. Day broke upon us when we were about ten miles above the city, and we were compelled to leave our boat from fear of being apprehended. This was an anxious time. However, we had got so far away that we knew there was no danger of being discovered by the hounds, and we thought we would go on foot. When we got within seven miles of Cincinnati, we came to the Miami River, and we could not reach the city without crossing it.

This was a great barrier to us, for the water appeared to be deep, and we were afraid to ask the loan of a boat, being apprehensive it might lead to our detection. We went first up and then down the river, trying to find a convenient crossing-place, but failed. I then said to my company, "Boys, let us go up the river and try again." We started, and after going about a mile we saw a cow coming out of a wood, and going to the river as though she intended to drink. Then said I, "Boys, let us go and see what the cow is about, it may be that she will tell us some news." I said this in order to cheer them up. One of them replied, in rather a peevish way, "Oh, that cow can't talk;" but I again urged them to come on. The cow remained until we approached her within a rod or two; she then walked into the river, and went straight across without swimming, which caused me to remark, "The Lord sent that cow to show us where to cross the river!" This has always seemed to me to be a very wonderful event.

Having urged our way with considerable haste, we were literally saturated with perspiration, though it was snowing at the time, and my companions thought that it would be highly dangerous for us to proceed through the water, especially as there was a large quantity of ice in the river. But as it was a question of life or death with us, there was no time left for reasoning; I therefore advanced—they reluctantly following. The youngest of the Lightfoots, ere we reached halfway over the river, was seized with violent contraction of the limbs, which prevented further self-exertion on his part; he was, therefore, carried the remainder of the distance. After resorting to continued friction, he partially recovered, and we proceeded on our journey.

We reached Cincinnati about eleven on Sunday morning, too late for the stage that day; but having found some friends, we hid ourselves until Monday evening, when we recommenced our long and toilsome journey, through mud, rain, and snow, towards Canada. We had increased our distance about one hundred miles, by going out of our road to get among the Quakers. During our passage through the woods, the boy before referred to was taken alarmingly ill, and we were compelled to proceed with him on our backs; but finding this mode of conveying him exceedingly irksome, we constructed a kind of litter with our shirts and handkerchiefs laid across poles. By this time we got into the State of Indiana, so that we could travel by day as long as we kept to the woods. Our patient continued to get worse, and it appeared, both to himself and to us, that death would soon release him from his sufferings. He therefore begged to be left in some secluded spot, to die alone, as he feared that the delay occasioned by his having to be carried through the bush, might lead to the capture of the whole company. With very considerable reluctance we acceded to his request, and laid him in a sheltered place, with a full expectation that death would soon put an end to his sufferings. The poor fellow expressed his readiness to meet the last struggle in hope of eternal life. Sad, indeed, was the parting; and it was with difficulty we tore ourselves away.

We had not, however, proceeded more than two miles on our journey, when one of the brothers of the dying man made a sudden stop, and expressed his inability to proceed whilst he had the consciousness that he had left his brother to perish, in all probability, a prey to the devouring wolves. His grief was so great that we determined to return, and at length reached the spot, where we found the poor fellow apparently dying, moaning out with every breath a prayer to heaven. Words cannot describe the joyousness experienced by the Lightfoots when they saw their poor afflicted brother once more; they literally danced for joy. We at once prepared to resume our journey as we best could, and once more penetrated the bush. After making some progress, we saw, at a little distance on the road, a waggon approaching, and I immediately determined to ascertain whether some assistance could not be obtained.

I at length circumvented the road, so as to make it appear that I had been journeying in an opposite direction to that which the waggon was taking. When I came up with the driver, I bade him good day. He said, "Where is thee going?" "To Canada." I saw his coat, heard his *thee* and *thou,* and set him down for a Quaker. I therefore plainly told him our circumstances. He at once stopped his horses, and expressed his willingness to assist us. I returned to the place where my companions were in waiting for me, and soon had them in the presence of the Quaker. Immediately on viewing the sufferer he was moved to tears, and without delay turned his horses' heads, to proceed in the direction of his home, although he had intended to go to a distant market with a load of produce for sale. The reception we met with from the Quaker's family overjoyed our hearts, and the transports with which the poor men looked upon their brother, now so favourably circumstanced, cannot be described.

We remained with this happy family for the night, and received from them every kindness. It was arranged that the boy should remain behind, until, through the blessing of God, he should recover. We were kindly provided with a sack of biscuit and a joint of meat, and once more set our faces in the direction of Lake Erie.

After proceeding some distance on our road, we perceived a white man approaching, but as he was travelling alone, and on foot, we were not alarmed at his presence. It turned out that he had been residing for some time in the South, and although a free white man, his employers had attempted to castigate him, in return for which he had used violence, which made it necessary that he should at once escape. We travelled in company, and found that his presence was of signal service to us in delivering us out of the hands of the slave-hunters who were now on our track, and eagerly grasping after their prey. We had resolved on reaching the lake, a distance of forty miles, by the following morning; we, therefore, walked all night.

Just as the day was breaking, we reached a wayside tavern, immediately contiguous to the lake, and our white companion having knocked up the landlord, ordered breakfast for six. Whilst our breakfast was in course of preparation, we dosed off into slumber, wearied with our long-continued exertion.

Just as our breakfast was ready, whilst half-asleep and half-awake, an impression came forcibly upon me that danger was nigh, and that I must at once leave the house. I immediately urged my companions to follow me out, which they were exceedingly unwilling to do; but as they had promised me submission, they at length yielded to my request. We retired to the yard at the side of the house, and commenced washing ourselves with the snow, which was now up to our knees. Presently we heard the tramping of horses, and were at once warned of the necessity of secreting ourselves. We crept beneath a pile of bushes, close at hand, which permitted a full view of the road. The horsemen came to a dead stop at the door of the house, and commenced their inquiries; my companions at once recognised the parties on horseback, and whispered their names to me. This was a critical moment, and the loud beatings of their hearts testified the dreadful alarm with which they viewed the scene. Had we been within doors, we should have been inevitably sacrificed. Our white friend proceeded to the door in advance of the landlord, and maintained his position. He was at once interrogated by the slave-hunters whether he had seen any negroes pass that way. He said, yes, he thought he had. Their number was demanded, and they were told about six, and that they were proceeding in the direction of Detroit; and that they might be some few miles on the road. They at once reined their horses, which were greatly fatigued, through having been ridden all night, and were soon out of sight. We at length ventured into the house, and devoured breakfast in an incredibly short space of time. After what had transpired, the landlord became acquainted with our circumstances, and at once offered to sail us in his boat across to Canada. We were happy enough to have such an offer, and soon the white sail of our little bark was laying to the wind, and we were gliding along on our way, with the land of liberty in full view. Words cannot describe the feelings experienced by my companions as they neared the shore—their bosoms were swelling with inexpressible joy as they mounted the seats of the boat, ready, eagerly, to spring forward, that they might touch the soil of the freeman. And when they reached the shore, they danced and wept for joy, and kissed the earth on which they first stepped, no longer the SLAVE—but the FREE.

After the lapse of a few months, on one joyous Sabbath morning, I had the happiness of clasping the poor boy we had left in the kind care of the Quaker, no longer attenuated in frame, but robust and healthy, and surrounded by his family. Thus my joy was consummated, and superadded were the blessings of those who were ready to perish, which came upon me. It is one of the greatest sources of my happiness to know, that by similar means to those above narrated, I have been instrumental in delivering one hundred and eighteen human beings out of the cruel and merciless grasp of the slaveholder.

Mr. Frank Taylor, the owner of the Lightfoots, whose escape I have just narrated, soon after he missed his slaves, fell ill, and became quite deranged; on recovering, he was persuaded by his friends to free the remainder of the family of the Lightfoots, which he at length did, and after a short lapse of time, they all met each other in Canada, where they are now living.

# CHAPTER XVIII

## HOME AT DAWN

Condition in Canada—Efforts in Behalf of My People—Rev. Mr. Wilson—A Convention of Blacks—Manual-Labour School

I did not find that our prosperity increased with our numbers. The mere delight the slaves took in their freedom, rendered them, at first, contented with a lot far inferior to that to which they might have attained. Their ignorance often led them to make unprofitable bargains, and they would often hire wild land on short terms, and bind themselves to clear a certain number of acres. But by the time they were cleared and fitted for cultivation, and the lease was out, the landlords would take possession of the cleared land and raise a splendid crop on it. The tenants would, very likely, start again on just such another bargain, and be no better off at the end of ten years than at the beginning. Another way in which they lost the profits of their labour was by raising nothing but tobacco, the high price of which was very tempting, and the cultivation of which was a monopoly in their hands, as no white man understood it, or could compete with them at all. The consequence was, however, that they had nothing but tobacco to sell, and soon there was rather too much of it in the market, and the price of wheat rose, while their commodity was depressed; hence they lost all they should have saved, in the profit they gave the trader for his corn and stores.

I-saw the effect of these things so clearly, that I could not help trying to make my friends and neighbours see it too; and I set seriously about the business of lecturing upon the subject of crops, wages, and profit, just as if I had been brought up to it. I insisted on the necessity of their raising their own crops, saving their own wages, and securing the profits of their own labour, using such plain arguments as occurred to me, and were as clear to their comprehension as to mine. I did this very openly; and frequently, my audience consisted in part of the very traders whose inordinate profits upon individuals I was trying to diminish, but whose balance of profit would not be ultimately lessened, because they would have so many more persons to trade with, who would be able to pay them a reasonable advance in cash, or its equivalent, on all their purchases. The purse is a tender part of the system; but I handled it so gently, that the sensible portion of my natural opponents were not, I believe, offended; while those whom I wished to benefit, saw, for the most part, the propriety of my advice, and took it. At least, there are now great numbers of coloured fugitives, in this region of Canada, who own their farms, are training up their children in true independence, and giving them a good elementary education, who had not taken a single step towards such a result before I began to talk to them.

While I remained at Colchester, I became acquainted with a Congregational missionary from Massachusetts, by the name of Hiram Wilson, who took an interest in our people, and was disposed to do what he could to promote the cause of improvement which I had so much at heart. He cooperated with me in many efforts, and I have been associated with him for over thirty years. He has been a faithful friend, and still continues his important labours of love in our behalf. Among other things, he wrote to a Quaker friend of his, an Englishman, by the name of James C. Fuller, residing at Skeneateles, New York, and endeavoured to interest him in the welfare of our struggling population.

He succeeded so far, that Mr. Fuller, who was going on a visit to England, promised to interest his friends there, to induce them to aid us. He came back with fifteen hundred dollars which had been subscribed for our benefit. It was a great question how this sum, which sounded vast to many of my brethren, should be appropriated. I had my own decided opinion as to what it was best for us all to do with it. But, in order to come to a satisfactory conclusion, it was thought expedient to call a convention of delegates from every settlement of blacks that was within reach; that all might see that the ultimate decision was sanctioned by the disinterested votes of those who were thought by their companions best able to judge what would meet the wants of the community. Mr. Wilson and myself, therefore, called such a convention, to meet in London, Upper Canada, and it was held in June, 1838.

I urged the appropriation of the money to the establishment of a manual-labour school, at which our children could gain those elements of knowledge which are usually taught in a grammar-school. I urged that the boys should be taught, in addition, the practice of some mechanical art, and the girls should be instructed in those domestic arts which are the proper occupation and ornament of their sex; and that such an establishment would not only train up those who would afterwards instruct others, but that it would gradually enable us to become independent of the white man for our intellectual progress, as we could be for our physical prosperity. It was the more necessary, as in many districts, owing to the insurmountable prejudices of the inhabitants, the children of the blacks were not allowed to share the advantages of the common school. There was some opposition to this plan in the convention; but in the course of the discussion, which continued for three days, it appeared so obviously for the advantage of all to husband this donation, so as to preserve it for a purpose of permanent utility, that the proposal was, at last, unanimously adopted; and a committee of three was appointed to select and purchase a site for the establishment. Mr. Wilson and myself were the active members of this committee, and after traversing the country for several months, we could find no place more suitable than that upon which I had had my eye for three or four years, for a permanent settlement, in the town of Dawn.

We therefore bought two hundred acres of fine rich land, on the River Sydenham, covered with a heavy growth of black walnut and white wood, at four dollars the acre. I had made a bargain for two hundred acres adjoining this lot, on my own account; and circumstances favoured me so, that the man of whom I purchased, was glad to let me have them at a large discount from the price I had agreed to pay, if I would give him cash for the balance I owed him. I transferred a portion of the advantage of this bargain to the institution, by selling to it one hundred acres more, at the low price at which I obtained them.

In 1842 I removed with my family to Dawn, and as a considerable number of my friends were soon there about me, and the school was permanently fixed there, as we thought, the future importance of this settlement seemed to be decided. There are many other settlements which are prosperous; indeed, the coloured population is scattered over a territory which does not fall far short of three hundred miles in extent, in each direction, and probably numbers not less than twenty thousand persons in all. We looked to the school, and the possession of landed property by individuals, as two great means by which our oppressed and degraded race could be elevated to enjoy a participation in the blessings of civilisation, whereas they had hitherto been permitted to share only its miseries and vices.

My efforts to aid them, in every way in my power, and to procure the aid of others for them, have been constant. I have made many journeys into New York, Connecticut, Massachusetts, and Maine, in all of which States I have found or made many friends to the cause, as well as personal friends. I have received many liberal gifts for my people, and experienced much kindess of treatment; but I must be allowed to allude particularly to the donations received from Boston—by which we were enabled to erect a sawmill, and thus to begin in good earnest the clearing of our lands, and to secure a profitable return for the support of our school—as among those which have been most welcome and valuable to us.

Some of the trips I have made, have led to some incidents and observations which must be the theme of a future chapter.

# CHAPTER XIX

## LUMBERING OPERATIONS

Industrial Project—Find Some Able Friends in Boston—Procure Funds and Construct a
Sawmill—Sales of Lumber in Boston—Incident in the Custom House

The land on which we settled in Canada was covered with a beautiful
forest of noble trees of various kinds. Our people were accustomed
to cut them down and burn them on the ground, simply to get rid of
them. Often as I roamed through the forest, I was afflicted at seeing
such waste, and longed to devise some means of converting this
abundant natural wealth into money, so as to improve the condition
of the people.

Full of this subject, I left my home on a journey of observation
through the State of New York, and New England. I kept my
purposes to myself, not breathing a word of my intentions to any
mortal. I found in New York, mills where precisely such logs as those
in Canada were sawed into lumber, which I learned commanded large
prices. In New England I found a ready market for the black walnut,
white wood, and other lumber, such as abounded and was wasted in
Canada.

On reaching Boston, Mass., I made known these facts and my
feelings to some philanthropic gentlemen with whom I had become
acquainted. It cannot be improper for me to mention the names of
these gentlemen, who lent so ready an ear to my representations, and
placed so much confidence in my judgment, that they furnished me
with the means of starting what has since proved a very profitable
enterprise.

Rev. Ephraim Peabody introduced me to Samuel Elliot, Esq., who was kind enough to examine carefully into all my representations, and to draw up a sketch of them, which was afterwards presented to Amos Lawrence, Esq., and others. By means of this, many of the leading gentlemen of Boston contributed about fourteen hundred dollars, to aid me in this enterprise.

With this money I returned to Canada, and immediately set myself about building a sawmill in Camden (then Dawn). The improvement in the surrounding section was astonishing. The people began to labour in earnest, and the progress in clearing and cultivating the land was cheering.

But after the framework of my mill was completed and covered, my scanty funds were exhausted. This was a trying time. I had begun the work in faith, I had expended the money honestly, and to the best of my judgment, and now should the whole enterprise fail? I immediately returned to my Boston friends. Amos Lawrence, H. Ingersoll Bowditch, and Samuel A. Elliot, Esqs., listened to me again, and gave me to understand that they deemed me an honest man. They encouraged me in my business-enterprise, and the approval of such men was like balm to my soul. They endorsed a note for me and put it into the bank, by which I was enabled to borrow, on my own responsibility, about eighteen hundred dollars more. With this I soon completed the mill, stocked it with machinery, and had the pleasure of seeing it in successful operation. I ought here to add, that the mill was not to be my own private property, but to belong to the association, which established an excellent manual-labour school, where many children and youth of both sexes have been educated. The school was well-attended by coloured children, whites, and some Indians.

This enterprise having been completed to a great extent by my own labour and the labour of my own sons, who took charge of the mill, I immediately began to consider how I could discharge my pecuniary obligations. I chartered a vessel, and loaded it with eighty thousand feet of good prime black walnut-lumber, sawed in our mill, and contracted with the captain to deliver it for me at Oswego, N.Y. I entered into a contract there with a party to have it delivered at Boston, but the party having forwarded it to New York, failed to carry it any farther. There great efforts were made to cheat me out of the lumber, but, by the good friendship of Mr. Lawrence, of Boston, who furnished me the means of having it reshipped, I succeeded in bringing the whole eighty thousand feet safely to Boston, where I sold it to Mr. Jonas Chickering for forty-five dollars per thousand feet. The proceeds paid all expenses, and would have cancelled all the debts I had incurred; but my friends insisted that I should retain a part of the funds for future use. After that I brought another large load of lumber by the same route.

The next season I brought a large cargo by the River St. Lawrence, which came direct to Boston, where, without the aid of any agent or third party whatever, I paid my own duties, got the lumber through the Custom House, and sold it at a handsome profit. A little incident occurred when paying the duties, which has often afforded me a great deal of amusement. The Fugitive Slave Law had just been passed in the United States, which made it quite an offence to harbour or render aid to a fugitive slave. When the Custom House officer presented his bill to me for the duties on my lumber, I jokingly remarked to him that perhaps he would render himself liable to trouble if he should have dealings with a fugitive slave, and if so, I would relieve him of the trouble of taking my money. "Are you a fugitive slave, sir?" "Yes, sir," said I; "and perhaps you had better not have any dealings with me." "I have nothing to do with that," said the official; "there is your bill. You have acted like a man, and I deal with you as a man." I enjoyed the scene, and the bystanders seemed to relish it, and I paid him the money.

I look back upon the enterprise related in this chapter with a great deal of pleasure, for the mill which was then built, introduced an entire change in the appearance of that section of the country, and in the habits of the people.

# CHAPTER XX

## VISIT TO ENGLAND

Debt on the Institution—A New Pecuniary Enterprise—Letters of Recommendation to England—Personal Difficulties—Called an Impostor—Triumphant Victory over These Troubles

My interest in the Manual Labour School in Dawn, was the means of my visiting England. Those who have never engaged in such business, can have no idea of the many difficulties connected with so great an enterprise. In spite of all the efforts of the association, a debt of about seven thousand five hundred dollars rested upon it. A meeting of its trustees and friends, in the year 1849, was called to consider its condition, and to devise, if possible, some means for its relief. After a long discussion of the matter, it was finally determined to separate the concern into two departments, and put it under the charge of two parties, the one to take the mill and a certain portion of the land for four years, and to pay all the debts of the institution in that time; and the other party to take the other buildings and land, and to conduct the school.

A certain party was found willing to assume the school. But it was more difficult to find one who would be enterprising enough to take the mill for four years encumbered with a debt of seven thousand five hundred dollars.

At length I concluded to do it, provided that Mr. Peter B. Smith would assume an equal share of the responsibility, and attend to the business of the mill. He readily consented.

I decided to go to England, carry with me some of the best specimens of black walnut-boards our farm would produce and exhibit them in the world's great Industrial Exhibition, then in session at London, and perhaps negotiate there for the sale of lumber. I accordingly left for England, being readily furnished with very complimentary letters of introduction to such men as Thomas Binney, Samuel Gurney, Lord Brougham, Hon. Abbot Lawrence, then American Minister to England, from Rev. John Rolfe, of Toronto, Chief Justice Robinson, Sir Allen McNab, Col. John Prince, Rev. Dr. Duffield, of Detroit, Michigan; Judge Conant, of the same city; Hon. Ross Wilkinson, U. S. Judge, residing also in Detroit; Hon. Charles Sumner and Amos Lawrence, Esq., of Massachusetts. From the gentlemen above mentioned, I had in England a most cordial reception, and was immediately introduced to the very best society in the kingdom.

I regret exceedingly to make any allusions to personal difficulties, or to individuals who have pursued an unjust and unchristian course toward me or others, but I cannot give anything like a correct view of this part of my history, without, at least, a brief allusion to these difficulties.

It was undoubtedly the plan of certain individuals of the party who assumed the care of the school, probably from unworthy sectarian feelings, to obtain entire possession of the property of the association, or certainly, completely to destroy my influence over it and connection with it.

Much to my astonishment, therefore, when I had arrived in England, and had been cordially received by the men above mentioned, and had preached in the pulpits of Rev. Thomas Binney, Baptist Noel, William Brock, James Sherman, George Smith, and Dr. Burns, in London, and had already introduced my enterprise before a portion of the British public, I was confronted by a printed circular, to the following effect: "That one styling himself Rev. Josiah Henson was an impostor, obtaining money under false pretences; that he could exhibit no good credentials; that whatever money he might obtain would not be appropriated according to the wish of the donors, and that the said Josiah Henson was an artful, skilful, and eloquent man, and would probably deceive the public." This was a severe blow, but fortunately I had already requested my friends to appoint a committee of twelve persons to examine carefully into the merits of my enterprise, and particularly desired that this committee should appoint a sub-committee of three, and a treasurer, to receive every farthing contributed to me by the public, and to appropriate it only as they should deem proper. This committee had been appointed, and consisted of Samuel Gurney, Samuel Gurney, Junior, Samuel Morley, Esq., George Hitchcock, Esq., Rev. James Sherman, Rev. Thomas Binney, Rev. John Branch, Eusebius Smith, Esq., John Scobell, Secretary of the British and Foreign Anti-Slavery Society, Lord Ashley (now Earl of Shaftesbury), George Sturge, and Thomas Sturge. The sub-committee of three were, John Scobell, Rev. John Branch, and Eusebius Smith, who appointed Samuel Gurney, Junior, treasurer. Many of the above names are known throughout the world.

When the above attack was made upon me, a meeting of those interested in my cause was called, and my accuser, who was in the country, was requested to meet me face to face.

I believe all the difficulty arose from little petty jealousies, fostered, perhaps, by the unworthy influences of slavery, over the misguided people who were for a time misled by false representations.

We met before a company of English gentlemen, who heard all that my accuser had to say. They asked me for a reply. I simply restated to them the facts I had previously made known. I reminded them that a man who devotes himself to doing good, must and will be misunderstood and have enemies. I called their attention to the misinterpretation of their own motives made by their enemies. I related to them the parable of Christ about the wheat and the tares. My recommendatory letters were re-read—a sufficient reply to the allegation that I was an impostor.

They assured me of their entire confidence and satisfaction; but to be able to clear every aspersion on my character they determined, at their own expense, to send an agent to Canada, to make a full inquiry into the matter, and advised me to accompany him. Accordingly, their agent and myself started for Canada immediately. I had already collected nearly seventeen hundred dollars, which, of course, remained in the hands of the treasurer.

A mass meeting, of all interested in the matter, was called in the institution on the premises. A large assemblage met, and Rev. John Rolfe, of Toronto, presided. A thorough examination into the records of the institution was made. The originator of the slander against me, denied having made it; it was proved upon him, and the whole convention unanimously repudiated the false charges. The agent remained in Canada about three months, and before leaving, sent me a letter, informing me that whenever I should see fit to return to England, I should find in the hands of Amos Lawrence, Esq., of Boston, a draft to defray the expenses of the journey. Accordingly, in the latter part of 1851, I returned.

The ground was now prepared for me, and I reaped an abundant harvest. The whole debt of the institution was cancelled in a few months, when I was recalled to Canada by the fatal illness of my wife. Several very interesting occurrences happened during my stay in England, which I must relate in another chapter.

# CHAPTER XXI

## THE WORLD'S FAIR IN LONDON

My Contribution to the Great Exhibition—Difficulty with the American Superintendent—
Happy Release—The Great Crowd—A Call from the Queen—Medal Awarded to Me

I have already mentioned that the first idea which suggested to me the plan of going to England, was to exhibit, at the World's Great Fair, in London, some of the best specimens of our black walnut-lumber, in the hope that it might lead to sales in England. For this purpose, I selected some of the best boards out of the cargo which I had brought to Boston, which Mr. Chickering was kind enough to have properly packed in boxes, and sent to England in the American ship which carried the American products for exhibition. The boards which I selected were four in number, excellent specimens, about seven feet in length and four feet in width, of beautiful grain and texture. On their arrival in England, I had them planed and perfectly polished, in French style, so that they actually shone like a mirror.

The history of my connection with the World's Fair is a little amusing. Because my boards happened to be carried over in the American ship, the superintendent of the American Department, who was from Boston, insisted that my lumber should be exhibited in the American department. To this I objected. I was a citizen of Canada, my boards were from Canada, and there was an apartment of the building appropriated to Canadian products. I therefore insisted that my boards should be removed from the American department to the Canadian. But, said the American, "You cannot do it. All these things are under my control. You can exhibit what belongs to you if you please, but not a single thing here must be moved an inch without my consent."

This was quite a damper to me. I thought his position was rather absurd, and for the time it seemed impossible to move him or my boards.

A happy suggestion, however, occurred to me. Thought I, if this Yankee wants to retain my furniture, the world shall know who owns it. I accordingly hired a painter to paint in large white letters on the tops of my boards: 'This is the product of the industry of a Fugitive Slave from the United States, whose residence is Dawn, Canada." This was done early in the morning. In due time, the American superintendent came around, and found me at my post. The gaze of astonishment with which he read my inscription, was laughable to witness. His face was as black as a thunder-cloud. "Look here, sir," said he. "What, under heaven, have you got up there?"—"Oh, that is only a little information to let the people know who I am."—"But don't you know better than that? Do you suppose I am going to have that insult up there?" The English gentlemen began to gather around, chuckling with half-suppressed delight, to see the wrath of the Yankee. This only added fuel to the fire. "Well, sir," said he, "do you suppose I brought that stuff across the Atlantic for nothing?"—"I never asked you to bring it for nothing. I am ready to pay you, and have been from the beginning."—"Well, sir, you may take it away, and carry it where you please."—"Oh," said I, "I think, as you wanted it very much, I will not disturb it. You can have it now."—"No sir; take it away!"—"I beg your pardon, sir," said I, "when I wanted to remove it, you would not allow it, and now, for all me, it shall remain." In the meantime the crowd enjoyed it and so did I. The result was, that by the next day, the boards were removed to their proper place at no expense to me, and no bill was ever presented to me for carrying the lumber across the Atlantic.

In that immense exhibition, my humble contribution received its due share of attention. I had many interesting conversations with individuals among that almost innumerable multitude from every nation under heaven. Perhaps my complexion attracted attention, but nearly all who passed, paused to look at me, and at themselves, as reflected in my large black walnut mirrors.

Among others, the Queen of England, Victoria, preceded by her guide, and attended by her cortege, paused to view me and my property. I uncovered my head and saluted her as respectfully as I

could, and she was pleased with perfect grace to return my
salutation. "Is he indeed a fugitive slave?" I heard her inquire; and
the answer was, "He is indeed, and that is his work."

But notwithstanding such pleasant occurrences, the time wore
heavily away. The immense crowd, kept in as perfect order as a single
family, became wearisome to me, and I was not sorry, as related in a
preceding chapter, to go back to Canada, leaving my boards on
exhibition.

On returning to England the exhibition was still in progress. There
seemed no diminution of the crowd. Like the waters of the great
Mississippi, the channel was still full, though the individuals were
changed.

But among all the exhibitors from every nation in Europe, and
from Asia, America, and the Isles of the Sea, there was not a single
black man but myself. There were negroes there from Africa,
brought to be exhibited, but no negro-exhibitors but myself. Though
my condition was wonderfully changed from what it was in my
childhood and youth, yet it was a little saddening to reflect that my
people were not more largely represented there. The time will yet
come, I trust, when such a state of things will no longer exist.

At the close of the exhibition, on my return to Canada, I received
from England a large quarto bound volume containing a full
description of all the objects presented at the exhibition, the names
of the officers of all the committees, juries, exhibitors, prizes,
&c., &c. Among others, I found my own name recorded; and in
addition a bronze medal was awarded to me. I also received a
beautiful picture of the Queen and royal family, of the size of life,
and several other objects of interest.

These testimonials of honour I greatly prize. I fully succeeded in
my mission to England, and released myself from the voluntarily-
assumed debt in behalf of the manual-labour school. While in
England, I was permitted to enjoy some excellent opportunities to
witness its best society, which I propose to relate in the following
chapter.

# CHAPTER XXII

## VISITS TO THE RAGGED SCHOOLS

Speak at Sunday-School Anniversary—Interview with Lord Grey—Interview with the Archbishop of Canterbury, and Dinner with Lord John Russell, the Great Events of My Life

While in England I was frequently called upon to speak at public meetings of various kinds. I was deeply interested in the Ragged School enterprise, and frequently addressed the schools, and also public meetings held in their behalf. I attended most of the great anniversaries held in May and was called upon to speak at many of them. On several occasions I did what I could, to make known the true condition of slaves, in Exeter Hall and other places. On one occasion, I recollect, an eminent man from Pennsylvania was addressing the anniversary of a Sabbath School Union. He boasted of the great benefits of Sunday schools in the United States, and asserted that all classes indiscriminately enjoyed their blessings. I felt bound to contradict him, and after putting to the speaker a few questions, which he stammeringly answered, I told the immense meeting that in the Southern States, the great body of the coloured people were almost entirely neglected, and in many places they were excluded altogether; and that in the majority of the Northern States, the great mass of the coloured children were not sought out and gathered into Sunday schools. This created some little storm, but my own personal observation and experience carried conviction to the people.

Being thus introduced to the public, I became well acquainted with many of the leading men of England. Lord Grey made a proposition to me, which, if circumstances had permitted, I should have been glad to have accepted. It was to go to India, and there superintend some great efforts made by the government to introduce the culture of cotton on the American plan. He promised to appoint me to an office, with a good salary. Had it not been for my warm interest in my Canadian enterprise, I should have accepted his proposal.

One of the most pleasing incidents for me now to look back upon, was a long interview which I was permitted to enjoy with the Archbishop of Canterbury. The elevated social position of this man, the highest beneath the crown, is well known to all those acquainted with English society. Samuel Gurney, the noted philanthropist, introduced me, by a note and his family-card, to his grace the archibishop. The latter received me kindly in his palace. I immediately entered into a conversation with him upon the condition of my people, and the plans I had in view. He expressed the strongest interest in me, and after about a half-hour's conversation, he inquired, "At what university, sir, did you graduate?" "I graduated, your grace,"said I, in reply, "at the university of adversity." "The university of adversity," said he, looking up with astonishment; "where is that?" I saw his surprise, and explained. "It was my lot, your grace," said I, "to be born a slave, and to pass my boyhood and all the former part of my life as a slave. I never entered a school, never read the Bible in my youth, and recieved all of my training under the most adverse circumstances. This is what I mean by graduating in the university of adversity." "I understand you, sir," said he. "But is it possible that you are not a scholar?" "I am not," said I. "But I should never have suspected that you were not a liberally educated man. I have heard many negroes talk, but have never seen one that could use such language as you. Will you tell me, sir, how you learned our language?" I then explained to him, as well as I could, my early life; that it had always been my custom to observe good speakers, and to imitate only those who seemed to speak most correctly. "It is astonishing," said the archbishop. "And is it possible that you were brought up ignorant of religion? How did you attain to the knowledge of Christ?" I explained to him, in reply, "that a poor ignorant slave mother had taught me to say the Lord's Prayer, though I did not then know how, truly, to pray." "And how were you led to a better knowledge of the Saviour?" I answered that it was by the hearing of the Gospel preached. He then asked me to repeat the text, and to explain all the circumstances. I told him the text of the first sermon I had heard, was, "He, by the grace of God, tasted death for every man." "A beautiful text was that," said the archbishop, and so affected was he by my simple story, that he shed tears freely.

I had been told by Samuel Gurney that perhaps the archbishop would give me an interview of a quarter of an hour; I glanced at the clock and found that I had already been there an hour and a half, and arose to depart. He followed me to the door, and begged of me if ever I came to England to call and see him again; and shaking hands affectionately with me, while the tears trembled in his eyes, he graciously put into my hands a bank-note for £50, and bade me adieu. I have always esteemed him as a warm-hearted Christian.

Thus ended the interview with the venerable Archbishop Sumner, of England. On my second visit to England, I had an invitation, in company with a large number of Sabbath School teachers, to spend a day in the beautiful grounds of Lord John Russell, then Prime Minister of England. His magnificent park, filled with deer, of varied colours, from all climes, and sleek hares, which the poet Cowper would have envied, with numberless birds, whose plumage rivalled the rainbow in gorgeous colours, together with the choicest specimens of the finny tribe, sporting in their native element, drew from me the involuntary exclamation: "Oh, how different the condition of these happy, sportive, joyful creatures, from what was once my own condition, and what is now the lot of millions of my coloured brethren in America!" This occupancy of the elegant grounds of England's Prime Minister, for the day, by a party of Sabbath School teachers, was a picnic, with this difference, that, instead of each teacher providing his own cakes, and pies, and fruit, they were furnished by men and women, who were allowed to come on to the grounds, with every variety of choice eatables for sale. After strolling over these charming grounds, enjoying the beautiful scenery, the happy gambols of the brute creation, and the conversation of the many intelligent men and women with whom we came in contact, we were most unexpectedly, at five o'clock, sent for to visit the elegant mansion of the proprietor. There we found what I will call a surprise-party, or at any rate, we were taken by surprise, for three hundred of us were ushered into a spacious dining hall, whose dimensions could not have been less than one hundred feet by sixty, and here were tables, groaning under every article of luxury for the palate, which England could supply, and to this bountiful repast we were all made welcome. I was invited to take the head of the table; I never felt so highly honoured. The blessing was invoked by singing the following verse:

> "Be present at our table, Lord,
>   Be here and everywhere adored:
>   These creatures bless,
>   And grant that we may feast
>   In Paradise with Thee!"

After dinner, various toasts were proposed, on several subjects, and in my humble way I offered the following:

"First to England. Honour to the brave, freedom to the Slave, success to British emancipation. God bless the Queen!"

Cheers and laughter followed the reading of this toast, succeeded by the usual English exclamations, *"Up, up, up again!"* I again rose and gave, To our most Sovereign Lady, the Queen:

"May she have a long life, and a happy death. May she reign in righteousness, and rule in love!"

And to her illustrious consort, Prince Albert:

"May he have peace at home, pleasure abroad, love his Queen, and serve the Lord!"

Among the distinguished persons who made speeches on this joyous occasion, were Rev. William Brock, Hon. Samuel M. Peto, and the brother-in-law of Mr. Peto, with his accomplished and beautiful lady. Thus ended one of the pleasantest days of my life.

# CHAPTER XXIII

## CLOSING UP MY LONDON AGENCY

My Narrative Published—Letters from Home Apprising Me of the Sickness of My Wife—Departure from London—Arrival at Home—Meeting with My Family—The Great Sorrow of My Life, the Death of My Wife

The dinner at Lord John Russell's, as detailed in the previous chapter, was in the month of June, 1852; from that time to the 1st of August, I was busily employed in finishing up all matters connected with my agency, in which I was very successful, having accomplished the objects of my mission. During the month of August, I was engaged in publishing a narrative of incidents in my slave-life, which I had been urgently requested to do by some of the noblest men and women in England. Just as I had completed the work, I received, on the 3rd of September, a letter from my family in Canada, stating that my beloved wife, the companion of my life, the sharer of my joys and sorrows, was at the point of death, and that she earnestly desired me to return immediately, that she might see me once more before she bade adieu to earth. This was a trying hour for me. I was in England, four thousand miles from my home. I was not long in deciding to go home. On the morning of the 4th of September, having received the letter from home at four o'clock on the afternoon of the 3rd, I was on my way from London to Liverpool, and embarked from Liverpool on the 5th, in the steamer Canada, bound for Boston. On the 20th of the same month I arrived at my own Canadian home. Those who have been placed in similar situations, can realise what must have been my feelings as I drew near my humble dwelling. I had heard nothing since the information contained in the letter which reached me at Liverpool. I knew not whether my dear wife, the mother of my children, she who had travelled with me, sad, solitary, and footsore, from the land of bondage, who had been to me a kind, affectionate, and dutiful wife for forty years, was still alive, or whether she had entered into her rest.

A merciful Father had, however, kindly prolonged her life, and we were permitted once more to meet. And oh! such a meeting! I was met in the yard by four of my daughters, who rushed to my arms, delighted at my unexpected return. They begged me not to go in to see mother, until they should first go and prepare her for it, thinking very wisely that the shock would be too great for her poor shattered nerves to bear. I consented that they should precede me. They gradually prepared her mind for our meeting. When I went to her bedside, she received and embraced me with the calmness and fortitude of a Christian, and even chided me for the strong emotions of sorrow which I found it utterly impossible to suppress. I found her perfectly calm and resigned to the will of God, awaiting with Christian firmness the hour for her summons. She was rejoiced to see me once more, while at the same time she said that perhaps she had done wrong in allowing me to leave England when my business-prospects were so flattering. I told her that I was more than satisfied, that I was truly thankful to my Heavenly Father for granting us this interview, no matter what the pecuniary sacrifice might be. We talked over our whole past life as far as her strength would permit, reviewing the many scenes of sorrow and trouble, as well as the many bright and happy days of our pilgrimage, until exhausted nature sought repose, and she sunk into a quiet sleep.

The day following she revived; my return seemed to inspire her with the hope that possibly she might again be restored to health. It was not, however, so to be; but God in His mercy granted her a reprieve, and her life was prolonged a few weeks. I thus had the melancholy satisfaction of watching day and night by her bed of languishing and pain, and was permitted to close her eyes when the final summons came. She blessed me, and blessed her children, commending us to the ever-watchful care of that Saviour who had sustained her in so many hours of trial; and finally, after kissing me and each one of the children, she passed from earth to heaven without a pang or a groan, as gently as the falling to sleep of an infant on its mother's breast.

"Who would not wish to die like those
Whom God's own Spirit deigns to bless!
To sink into that soft repose,
Then wake to perfect happiness!"

I can truly and from an overflowing heart say, that she was a sincere and devoted Christian, a faithful and kind wife to me, even to the day of her death arranging all our domestic matters, in such a manner as to contribute as largely as possible to my comfort and happiness.

# CHAPTER XXIV

## MY BROTHER'S FREEDOM

Am I My Brother's Keeper?—Efforts to Secure His Freedom—Attempts to Raise the Money—Union of His Family

I received numerous tokens of regard from many philanthropic gentlemen while I was in London, which I shall never forget; but I was particularly touched by the special kindness of Samuel Morley, Esq., and George Hitchcock, Esq., of St. Paul's Churchyard. These two gentlemen invited me to dine with them every day at half-past one. I gratefully accepted their invitation, and dined alternately with these gentlemen, always receiving a very warm welcome from them. The spirit of manhood, one of the strongest elements of my mind, was in no instance wounded, for I was invariably received and entertained as a respected guest. One day I was sitting at Mr. Morley's table, and was about to partake of his bountiful supply of nourishing food, when suddenly my mind reverted to the past. I remembered the trying scenes of my eventful life, and that my only brother was still bound in the iron chains of slavery, deprived of all the comforts of life, dragging out an abject, miserable existence, while I was surrounded with luxuries, and sitting at the sumptuous table of one of the first men in the kingdom. I could almost hear the clanking of his chains, and, in my mind's eye, see him with scarcely a crust of bread to satisfy his hunger, or a glass of water to quench his thirst. I was so forcibly impressed with my vision, that I rose from the table without eating a mouthful of food.

Struck with my unusual appearance, for I had always been cheerful and happy, Mr. Morley said, 'What is the matter, Josiah? Has anything occurred to disturb your peace of mind?"

At first I could not control my emotions sufficiently, to reply. He added, "Come, come, Josiah, do help yourself and make yourself at home."

Soon I summoned the courage to tell him the cause of my agitation, and asked him "to excuse me from eating my dinner on that day, for I had no appetite."

I then and there resolved in my own mind, that as soon as I returned to America, I would make every possible effort to secure to my brother the blessed freedom I enjoyed.

Slavery had no power to eradicate the social ties that bound the different members of a family together, and though families were often torn asunder, yet memory generally kept the affections warm and abiding.

I had made several efforts to induce my brother to run away previous to my going to England. Mr. William L. Chaplain, of New York, saw him in his southern home, and tried to induce him to take the underground railroad—that is, to run away. But he found my brother's mind so demoralised or stultified by slavery, that he would not risk his life in the attempt to gain his freedom, and he informed me of this fact. Still I could not rest contented, and Mr. Chaplain promised to make another effort, as he intended to visit the neighbourhood again. He laboured with my brother the second time, with no good result, and then he endeavoured to assist Mr. Toomb's slaves, who had resolved to escape from Georgia to Canada. Mr. Chaplain was detected, and thrown into prison to await a trial. He was released on bail, three times the amount of the value of the slaves. The Hathaways, benevolent Quakers of Farmington, New York, Asa B. Smith, and William R. Smith, his son, of the same town, paid the bail, which they desired Mr. Chaplain to forfeit, as they knew that the result of the trial would be that he would be hung. I will here add that the Smiths had to sell their farms, and were pecuniarily ruined for the time, and it is with pleasure that I make this record of their generosity in the Anti-Slavery cause.

On my return to Canada, the release of my brother was my uppermost thought. Whenever I have adopted the language of the prodigal son, who said, "I will arise, and go to my father,"—that is, when I have uttered in my heart the words, "God helping me, I will,"—I have somehow had the ability to accomplish my undertaking. Though I may have been obliged to change my plans and course of action, and pursue others more feasible, yet, ultimately, the end has been most marvellously attained. All my previous plans to rescue my brother had failed, but I was not at all disposed to relinquish the project. By the aid of friends, I learned that the mistress to whom my brother belonged would give him his freedom-papers for 400 dollars, and I concluded that I must raise 550 dollars, or about £110, so that I should be able to take him to my home in Canada. I consulted some of the Anti-Slavery friends in Boston, particularly Amos Lawrence, Esq., and they agreed to publish the story of my life, as I had suggested to them, that I might be able, from its sale, to raise a sufficient sum of money to buy my brother's freedom. I took a package of the books on my back and travelled in the New England States, and succeeded in interesting the people, so that I was enabled to raise the money I required. Then, through the negotiation of Mr. Charles C. Berry, cashier of the City Bank in Boston, Massachusetts, who had friends at the South, I joyfully sent the ransom. Soon my brother came from Maryland to Baltimore; thence by sea to Boston, where I met him and took him to my home in Canada, and kept him there for fifteen years. When President Lincoln's Proclamation of Emancipation gave freedom to all the slaves in America, my brother's eldest son came to Canada to see his father, and the meeting would have done President Lincoln's heart good if he had witnessed it.

The son went back and remained with his mother and brothers for three years. Then he came to Canada to take my brother to rejoin his wife and family in New Jersey; for after the Emancipation Act was enforced, my brother's mistress removed from Maryland to New Jersey, where her husband bought a large dairy-farm. She had in vain endeavoured to suit herself with ordinary white servants. Then she persuaded my brother to bring his family to her farm, and they have remained with her to this day as hired servants, receiving excellent wages for their faithful services. My brother's eldest son superintends her dairy, and is the head-man, in whom great confidence is placed. My brother is now ninety-one years of age, and is the only living relative I have, excepting my wife and children.

# CHAPTER XXV

## MRS. STOWE'S CHARACTERS

My Visit to Mrs. Stowe—Why I Am Called "Uncle Tom"—Her Interest in My Life-Story—
Her Famous Book—Is It an Exaggeration?—Mrs. Stowe's Key

I was in the vicinity of Andover, Mass., in the year 1849, where Mrs. Harriet Beecher Stowe resided. She sent for me and my travelling companion, Mr. George Clark, a white gentleman, who had a fine voice for singing, and usually sang at my meetings to add to their interest. We went to Mrs. Stowe's house, and she was deeply interested in the story of my life and misfortunes, and had me narrate its details to her. She said she was glad it had been published, and hoped it would be of great service, and would open the eyes of the people to the enormity of the crime of holding men in bondage. She manifested so much interest in me, that I told her about the peculiarities of many slaveholders, and the slaves in the region where I had lived for forty-two years. My experiences had been more varied than those of the majority of slaves, for I was not only my master's overseer, but a market-man for twenty-five years in the market at Washington, going there to sell the produce from my master's plantation.

After Mrs. Stowe's remarkable book, "Uncle Tom's Cabin," was published, and circulated in all parts of America, read openly at the North, and stealthily at the South, many thought that her statements were exaggerations. She then published the Key to her book, to prove that it was impossible to exaggerate the enormities of slavery, and she therein gave many parallel cases, and referred to my published life-story, as an exemplification of the truth of the character of her Uncle Tom. From that time to the present, I have been called "Uncle Tom," and I feel proud of the title. If my humble words in any way inspired that gifted lady to write such a plaintive story that the whole community has been touched with pity for the sufferings of the poor slave, I have not lived in vain; for I believe that her book was the beginning of the glorious end. It was a wedge that finally rent asunder that gigantic fabric with a fearful crash.

Though she made her hero die, it was fit that she did this to complete her story; and if God had not given to me a giant's constitution, I should have died over and over again long before I reached Canada. I regard it as one of the most remarkable features of my life that I have rallied after so many exposures to all kinds of hardships. I am grateful to God for His abundant mercies to me in bringing me out of Egypt into the promised land, and I hope to be His faithful servant to my dying hour.

The white slaves, George Harris, and his wife Eliza, were my particular friends. George Harris, whose real name is Lewis Clark, is about three parts white. He has travelled and lectured with me in the New England States. He is a very ingenious and intelligent man, as Mrs. Stowe represented him. He and his wife lived in Canada for a long time after their escape from slavery, and finally moved to Oberlin, Ohio, to educate their children, for there is still a great prejudice, in certain localities of Canada, with regard to admitting children who have one drop of black blood in their veins, into the schools where white children are taught; yet the coloured people of those districts pay their proportion of taxes and school-rates.

Many people thought that Mrs. Stowe's interesting description of Eliza was a great exaggeration, and that it was impossible for a slave woman to escape in such a manner. That Mrs. Stowe had a real incident for her character will be evident from the following quotation from the published "Reminiscences of Levi Coffin," in which he gives the truthful version of this thrilling incident as told him by the woman herself:

"She said she was a slave from Kentucky, the property of a man who lived a few miles back from the Ohio River, below Ripley, Ohio. Her master and mistress were kind to her, and she had a comfortable home, but her master got into some pecuniary difficulty, and she found that she and her only child were to be separated. She had buried two children, and was doubly attached to the one she had left, a bright, promising child, over two years old. When she found that it was to be taken from her, she was filled with grief and dismay, and resolved to make her escape that night, if possible. She watched her opportunity, and when darkness had settled down, and all the family had retired to sleep, she started with her child in her arms and walked straight toward the Ohio River. She knew that it was frozen over at that season of the year, and hoped to cross without difficulty on the ice; but when she reached its banks at daylight she found that the ice had broken up and was slowly drifting in large cakes. She ventured to go to a house near by, where she was kindly received and permitted to remain through the day. She hoped to find some way to cross the river the next night, but there seemed little prospect of any one being able to cross in safety, for during the day the ice became more broken and dangerous to cross. In the evening she discovered that pursuers were near the house, and with desperate courage she determined to cross the river or perish in the attempt. Clasping her child in her arms, she darted out of the back door, and ran toward the river, followed by her pursuers, who had just dismounted from their horses when they caught sight of her. No fear or thought of personal danger entered Eliza's mind, for she felt that she would rather be drowned than be captured and separated from her child. Clasping her babe to her bosom with her left arm, she sprang on to the first cake of ice, then from that to another and another. Sometimes the cake she was on would sink beneath her weight, then she would slide her child on to the next cake, pull herself on with her hands, and so continue her hazardous journey. She became wet to the waist with ice-water, and her hands were benumbed with cold, but as she made her way from one cake of ice to another, she felt that surely the Lord was preserving and upholding her, and that nothing could harm her.

"When she reached the Ohio side near Ripley, she was completely exhausted and almost breathless. A man who had been standing on the bank watching her progress with amazement, and expecting every moment to see her go down, assisted her up the bank. After she had recovered her strength a little, he directed her to a house on the hill in the outskirts of the town. She made her way to the place, and was kindly received and cared for. It was not considered safe for her to remain there during the night, so, after resting awhile, and being provided with food and dry clothing, she was conducted to a station on the underground railroad, a few miles farther from the river. The next night she was forwarded on from station to station to our house in Newport, where she arrived safely and remained several days.

"Other fugitives arrived in the meantime, and Eliza and her child were sent with them by the Greenville branch of the underground railroad to Sandusky, Ohio. They reached that place in safety, and crossed the lake to Canada, locating finally at Chatham, Canada West."

Eliza died in Oberlin this year, but her husband is still an active, enterprising man. His brother's complexion is so nearly white, that it is almost impossible for any one, who is not acquainted with his history, to perceive that he has any coloured blood. He is in the Custom House in Boston, Mass.

There was on our plantation a negro girl, Dinah, who was as near like Mrs. Stowe's Topsy as two peas in a pod. Dinah was clear-witted, as sharp and cunning as a fox, but she purposely acted like a fool, or idiot, in order to take advantage of her mistress. When the latter said, "Dinah, go and do your work," she would reply with a laugh, "Yes, yes; when I get ready;" or, "Go, do it yourself." Sometimes she would scream out, "I won't; that's a lie—catch me if you can;" and then she would take to her heels and run away. She was so queer and funny in her ways, that she was constantly doing all kinds of odd things, but escaped the whipping that other slaves, who did not behave half so badly, had received daily, because her mistress thought she was an idiot.

There was a gentleman, Mr. St. Clair Young, who lived in the neighbourhood of my old home. He was as kind-hearted as Mrs. Stowe's St. Clair. Soon after I left the district, I learned that he became a converted man, gave his slaves their freedom, sold his land, moved into Indiana, and preached as a Methodist minister.

It is a fact, that as soon as the conscience of a slaveholder was aroused, he was obliged to give up his slaves or his religious convictions; for these were so antagonistic they could not agree. Mr. St. Clair Young had a sweet little girl who could easily have been the original of precious little Eva. The children of slaveholders were often kind-hearted, good-tempered, and were genial companions during their childhood, before they were old enough to exercise authority. Then, under the influence of their circumstances, slavery would often turn the mildest disposition into a cross one, the same as thunder will turn sweet milk.

Bryce Litton, who broke my arm and maimed me for life, would stand very well for Mrs. Stowe's cruel Legree. Litton was the most tyrannical, barbarous man I ever saw, and I have good reason to know that his revengeful and malicious spirit would have led him to perform the most cruel acts. He lived a miserable life, like a hog, and died like a dog a few years after I left that part of the country. He was universally detested even among slaveholders, for when an overseer far exceeded the bounds of what they termed humanity, he was a marked man, his society was avoided, and his career was by no means a pleasant one. Even slaveholders, like thieves, had a certain code of honour.

Mrs. Stowe's book is not an exaggerated account of the evils of slavery. The truth has never been half told; the story would be too horrible to hear. I could fill this book with cases that have come under my own experience and observation, by which I could prove that the slaveholder could and did break every one of the ten commandments with impunity. A slave was not allowed to testify against a white man in a court of justice, hence he had to bear all the cruelties his master was pleased to inflict. I could give statements of facts that would appal a generous and kind-hearted soul.

After my successful visit to England, I travelled in Canada, and in Maine, New Hampshire, Vermont, Massachusetts, Connecticut, and Rhode Island. In all these States I was cordially welcomed as a speaker in the pulpits of the Congregationalists, Presbyterians, Methodists, Baptists, and Universalists. I held many meetings, and discussed the subject of slavery in all its bearings on society. At that time, slavery was considered to be a permanent institution of the South, and it was supposed that nothing but an earthquake would have the power to break up the foundations of the system. It is a mistaken idea that the majority of the slaveholders would have sold their slaves if the government had offered to buy them. They liked the system, had grown up with it, and were not disposed to part with it without a struggle. Anti-slavery ideas were not popular at the South, nor generally at the North. On this account, those who had sufficient moral courage to discuss the merits and demerits of the system, were accustomed to hold meetings and conventions for this purpose. I was constantly travelling and doing all I could to help to change the public sentiment of the North.

# CHAPTER XXVI

## THE MANUAL LABOUR SCHOOL AT DAWN

Troubles—Misplaced Confidence—Eyes Opened—Lawsuit—Wilberforce University

Difficulties had arisen in the management of the Manual Labour Institution at Dawn, before I visited England in 1851. Debts had accumulated, and I had pledged myself to take the sawmill and part of the land, and clear off the debts as I have before explained. The school was established with the express idea that it was not to promulgate sectarianism. But those who had obtained control over it, were inclined to drift it into a particular sect. I opposed this, and hence incurred their disapprobation. Soon after I visited England, and began to raise a fund for the benefit of the school; but, as I before stated, the dominant party attempted to counteract my efforts by slandering me. My committee in London proposed that a gentleman should visit Canada, and ascertain the facts respecting my personal character. Mr. Samuel Morley suggested that I should go to Canada with the gentleman. He said, "If things are as you say, Josiah, we will provide a way for you to return, and you can then finish your work here. But if you are an impostor, as your enemies have represented, you will then be at home with your family; you will not want to come back and we shall not want to see you. If it were proved you were here getting money on false pretences, nothing would save you from being sent to Van Diemen's Land."

When we reached Canada, there was a convention called on the premises where the school was located; careful inquiries were made, and no charges were found against me. After this English gentleman had ascertained all the particulars, he returned to England, made a favourable report to my committee, and remained in England for a year or two.

Before he left America, he arranged with Amos Lawrence, Esq., of Boston, that I was to go to England when I was ready, and deposited the money with him for my passage. Accordingly, in the winter of 1851, the same year, I was back in England; I finished my work, raised about £1,000 for the school, and left this money, which was sufficient to defray all the debts of the school, in the hands of the treasurer, Mr. Gurney, of London. The English gentleman told the trustees of the school at Dawn, "that the spot could be made the brightest spot in the garden of the Lord, if there were only an efficient manager at its head to control it." All but one of the trustees agreed to assign the institution to him to manage. He promised to clear it from debt, and represented to the trustees "that the committee in London whom I had selected, would be responsible for him, or would aid him in placing the school on a permanent foundation, and in making it a glorious moral lighthouse, a beacon whose illumination should be perpetual."

This looked reasonable, and I agreed with the trustees when they conferred upon him the assignment, for I knew that he was respected in London, had been sent to the West Indies to inquire into the condition of slavery there, and that his reports had helped to secure the emancipation of the slaves in the West Indies.

He presented the case to the committee in London, and when he told them he expected they would endorse him, Samuel Morley said, "We did not authorise you to represent that we would shoulder the responsibility of the school, and we cannot do it." It was decided that the committee would be interested in the welfare of the school, but that they would not incur any pecuniary risks for it.

In about two years the gentleman returned to Canada, and took with him the funds I had raised for the school debts. He bought up the debts, giving to some 62 cents in the dollar, to others the full amount. Then, his family being with him, he took possession of the premises, and the charge of the institution in earnest. He said, "I am going to renovate this place, 'de novo.'" I shall never forget those words, they sounded so grandly to my ears.

I soon found he intended to commence at the beginning. I had great faith in his integrity, and believed every word he uttered, and at that time would have pledged myself to carry out his ideas to the uttermost. As the land was in splendid condition, he probably anticipated having by-and-by a model farm, which would bring a large annuity.

It is my candid opinion that, in the beginning, he intended to benefit the coloured race, and to have a splendid school which should be the pride of the neighbourhood. If he had been a practical instead of a theoretical farmer, he doubtless would have accomplished those blessed results. He soon began to buy the most expensive cattle in the market, at fancy prices, and without any reference to the fact that he had not sufficient fodder to feed them after he had them in his stables. He also bought expensive farming utensils to work the farm scientifically, and then pulled down the school-buildings, as they were too primitive to suit his magnificent ideas, and he promised to erect more substantial and commodious buildings. I upheld him in all these suggestions, for I had a kind of respect for the man that almost amounted to veneration.

At his request, I often went to market with him, and he generally asked my judgment about the fine cattle that he was constantly adding to his stock. I sometimes ventured to suggest that they would require a great amount of grain during the long Canadian winter. But he invariably declined to take my advice in this respect, and I concluded he knew what he was doing, and must have had experience, or he would not have pursued such a reckless course.

One year passed away, and there were no school buildings and no school. Our people said, "Surely he will commence building next year." The second year passed away, and again I silenced the questionings and murmurings; for I still had confidence in his integrity of purpose. The third year passed, and then the coloured people began to tell me "I was in league with him, and that in some way he and I were gaining pecuniary advantages from the cultivation of that splendid tract of three hundred acres of land on the Sydenham River."

By-and-by his finances became involved, and he borrowed of me several hundred dollars to meet his bills, and the fourth year passed; still there was no school. He supported his family and his brother-in-law's family from the farm that belonged to our coloured people. True, the family of his brother-in-law, from their straitened circumstances, frequently came to my house for food, and my wife gave them the best we had. The fifth, sixth, seventh, eighth, and ninth year passed, and we had no school, and not an individual could make any change. He had no title to the land, so he had no power to sell this, and it was a most fortunate thing. I had repeatedly said to him, "The people are growling." He replied, "Let them growl." He invariably refused to discuss the question. At length, when nine years had passed, I began to doubt the man's intentions, and I thought I would have a serious conversation with him on the subject, and ascertain what he proposed doing. I said to him as politely as I could, "The people about here are beginning to talk very hard about you and myself, and I do not want to let them have any cause to think ill of us. If you will be so kind as to give me some intimation when you propose to commence the school-buildings I can satisfy them." He curtly replied, "When I get ready; when I please." I said, meekly, "It is quite unfortunate for me, for my honour is impeached, as I have always defended you."

"What's your honour to me? I don't care what they say." He added, in a very dignified manner, "I did not come here for the coloured people to dictate to me."

I replied, "If you really do not intend to build us a school, you ought to leave the farm, and let us manage for ourselves."

With some excitement he said, "Pay me what I have expended during the many years I have tried to make this place meet its expenses, and I will go at once."

The scales fell from my eyes; I saw through the man's motives. I went to the coloured people and told them, sadly, "that I had been greatly deceived, that we should never have a school until we gained possession of the property, and that if I had a power of attorney to act for them I would consult an able lawyer, and ascertain what could be done." A convention of the coloured people of the region was called. I was given by them the power of attorney to examine the subject and act for them. I went immediately to London, Canada, and laid the case before Lawyer Wilson, since made a judge, and Lawyer McKenzie, two eminent lawyers. They promised to weigh the matter very carefully, and to let me know the result. In about three months they sent me word "that if I could find two substantial men, one coloured and one white, who owned freehold property unencumbered, and were willing to pledge themselves to pay the costs, that they would undertake the case." They said "I must keep in the background, while the two men should be the ostensible 'relators.' " I found the men that same night, and pledged myself to them "that I would pay the costs if they would allow their names to be used." The attorney-general brought the suit for non-fulfilment of trusts and for maladministration of the affairs of the school. A clever lawyer of Toronto defended the gentleman, and the war commenced in earnest. In the beginning I paid two hundred dollars, and borrowed money from time to time by mortgaging, first one house and lot, then three houses and lots, then re-mortgaged them, then sold several lots to pay the mortgages, then re-mortgaged, and was constantly called upon to pay disbursements to the lawyers. It was an anxious, perplexing period, for the case was taken from court to court, till *seven* years had elapsed, when at last, wearied and exhausted, the lawyer offered to give it up as a non-suit if his expenses during these seven years could be paid. To this we all agreed, and the important case was decided in our favour. Then the Court of Chancery appointed a new board of trustees, granted a bill to incorporate the institution as the Wilberforce University, also the power to sell the land, which brought about 30,000 dollars, £6,000, in cash, with a stipulation that the University should be erected on a plot of ground in the same county. The town of Chatham, Canada, was selected, and for four years the school has been *self-sustaining,* and has been attended by many pupils.

Thus ended seven years of perplexity and excitement. During them I learned many practical lessons.

In the beginning of the contest the gentleman left the premises, but installed his son as master over them. I had leased a plot of ground on the school-farm, and had ploughed it for several years. When this young gentleman heard that my men were ploughing the ground, he sent word to them "to be off his premises." I said to my men, "Go to your ploughing to-morrow morning, and I will be there to sustain you."

The next morning my men began their work. Soon the young gentleman appeared on the spot with several of his men. He commanded mine "to leave at once." I was at hand, and said, "I leased this land from your father, and as long as he retains the possession of the whole farm I have a legal right to work this plot, and I shall defend that right."

He mildly said, "Why, Mr. Henson, is that you? I thought you were a praying man, not a fighting man?"

I replied, "When it is necessary I can fight, as I have done for Canada when she was in trouble. I intend to respect the rights of others, and they must respect mine." He soon became angry; first came words, then blows. I could not prevent him from bruising his head several times against my heavy walking-stick, which I held before me to ward off the blows he attempted to level at me. When he was tired of that kind of play, he went off muttering a threat, "that he would have a writ served upon me immediately." I at once had my fastest horse harnessed to my waggon, and rode off to the nearest magistrate accompanied by a constable. The magistrate readily gave me a writ for the young gentleman. When we were returning we met him within a mile from the railroad station. He had intended to go and see his father, and then have a summons sent out for me. The constable alighted, touched him on the shoulder, and said, "You are my prisoner, in the name of the Queen, for assault and battery on Josiah Henson on his own premises."

He was crestfallen and very angry, especially when he was obliged to walk between ten and fifteen miles to Dresden to the court to have his trial. His lawyer removed the trial from one court to another, till at London, Canada, he was compelled to pay costs and a bonus to end the suit. He gave me no further trouble, for he perceived that I had a practical knowledge of the common laws of the country. This incident shows how important it was for the coloured people to be able to defend their natural and inalienable rights after they became freemen and citizens of Canada.

# CHAPTER XXVII

## IDOLS SHATTERED

### The Fate of the Sawmill—How the Grist-Mill Vanished in the Night

As so many of my friends have been interested in the history of the sawmill that was erected on our school-premises, a few words about its fate may be appreciated. It was a great undertaking to secure the money necessary to purchase the materials for the mill, and the building of it, and a great responsibility to work it successfully. It would have continued to have been a very profitable investment, as it was at first, had it been properly managed; for the River Sydenham is navigable for vessels, and we could send the lumber by water to Detroit, or to almost any part of the United States.

Though there was no school on the premises, the mill was leased to a man who employed forty or fifty men, and they worked faithfully, sawed many thousand feet of lumber, and the lumber was shipped from time to time to different ports. After several prosperous years there came a period of depression, simply because the man who leased the mill did not attend to his business carefully. At length he had a lot of timber sawed, filled three vessels with it, and these sailed for some unknown port. The man disappeared and left his workmen in a starving condition, with their wages in arrears. He gave out the word that he was going off to lay in supplies for the future. The men had no money and could not procure the necessaries of life. They waited till they were convinced their master did not intend to return; then they vented their angry and revengeful feelings on the mill itself, and tore up even its foundations. Thus they ruthlessly destroyed this valuable building, the establishment of which had cost me so many anxious hours, and had proved to be such a valuable

*125*

piece of property in my hands. When it was gone, I felt as if I had parted with an old idolised friend.

Though Canada was the land of freedom to the fugitive slaves, yet they met with so much prejudice at first, on account of their colour, that it was with difficulty they could procure the common comforts of life. When they endeavoured to have their corn ground they found it no easy matter. A man would often walk three and four miles with two or three bushels on his shoulders, through paths in which the mud was knee-deep, leave his corn at the mill, and then go repeatedly after it in vain; he would be put off with a variety of excuses till he was quite discouraged, and would conclude that it was almost useless for him to raise any grain; and yet there was no other way for him to have a bit of bread or corn-cake. I was tired of hearing these complaints, which became real grievances, and without having a spare dollar in my pocket, I determined that, as the only remedy was to have a grist-mill, independently of any already established, I would erect one and help the coloured people out of their difficulties.

Accordingly, I went to Boston, Mass. among my devoted friends, and told them of the necessities of the case, and by their generous help, which, thank God, has never failed me in an hour of need, I soon collected 5,000 dollars, or £1,000, obtained a plan, arranged for its building, introduced steam-power to work it, and in a short time we ground the corn for the entire neighbourhood, and this venture was a decided success.

When the lawsuit commenced, I did not wish to have any trouble with the young gentleman who was placed on the school-premises, about the gristmill, which I had rented to a man. A short time previously, I, therefore, proposed to sell the mill, as it belonged to me personally; but I agreed to move it from the grounds of the institution, as I had no lease of the land on which it was built, so I was obliged to resort to strategem to accomplish my purpose. My son-in-law was the miller, and acceded to my proposition, which was that twenty men should be secreted in the mill one Sunday night, and as soon as the hour of midnight had struck, these men should carefully take down the mill and remove every vestige, foundation, engine, and timber, a short distance on to the road, which was the common highway. By ten o'clock on Monday morning the mill had vanished, as if by magic, from its old resting-place, and by noon it was carried off, in ten or twelve teams that were in readiness, to Dresden. It was erected speedily, and it remains there to this day, in splendid working order.

# CHAPTER XXVIII

## FUGITIVE SLAVES ENLISTING IN THE STATES

Taking up Arms for My Country—Civil War in America—Risk of Imprisonment for Seven Years—Special Providence Saves Me

During the Canadian rebellion I was appointed a captain to the 2nd Essex Company of Coloured Volunteers. Though I could not shoulder a musket, I could carry a sword. My company held Fort Maldon from Christmas till the following May, and also took the schooner Ann and captured all it carried, which were three hundred arms, two cannons, musketry, and provisions for the rebel troops. This was a fierce and gallant action, and it did much towards breaking up the rebel party, for they could not obtain provisions while we held the fort, which we continued to do till we were relieved by the colonel of the 44th Regiment from England. The coloured men were willing to help defend the government that had given them a home when they had fled from slavery.

My sword had been turned into a ploughshare. When the civil war in America broke out, somehow the coloured people in Canada had an idea that the result of it would be the abolition of slavery. If I could have carried a gun, I would have gone personally, but I thought it was my duty to talk to the people. I told them "that the young and able-bodied ought to go into the field like men, that they should stand up to the rack, and help the government." My oldest son, Tom, who was in California, enlisted on a man-of-war in San Francisco, and I suppose he must have been killed, as I have not heard from him since that time.

My son-in-law, Wheeler, enlisted in Detroit. I advised the people, in general terms, to do the same, and said that if any of them wished to go to enlist early, so as to secure the bounty offered, I would provide for their families till they could send the bounty-money to them. A number went, and some lost their bounty-money through "sharpers" lying in wait for them. So I proposed to go with a second lot, that they need not be annoyed in this way. There was one man, named John Alexander, who had decided to be of this second company. I therefore sent some pork and clothing from the stores to his wife and family, as they were poor. At the last he gave me the slip, and during my absence he traitorously and untruthfully declared "that I had tried to induce him and others to enlist." He even testified to this statement before a magistrate, and my wife telegraphed to me "to remain in Boston and not return, for a writ was ready to take me as soon as I appeared in Dresden, and if the charge was proved, the penalty, by the Foreign Enlistment Act, would be seven years' imprisonment." At first I thought I would remain away till the excitement had subsided. Then I reflected that what I had done was for the cause of Christ, and with good motives; that the war was a righteous war; that the coloured people ought to take some part in it. I said to one of my companions, "God helping me, I will not run away when I have done no wrong."

I soon returned to Dresden, and rode in a waggon to my own door in the most public manner; for I was not ashamed to be seen. This was on a Thursday afternoon about four o'clock. My family were highly excited, and with tears in their eyes, begged me to go away; but I said, "I must remain and have this slander cleared up publicly, as the whole community had been discussing it." The next morning, Friday, before seven o'clock, the constable, an old friend, came to my home. I was sitting on the fence talking to my son-in-law. The constable said, pleasantly, "Good morning, Mr. Henson; have you any potatoes to sell?" "Good morning," I answered. "Yes, sir, I have some." "I should like to buy a few if you can spare any." "How many do you want?" "Ten or fifteen bushels." "I can spare one hundred bushels." "Oh, I do not want so many." "Very well; I suppose it is only one good black potato about my size that you want, and you can have it if you will come and get it."

He at once came forward, put his hand on my shoulder, and said, "Mr. Henson, you are my prisoner in the name of the Queen. Here is a writ for you."

"All right, Bill." His name was William Nellis. "Let me have a bit of breakfast, and then you can have me." We went into the house, where my wife and children were crying. I invited the constable to eat, but he declined, saying he had eaten his breakfast. We talked for half an hour. Then I took my hat and said to him, "I am ready; how are we going? The writ says you must take me."

The constable said, "If you will have your horse and waggon prepared, I'll pay for it." "I will do no such a thing; you must take me, and if you have no other way, go get a wheelbarrow, for I will not walk with you." He argued with me for an hour or two, till it was nearly noon. Then I said, "You can go your way when you like, and you may tell the squire I will soon be there."

I found that two clever magistrates had arranged everything before I came home. I was not allowed to make a defence or to have a lawyer to plead my case. One of the magistrates was prejudiced against me on account of the interest I had taken in the suit against the school-trustees; the other, Squire Terrace, was my friend. But both were obliged to decide legally, and if they had agreed as to the interpretation of the law, there would have been no opportunity for me to appeal from the magistrate's court. They did not agree, and the case was referred to the next magistrate. When he had heard the statements, he could not decide, and it was proposed to consult the county attorney, Mr. McLean, of Chatham, who was a friend of mine. I had worked faithfully for his grandfather, and was esteemed by the family as a man who conscientiously kept his word, and tried to discharge every known duty. Mr. McLean said, "I am surprised to find these charges against Mr. Henson. He is a common-sense man, and knows the laws better than the majority of the people. There must be a screw loose somewhere in this affair. If what John Alexander has declared on oath be true, nothing will prevent Mr. Henson from seven years' imprisonment in Kingston under the Foreign Enlistment Act, which does not allow a man to entice or persuade another to enlist in the army. Mr. Henson, give me your version of the case."

I then told the whole truth, word for word, and did not dodge a single hair. I admitted that I had given John Alexander's wife provisions, and said "I would give them to any one, white or black, if I had them to give, and the individual needed them; but I did not suppose the man would turn my generosity against me in this base manner." I perceived that this was the only proof they had, and the man called it bribery on my part to get him to enlist.

Squire McLean said, "We all know Mr. Henson's character, that he is an honest, upright, Christian man. Now what is the character of his accuser? Today is Saturday; I will defer my decision till Monday morning, and in the meantime inquiries can be made respecting the veracity of John Alexander."

How I should get released from the legal net that was spread over me I did not know, but I trusted in God; I knew He had delivered me many, many times before from the lions' den, and, like Daniel of olden times, I now put my faith in Him. In my heart I cried out, "Oh, Lord, deliver me, but in prison, or under the free air of heaven, I will praise Thy great and holy name."

Still in the custody of the constable, I was allowed to go home on Saturday afternoon. A man called that night at my house and said to me, "There is a man loading his boat up the river, a bit; he comes from the same district where John Alexander lived before he prowled about Dresden. This Smith says Alexander is a thief, that he stole a lot of clothes from a line in a yard there, and other things, and a writ was taken out to apprehend him, but he ran away, and is now trying to send an innocent man to prison by telling a lot of lies, and he ought to be stopped."

As soon as this man left my house the constable gave me permission to call on Squire Terrace. This was Saturday evening. I gave him the drift of what the man had told me of Smith's knowledge of John Alexander. The squire said, "Go home and be quiet over Sunday, for Monday morning before the sun rises I will be at the river, and if I can find that Smith, and he will testify as you have represented, I will have him in court on Monday morning by nine o'clock."

I remained quiet during Sunday, and my soul was full of joy and rejoicing, for this unlooked-for providence of God which I was sure would deliver me.

"Suppose he should not be found?" said one of my family. I answered, "But he will, I am certain." Though my fate hung upon a thread that might easily be cut, I anticipated no evil results.

Early on Monday morning Squire Terrace was at the river's bank; he saw the boat half a mile off; he hailed it, and said, "Is there a man named Smith on that boat?" "I'm the man, sir." "Come ashore, I want to speak to you." This Smith then told the magistrate that he had worked with Alexander, and that "he was a mean, lying thief, and he could prove it." "Enough; I subpoena you to appear at the court this morning by nine o'clock to testify in this case," Squire Terrace answered.

The time came. It was understood at court that a witness would testify to the character of John Alexander, who was present in an exultant frame of mind. The witness was called. The attorney said, "You have worked with John Alexander; is he a trustworthy man? Has he a good, reliable character?" Smith said, "He is one of the greatest rogues out of prison." Alexander was about to interrupt him; but Smith looked him square in the face, and said, "You know if you stepped your foot where you used to work with me, you'd be hustled off to prison, where you ought to go if you got your deserts." Squire McDonald exclaimed, "What do you say? Is the man a rogue—has he no character?"

"He has none, sir; but was obliged to 'cut sticks,' as we say up in the country—that is, he gave 'leg bail' and ran away."

"Well," said Squire McDonald, "if John Alexander has no character, Mr. Henson has his acquittal." He was as much astounded at the appearance of the witness as my accuser was. It is needless to say that my friends and family rejoiced with me at this signal deliverance. I sent John Alexander word "that the world, or that part of it where I lived, was too small for him and me; that if he crossed my path I was afraid I should be tempted to shoot him." He was in terror, for he knew he deserved shooting, or a severe castigation. At last he sent by a couple of friends a humble request for me to forgive him; I told them he must come to me personally and acknowledge his contemptible meanness in the presence of three of my friends, whom I named. He came at an appointed time, and on his knees he confessed his sin and ingratitude to me for my kindness to his family, and in the name of the Lord begged my forgiveness.

I said, "It was about the meanest thing you could do to defame me in my absence, when my character was one of the most precious things I had to cherish. You ought to be hung, and I have been tempted to dispatch you; but I leave you in the hands of the Lord; vengeance belongeth to Him, and not to me. I forgive you. Go and sin no more."

Not very long after, there was another peculiar incident, connected with the civil war, which threatened to give me some trouble. Many in the States, both white and coloured, enlisted merely to receive the bounty, and then they "jumped the bounty," as it was termed—that is, they took the money and did not go into the army. A friend of mine, Alexander Pool, a coloured man of my neighbourhood, told me "that his son and wife's brother were talking about running away to join the army, but he thought he ought to get a bounty for them, and he wished I would take them to Detroit and advise them what to do." I replied, "I do not intend to subject myself to another trial on that score. I don't care whether they enlist or not; still, if they are going to the war, you ought to get some of their bounty, and it would enable you to pay for your land, but I can't enlist them."

He repeatedly asked my advice about the way to get to Detroit, and at length solicited me to accompany them there, and he offered to pay my expenses and for the time I lost. I said to the lads, "It is not my wish that you should enlist, but for your father's sake I will go to Detroit with you to protect you from the sharpers." We went, and they entered their names as Martin Pool and Basil Pool, and represented themselves as two brothers. I thought by this that probably their idea had been to run away, but the officer took possession of them and handed me a packet of money in an envelope directed to their father. I took from this package one hundred dollars and sent to the two lads. I took the remainder, eleven hundred dollars, to their father. He gave me four hundred for my expenses and trouble. The father had never seen so much money as he now had in his possession, but instead of using it for a good purpose he squandered it in dissipation. These lads went to the war, were in several battles, came back, and got their discharge. They demanded some of their bounty-money from their father. He pretended he had not received any. They said, "I must have kept it," and were very angry. They demanded it of me; but I indignantly told them "that they might go back to their father and ask him for it." They consulted a lawyer, who sent them to Squire McDonald, the same magistrate who conducted my case with John Alexander. He said, "I am surprised that Mr. Henson should have had anything to do with enlisting men, for he knows the law in such a case. I would advise you to make no stir in the matter, but to go with me to see him. Perhaps I can induce him to pay you something down, and then by instalments in the future to make up the difference. He called upon me with these lads, and said, "I am amazed to find that you have enlisted these young men and appropriated their bounty. I have called to suggest to you, Mr. Henson, to pay them something to-day, and then you can arrange to make up the balance at a more convenient time."

I replied, "Squire McDonald, I know nothing of what you refer to. I have not done what these men say." I turned to them and said, "I suppose you have your discharge-papers with you?" "Oh, yes," Basil Davis answered, eagerly, not suspecting in the least my purpose in wishing to see them. He pulled his out of his pocket. I turned to Squire McDonald and said, "You had better look after this man, he enlisted and was discharged under a false pretence; why didn't he use his right name, unless it was to enable him to run off and 'jump the bounty?' and now, because he could not succeed in escaping, but had to serve in the war, he must come back and vilify my name; you had better look after him."

The squire and his clients soon left me in peace. As their shadows were retreating I could not help laughing out loud and exclaiming, "Though there are more ways to kill a dog than feeding him on sweet cake, it will take cleverer lads to get the better of Father Henson than those who have just paid me a visit." I, however, learned another lesson, and thought that in the future I had better let coloured volunteers gain wisdom and experience for themselves, without giving them either advice or personal assistance.

# CHAPTER XXIX

## EARLY ASPIRATIONS CHECKED

Desire to Learn to Spell Nipped in the Bud—Superstition—Insurrection—Preaching and Its
Penalty—Negro Songs

Sharp flashes of lightning come from black clouds, sprightly words of
wit come from those who live in dark hovels, and bright gleams of
intelligence come from children brought up in the most abject
ignorance of books. It has often been a mystery to me how I gained a
practical knowledge of figures, enough to sell all the produce of four
farms during twenty-five years in the market at Washington, for I had
to compute fractions and make great estimates, and yet I never
studied arithmetic. I came in contact with many of the most
intelligent gentlemen in Washington, for I used to take great pride in
selecting the best butter for some of the best families, and was
delighted to take it to their houses. They manifested a great interest
in me, and when they conversed I listened attentively and remembered their phrases and sentences, and in this way I learned to speak
more correctly than the majority of the slaves, or even the poor
whites of the district. I never said "go dar," or "gib me," and other
negro phrases, for I was anxious to imitate those whom I respected as
gentlemen. I also gained a very good practical knowledge of law from
hearing clever lawyers talk and explain their cases. If I had been a
white boy and been blessed with the opportunities to study law in
my youth, I think I should have been delighted with its study and
practice. The knowledge I "picked up" has enabled me in several
instances to protect my own rights and those of my people.

I shall never forget my first attempts to learn to spell. I was about
thirteen years of age, when I nearly lost my life because I made an

135

effort to gain this kind of knowledge. The schools for the white children were generally four or five miles apart, and a negro boy was accustomed to drive his master's children in a waggon to school in the morning, and to go for them in the afternoon. A negro boy, William, belonging to Lewis Bell, was a bright, clever lad. He learned to read and to spell by hearing his master's boys talk about their lessons while they were riding to and from school. I was so pleased to hear William read, that he told me if I would buy a Webster's spelling-book in the store at Washington he would soon teach me. I had already made some ink out of charcoal, and had cut a goose quill so that it looked like my master's pen, and I had begun to make scratches on odd bits of paper I had picked up in the market. I had noticed that all the butter I sold was stamped with two letters, "I. R.," and after awhile I learned that those letters stood for my master, Isaac Riley, and I tried and tried to imitate those marks, and they were really the first letters I ever wrote.

It seemed to me if I took some of the apples that fell from the trees in the orchard and sold them I should be able to get the money for the spelling-book. I did this. Early the next morning I was about to harness the horse for my master; the horse was frisky and ran, and I ran to catch him, when my hat fell off and the book in it dropped on to the ground. After I had harnessed the horse my master exclaimed, "What's that?" "A spelling-book." "Whose is it?" "Mine." "Where did you get it?" "Bought it, sir, when I went to market." "How much was it?" "Eleven cents." "Where did you get the money?" "I sold some apples out of our orchard." "Our orchard!" he exclaimed, in a passion. "I'll teach you to get apples from our orchard for such a vile purpose, so you'll remember it. Give me that book." I stooped to pick it up, and as I saw his big cane coming down I dodged. "Pick up that book," he cried, using an awful oath. At last I was obliged to do it, when he beat me across the head and back till my eyes were swollen and I became unconscious. My poor mother found me in this state, and it was some time before I was able to be about my work again. When my master saw me after I recovered, he said, sneeringly, "So you want to be a fine gentleman? Remember if you meddle with a book again I'll knock your brains out." The wonder to me is, why I have any brains left. I shall carry to my grave a scar my master made that day on my head.

I did not open a book again till after I was forty-two years of age and out of the land of slavery. There was so much excitement when it was understood by the masters that Lewis Bell's slave, William, was intending to teach their slaves, that William was sent to Georgia and sold, for the masters in our neighbourhood said, "We will not have our niggers spoiled by that rascal."

Many a time, when I was a young man, I have driven chickens and pigs into the woods and killed them in the night, and then taken them to the cabins of the feeble, sickly women, who had to work during the day under a hot sun, without having sufficient food to nourish them and their little babies.

I used to reason that the slaves were the property of their masters, and so were the pigs, and if accidentally the pigs got a sore throat, and I induced them to wander away, it was only taking a part of master's property, the pigs, to make the other part of his property, the women, more valuable. For the same reason, when I had a row to hoe between the rows of two women, I have often made them sit down and rest while I would hoe all three rows, and would give them a loud warning to get up if I perceived master was coming; in this way I have saved many women from beatings with the lash.

It is a singular fact that the law did not recognise it as stealing if a slave took any food from his master. If he stole a chicken from another plantation he could receive by law sixteen stripes at the public whipping-post, twenty stripes for a turkey, twenty-five or thirty for a pig, thirty-nine for a sheep, which was the highest. It is not surprising that slaves took all the food they could find, for their life was one of incessant toil, and they were scantily supplied with the poorest fare, which could not possibly give them strength. When removed from the debasing influences of slavery, the fugitives, as a general thing, had as keen perceptions of the sense of property as the white population. It has been an exceptional thing for a coloured man to steal after he reached Canada; and stealing is regarded by him as a disgraceful sin. He knows he can enjoy the proceeds of his own labour in the land of freedom, and all the fugitives in Canada can earn their own livelihood if they will exert themselves. At first they had to live on roots and herbs; but after a few years they began to own their own farms, to raise all kinds of grain and vegetables, and to cultivate a great variety of fruit-trees. All may now sit under their own vine and fig-tree. Some have asked me "if those who have been accustomed to a hot climate at the south, do not find the cold Canadian winters long and unpleasant?" I have only one reply to make to that query, *"that cool freedom is far better than hot oppression."* It is easy to protect ourselves against the inclemency of the weather, but we could not ward off the blows of a cruel master, who was well aware that it was necessary to crush the manhood of the slave, to make him subservient to his master's selfish interests.

Superstition and ignorance are generally found in company together. Sixty years ago the whites in Maryland and Virginia were very ignorant. With the exception of the few who were educated at the north and the professional gentlemen, not one man in 500 could write his name decently. There can be seen at the present day many state-records and documents in which the people have signed their names by making a cross or a mark. It is not strange that among such people many were exceedingly superstitious. It is well known that blacks as a class were very superstitious, and believed in all kinds of conjurations.

As a lad I was useful, very clever, and was often called my master's "Man Friday," after Robinson Crusoe's faithful servant. I soon perceived the weak points in the character of my mistress, and that she was very timid. She would sometimes complain if I did not get as good prices for the provisions as she desired, and I would hear of this through some of the servants, or by putting my ear down to the doorsill of the room where she was fretting to my master. The next morning I would talk to a little ball I had suspended to a delicate string which I held in my fingers. A short distance off no one could see the string, and as I talked to the ball it appeared to bound up and then go down again without being touched. "So Missis Riley thinks I didn't get enough for her butter?" Up would come the ball. "I got all it was worth?" Down the little ball would go. It was astonishing what a reputation for cleverness that ball obtained in my hands. "Why, it knows everything," I once heard my mistress say. If a dog howled, or a hen made an unusual noise, there was some meaning attached to it, and an interpretation made. The negroes often imagined they had frogs in their ankles or spiders in their throats, and the spell had to be broken by some doctor who understood how to take advantage of this peculiar feature of the negro's mind. Education soon clears away all this belief in witchcraft.

In many districts the blacks far outnumbered the whites. Sometimes one planter had 400 negroes on an extensive plantation. The year before Nat Turner's insurrection, for which he lost his life, there was an extensive organisation among the blacks who represented a district of fifty miles in extent, in the neighbourhood where I lived. The plans were well-laid, every detail had been well-considered, even the time when the blow was to be struck had been appointed.

It was to be at eleven o'clock at night, when the moon was full at that time. Certain slaves were to fire the barns and stables in all the different plantations comprised within the area, at the same hour. Then others were to be stationed at the houses, and as the masters rushed out to ascertain what the matter was, the slaves were to kill them and then kill the entire families, and burn up their houses. "Not one white shall be left to tell the tale!" exclaimed an excited slave. I could not agree with the leaders, and yet I felt that the evils of slavery could not be exaggerated, and that we had a right to our freedom. Little by little the light came to my soul, till I was convinced that it was not a feasible or Christian plan of procedure; so I began to raise doubts and queries, to discuss the subject, and finally, I had the moral courage to speak my mind plainly. I said, "Suppose we should kill one thousand of the white population, we should surely lose our own lives, and make the chains of those in bondage heavier and more securely riveted. No, let us suffer in God's name, and wait His time for Ethiopia to stretch forth her hands and be free." At last I prevailed on them to abandon the project. It is certain that the slaves had provocation enough to rise and take the places of their masters. I saw at one time, a faithful fellow-workman receive 500 lashes on his bare back, simply because, when he was a little tardy, he resisted being beaten by a cane over the head. He was nearly dead when he was given into my care for me to look after his condition.

After I began to preach, I just escaped receiving thirty-nine lashes at the public whipping-post in Alexandria, near Washington, simply for asking the Mayor to give me permission to comply with a request to preach there. He indignantly ordered me to be taken to prison on the Saturday, and to receive the whipping on the Monday or to pay a fine of 25 dollars. I had no money, and I prayed to God to show me what to do. At last I found some one to send to my master's young brother. He came to see me in jail, and by giving him my watch, worth 45 dollars, he paid the fine and I was released. Before we left the city, however, the blacks collected around me, and the Lord opened my mouth, and I had the moral courage to give them such a sermon as they had not heard for a long time. As soon as I had finished my sermon, my young master, who was ready with his waggon, hurried me into it, and we rode out of the city in great haste, for, as he told me, the law would not allow me to preach openly to a number of slaves in that district.

Under very different influences, I was talking or preaching to a very large audience of intelligent white ladies and gentlemen in Tremont Temple, Boston, Mass., after I had escaped from slavery. I had nearly finished my discourse, when, wrought up to the highest pitch of excitement, I exclaimed, "I wish I had the entire control of the southern slaveholders for twenty-four hours!" A man at the extreme end of that large hall jumped up, and said, excitedly, "Mr. Chairman, may I ask the speaker one question?" The gentleman who presided, fearing that the man intended to raise a row, said, mildly, "Mr. Henson has the platform, and no one must interrupt him without his permission." I said, "The gentleman at the back of the house may ask me the question." He rose, and, in an excited manner, rather sneeringly asked, "And pray, what would you do with them?"

There was a breathless silence, and all my friends were anxious, not knowing how much I might be agitated by my past memories of the cruelty of slaveholders, and that I had cause for revengeful feelings, if I did not manifest them. I said, in as loud and deep a voice as I could command, "First, I would have them all thoroughy converted to God; and secondly, I would send them immediately to heaven, before they had one minute's time to backslide." I then sat down, and there was such an uproar of cheers and hurrahs as I had never heard at any meeting.

I may as well close this chapter by giving a sample of the songs the slaves sing when the family is about to separate because some of the members have been sold to new masters. Sometimes they sing these plaintive melodies, clanking their chains to keep time with their voices.

When I was down in Egypt's land,
Close by the river,
I heard one tell of the promised land,
Down by the river side.

*Chorus.*    We'll end this strife,
Down by the river,
We'll end this strife,
Down by the river side.

I never shall forget this day,
Down by the river,
When Jesus washed my sins away,
Down by the river side.

*Chorus.*

'Twas just before the break of day,
Down by the river,
When Jesus washed my sins away,
Down by the river side.

*Chorus.*

Cheer up, cheer up, we're gaining ground
Down by the river.
Old Satan's kingdom we'll pull down,
Down by the river side.

*Chorus.*

Shout, dear children, for you are free,
Down by the river,
Christ has brought to you, liberty,
Down by the river side.

*Chorus.*

# CHAPTER XXX

## MY FAMILY

A New Light in My Desolate Home—My Children—My Third Visit to England—Mr. Hughes

My heart and home were desolate after I lost the wife who had been my faithful companion in slavery, and had escaped with me to Canada. For four years it seemed to me her place could not be filled. I kept company with no one; I never walked out with any woman, and I thought it would be so to the end; but I was so lonely, so utterly miserable, that at last I decided that I would try to find another companion. I had travelled extensively, and had made many acquaintances, but I knew of but one woman whom I cared to have for a wife. She was a widow, an estimable woman, one who had been a faithful teacher in the Sunday School, and quite a mother in the church to which she belonged. She had been brought up by a Quaker lady in Baltimore, and had received a good education in the ordinary branches. Her mother had been a slave, but was such a superior laundress, that she earned enough to buy her freedom of her mistress, and then she earned enough to buy her husband's freedom. One of her daughters has lived for many years with a family, and she has travelled with them around the world.

I went to Boston and called upon the pleasant widow several times before I could summon the courage to ask her if she would be my wife. It was about two years before we were married in Boston by our bishop, who was holding a series of meetings at the time in the city. She has made me an excellent wife, and my cup has indeed run over with God's mercies. She had one son and two daughters. I have now seven living children. My eldest son, Tom, went to California, and I think was killed in the civil war, for I have not heard from him since he enlisted. Isaac, my second son, was a clever and godly lad. He was educated in a school in London for many years through the kindness of my London friends. He married, was ordained as a Wesleyan minister, and preached for about fifteen years. He died when only thirty-seven, and was universally beloved. My third son, Josiah, was very anxious to learn the shoemaker's trade, but I persuaded him to help me on my farm. At twenty-two he married a very capable young woman, and then he said, "I am determined now to have my own way, father; I've tried to stick to the farm, but I can't do so any longer; I know I can make my way." He left Canada, and went to Jackson, Michigan, where there was a great prejudice against employing coloured young men in the shoe-business. He found an English boot and shoe-maker there who agreed to teach him. He was bound to him for two years. His young wife was a good washer and ironer, and she went out to work by the day, and obtained excellent wages, and the young people were very happy. At the end of the two years his master said to me, "Young Josiah Henson is a clever fellow. He can make as good a boot as his master." My son then went to Adrian, where there was an anti-slavery college. He bought a couple of lots of ground in time. He worked at his trade during the winter, and in the spring went out to do lathing, plastering, and hanging paper in the houses of some of the best people. He was very fond of horticulture, and has cultivated a great variety of fruit trees. He has continued to do well, and now has property worth several thousand dollars. My fourth son, Peter, is a farmer, looks after my farm, and stays with me.

My four daughters are married; all of them can read and write very well, and one of them has been educated for two years in Oberlin. There has been a great change in the condition of the coloured people since I first went to Canada. Then, there was not a Bible or a hymn-book for a coloured individual to use for several hundred miles; and none of us could have read the Bible if we had possessed one; but now there are in every cabin the elements of education. When it was known I had preached at the South, I had urgent requests to labour in this way in Canada, and as a Methodist episcopal elder I have had a district of three hundred miles, over which I have travelled, held meetings, attended conferences, have established churches, and been interested in every movement that has been started for the improvement of our people.

We have had great assistance from the late Rev. Mr. Hughes, the Secretary of the Colonial and Continental Missionary Church Society in Canada (who died April 11th, 1876). For sixteen or seventeen years he worked most zealously as a missionary in Canada; he was always my devoted friend; he knew all my troubles with regard to the school, that my finances had been crippled by my mortgaging my property to pay the expenses of that lawsuit during seven years, and he proposed that I should again visit London in my old age, and he assured me that my old friends would rally to my assistance. It was a sad day to me when, only three months before I left Canada, I was summoned to his dying bedside. His last moments were peaceful, and his faith to the last was triumphant. He died as he had lived, a genuine Christian. In the last annual report of the Colonial and Continental Church Society, which has reached me since I came to London, he has kindly referred to my mission in London as follows: "Josiah Henson (Mrs. Stowe's 'Uncle Tom'), who, I think you are aware, resides near Dresden, proposes starting in a week or two for England. His principal object will be to try to raise money to clear off a heavy mortgage he had to give on his farm in order to meet the cost of the long lawsuit over the Dawn Institute property, and which but for him would have been entirely lost. Mr. Henson bore the whole expense of that suit, and when the case was settled it was found that the trustees, appointed by the Court of Chancery, had no power to refund him out of the estate. The proceeds of the sale of the Dawn property, nearly 30,000 dollars, constitute the greater part of the endowment of the Wilberforce Educational Institute. You will be pleased to learn that this institute is now in active operation, and if only wisely managed in the future will be a great blessing, in an educational point of view, to the coloured people of Canada. A voyage to England is no light undertaking for a man of Henson's extreme age, he being now eighty-seven. Though he is not by any means the man he was when in England twenty-five years ago, yet he still possesses extraordinary energy both of body and of mind, and knowing, as I do, his circumstances, and the hardship of his case, I sincerely hope he may be successful."

It may be well to add a few of many testimonials I received, when it was known I intended to visit England:

"We, the undersigned, beg to certify that we have known the Reverend Josiah Henson for a number of years; that he has resided, as we believe, in the County of Kent, Ontario, for the last forty-five years; that he has ever borne the highest character in this community, and is worthy of the confidence of the public.—Wm. Bryant Wells, Judge C. C. Co. Kent, Ontario; John Mercer, Sheriff, Kent; Wm. Douglas, Clerk of the Peace, Kent; H. Smythe, Mayor, Town of Chatham; Francis W. Sandys, A.M., Archdeacon of Kent, Ontario.— Chatham, 25th April, 1876."

"Memorial Church Rectory, London, Ontario, May 16, 1876.—To the Secretaries of the Colonial and Continental Church Society.— Dear Sirs,—In the last report to the Society, our lamented friend Mr. Hughes speaks of a proposed visit to England of the Rev. Josiah Henson (Mrs. Stowe's 'Uncle Tom') for the purpose of raising funds to clear off a mortgage which Mr. Henson had to give on his farm in order to meet the costs of a lawsuit over the Dawn Institute. The object of this note is to introduce him to you, hoping that you may be able to further his cause in England. He was well known to the friends of the coloured race twenty years ago, but the changes make it essential that he should have some who can recommend him in his present effort. You are already acquainted with the work of the Wilberforce Institute, which has been sustained at great personal expense by Mr. Henson. His experience as a slave, and as a preacher among the fugitives in Canada, makes his story extremely interesting. Mrs. Stowe, in her 'Key to Uncle Tom's Cabin,' gives a sketch of his life to confirm the character she has painted. On the authority of Mr. Hughes, who knew Mr. Henson for many years, and thought most highly of his work and character, I beg to introduce to you one who has been a great blessing to his coloured brethren in Canada. If you can give him any letters, or further his cause in any way, it will assist the movement with which the Colonial and Continental Church Society has been connected for many years.—Yours very sincerely, W. Harrison Tilley, Clerical Secretary to Corresponding Committee, Colonial and Continental Church Society."

"Dresden, Ontario, Canada, March 10, 1876.—Mr. Josiah Henson being about to proceed to England, has requested me to give him a letter testimonial. Mr. Henson is so highly respected throughout Western Canada, and also so well known to many influential persons, both in the United States and in England, that he scarcely needs anything of the kind from any individual. I have known Mr. Henson for more than sixteen years, and have great pleasure in bearing my testimony to his sterling Christian character. Mr. Henson's life has been an unusually active and eventful one. For many years he was a slave, and was most cruelly treated; and since his escape to Canada, now more than forty years ago, he has occupied a foremost place in all movements for the advancement of his people. Through his efforts for their good he has, unfortunately, suffered considerable pecuniary loss, and has been compelled in consequence to mortgage his farm. It is with the view of lifting this incumbrance that he has, in his extreme old age, resolved, in response to a cordial invitation given him, to visit England. I heartily commend him and his cause to the British public, and hope that he may have, in every respect, a 'prosperous journey by the will of God.'—Thos. Hughes, Missionary of the Church of England, Dresden."

# CHAPTER XXXI

## MY THIRD AND LAST VISIT TO LONDON

Meeting Old Friends and Making New Ones—"Christian Age"—Prof. Fowler's Description—My Mission Accomplished

After the lapse of twenty-five years I was delighted to be in London again. Many of the friends whom I had known during my former visit have passed away. I found that Samuel Morley, Esq., and George Sturge, Esq., remembered me most kindly, and that they were disposed to be my staunch, steadfast friends; they have been genuine friends to me during all these long years that have passed, and I hope to greet them when we have all passed over the River Jordan. They at once promised to aid me in removing the weight that was pressing down my spirits and embarrassing my declining years when I could not labour as formerly. They started a fund, and generously headed it, not only with their influential names, but each gave £50 towards it. May God bless them for their generosity, and for their abiding friendship to me. Sir Thomas Fowell Buxton, Bart., and R. C. L. Becavan, added £25 each to the fund, and many belonging to the Society of Friends added their subscriptions. I should like to record that I have always received the most generous treatment, both in America and England, from the members of the Friends' Society, and specially from George Sturge, Esq., who has interested himself to the extent of assuring me he would send me back to my Canadian home with a light heart. I am certain my heart will be *heavy with gratitude,* for it will be full of that emotion, and I shall pray to my dying day for blessings to rest upon one who has afforded me so much relief.

147

Among the new friends I have made are Professor and Mrs. Fowler, formerly of New York, now residing in London, and I have always felt at home in their pleasant office.

Professor Fowler, with his remarkable skill, gave me an analysis of my character from my head. I told him "I should have supposed my old master had beaten out all my brains," but he humorously remarked "that perhaps my skull was so thick, the blows did not penetrate."

The description he gave of me was published, with my portrait, in the *Christian Age,* a weekly paper, and notwithstanding there were 80,000 copies of this number circulated, a third edition had to be printed to meet the demand. I am sure Professor Fowler's description will be of interest, and therefore give it insertion here.

"The *organisation* of 'Uncle Tom' is as remarkable as his life and labours have been. His father was six feet in height, and was a very powerful, muscular man. He had a strong sense of justice and virtue, and an unflinching will. His son, Uncle Tom, is five feet seven inches in height.

"From his father he inherited a very strong osseous, muscular system, and a powerful constitution, as his physiology indicates and his most laborious life has proved. He has a large brain, twenty-three inches in circumference, with a predominance of brain in the superior coronal region, indicating great mental vigour, compass of mind, and availability of talent. His head is narrow, long, and high. The strength of his *social* nature centres in love to his wife and children, especially the latter, which he has proved to be intense, by his carrying two of his children on his back 600 miles, travelling on foot during the night, while fleeing from slavery and seeking his freedom on British soil in Canada. His head is very high in the crown and above the ears. No white man has a greater sense of liberty, love of freedom, manliness of feeling, and independence of mind, joined to a degree of firmness, perseverance, and determination of mind, not exceeded by a Cromwell or a Wellington, than Uncle Tom. His sense of *moral* obligations and love of truth are very strong.

"He is scrupulously honest, and his mind is as transparent as daylight. He is not inclined to double dealing, deception, and hypocrisy, undue selfishness or greed in his disposition, but he is cautious, looks ahead, and prepares for the future.

"He has by organisation, as well as by grace, a strong feeling of devotion, worship, and sense of dependence. As a Christian, some of his strongest religious feelings are his love of prayer and thankfulness, and his disposition to seek aid and consolation from a higher source than man in the hour of trouble. The exercise of his *veneration* was his comfort when a slave, and it has been a comfort to him through all the vicissitudes of life. *Benevolence* is also very large; he is full of the missionary element, delights to do good, and many years of his life have been spent in labours of love. He is liable to forget his own interests when he can make himself useful to others. In his mind, 'faith without works is dead.' He does not expect an answer to his prayers without he makes an effort in the right direction. He is active, industrious, and delights to be occupied; is always busy in one way or another; and is not afraid of hard work if necessary. His mind works slowly but quite safely. When he has an object he holds on to it till his end is accomplished. He is one of the real plodding kind. He has not the qualities to render him showy and imaginative, but he has good powers of imitation, and can easily adapt himself to a change of situation and circumstances. He has a vast amount of dry humour, and is very direct, practical, natural, and truthful in his style of talking. His intellectual faculties are of the most practical and common-sense kind.

"He has superior powers to draw correct conclusions and inferences, as he understands them. He deals mostly in facts, conditions, qualities, and bearings of things, and turns all his knowledge into useful channels. He has a remarkable gift for observing everything that is transpiring around him; has a superior memory of persons he sees, facts he hears, of places, events, and anecdotes; and his mind is like a great storehouse, in which he has collected a vast amount of interesting incidents. He has a good *capacity* to arrange, systematise, organise, and plan, with reference to definite results.

"He is a great lover of simple truths; acts and speaks just as he feels, and thinks instinctively; cannot assume a character and appear differently from what he really feels, and has a thorough abhorrence of hypocrisy or falsehood. He has great courage in times of danger, also great presence of mind and great self-control in the midst of excitement and opposition.

"He is not revengeful, but has any amount of contemptuous feeling towards those who act meanly. He is more direct in his style of talking than copious or wordy; yet, having but little restraint from *secretiveness,* and so much varied knowledge and experience, he finds it easy to talk when he has attentive listeners.

"Though in his eighty-eighth year, he appears to be at least fifteen years younger, for he is firm in step, erect in form, disposed to wait on himself, and prefers to walk rather than ride; is positive in his manner of speaking, social in his disposition, emotional in his feelings, tender in his sympathies, distinct in his intellectual operations, humorous in his conversation, and apt in his illustrations. While many at fifty years of age consider that there is no opportunity left for them to improve their condition, Uncle Tom, at eighty-eight, is buoyant, elastic, and still anxious to make improvements.

"I have been much gratified in making the acquaintance of 'Uncle Tom,' and hope the friends of the coloured race in England will send him back to Canada with sufficient means to enable him to live in comfort the remainder of his days."

Another of my new friends is Mr. John Lobb (the managing editor of the *Christian Age*). He has an extensive acquaintance with most of the evangelical ministers in London. He has arranged all my engagements, assisted me in addressing, at their request, very large audiences in public buildings, chapels, and places of worship. Indeed, he has on every public occasion rendered me material assistance as my *Chairman.* Under such obligations, I felt it to be a pleasant duty to make some acceptable acknowledgment, which I trust it will prove to be. I have therefore assigned the sole copyright of this work to Mr. John Lobb.

On my visit to London in 1851, I had made acquaintance with the family of Mr. Thomas Church, author of "Gospel Victories," and was glad to renew our friendship and love in 1876. I thank him for so ably assisting in my correspondence while in London.

I cannot omit to acknowledge my obligations to Dr. Macaulay, of the Religious Tract Society, and the able editor of a widely prized monthly, called the *Sunday at Home.* To other remembrances of kindness, I feel thankful for his excellent article in the October part for 1876, headed "Uncle Tom," and his confirmatory observations in favour of my history, and the object of my present visit to London.

# CHAPTER XXXII

## "UNCLE TOM" AND THE EDITOR'S VISIT TO
## HER MAJESTY THE QUEEN

As her Majesty's most gracious reception of Mr. Henson and Mr. Lobb has excited much interest throughout the country, and as incorrect accounts have appeared, we give the following extract from the *Times,* for the accuracy of which we can vouch.—Ed.

"On Monday, March the 5th, the Rev. Josiah Henson, the hero of Mrs. Stowe's story of 'Uncle Tom's Cabin,' left London on a visit to her Majesty at Windsor Castle. Mr. Henson travelled by South-Western train to Windsor, accompanied by Mrs. Henson, his second wife, and Mr. John Lobb, of the *Christian Age,* the Editor of Uncle Tom's Autobiography. The party reached the Castle at one, and were received by Sir T. M. Biddulph, K.C.B., who, after introducing them to Major-Gen. H. Ponsonby, invited them to partake of luncheon. At three her Majesty, accompanied by Prince Leopold and Princess Beatrice, appeared in the corridor leading to the Oak room, attended by the Hon. Horatia Stopford and the Countess of Erroll, ladies-in-waiting. Mr. Henson was then presented to her Majesty by Sir T. M. Biddulph. Her Majesty expressed pleasurable surprise at the coloured clergyman's strikingly hale and hearty looks, considering his great age. He was born, it will be remembered, on June 15, 1789. Her Majesty was also pleased to say that for many years she had been well acquainted with his history, and presented him with her photograph, signed 'Victoria Reg., 1877,' and mounted in a handsome ormolu frame. Mr. Henson thanked her Majesty on his own behalf for the great honour conferred upon himself, as well as on behalf of his coloured brethren in Canada and other portions of her Majesty's dominions—for her august protection when they were poor fugitive slaves, and for the unspeakable blessings they had at all times enjoyed under her rule. Mr. John Lobb was then presented by Sir T. M. Biddulph to her Majesty as the Editor of Mr. Henson's Autobiography, a copy of which had been graciously accepted by her Majesty, who was pleased to say that she had read it with the deepest interest. At her Majesty's gracious request the autographs of the Rev. Josiah Henson and Mr. J. Lobb with the date of the birth of each, were then inscribed in her Majesty's private album. Her Majesty had given special permission that all the household should see Uncle Tom, and they showed great interest in the veteran, many shaking him heartily by the hand. Uncle Tom and his friends were by the Queen's directions shown over the Castle, and taken through the private and state apartments by Sir John Cowell, eventually quitting the place at half-past four o'clock, highly pleased with the royal reception. While descending the Castle-hill, opposite the Albert Memorial Chapel, Mr. Henson was met by the Hon. and Very Rev. Gerald Wellesley, Dean of Windsor, and several gentlemen, with whom he entered into conversation, and in reply to a remark he said that he would soon be eighty-eight. Mr. Henson and his friends, after leaving the Castle, visited Mr. F. G. Cayley, in the High Street, Windsor. After tea, Mr. Henson addressed the *employés* of Mr. Cayley, about sixty in number, in touching terms. He appeared greatly impressed with the kindness shown him by her Majesty, and spoke of the good effect the royal example would have in Canada."

By her Majesty's desire, Mr. Lobb has forwarded to Windsor Castle *carte-de-visite* portraits of himself and Mr. Henson, which have since been duly acknowledged.

The following article is from the *Birmingham Daily Mail* of March 6th, 1877, and is, we think, worthy of preservation:—

"The hospitable doors of Windsor Castle have been thrown open during its long history to distinguished men of all creeds, and colours, and climes. Emperors and kings have banqueted within its walls; great warriors have received in its saloons the congratulations and thanks of their sovereign; men of letters have there been honoured with the homage which the most exalted rank pays without loss of dignity to genius. Science and literature, arms and arts, statecraft and divinity, have been *feted* in turns; dusky potentates from the far East, imperial rulers of a rival civilisation, ambassadors from the Court of Japan, and envoys rich in a blaze of barbaric gold, have been welcomed by its long succession of illustrious tenants. The records of the receptions given and the guests greeted in its venerable and historic halls would comprise much of the individual greatness of each reign—the greatness of achievement and the greatness of accident. Even within the forty years during which Queen Victoria has ruled over the land, what a long list of eminent men and women have been summoned to the Castle. Scarcely any one who has achieved, in any walk of life, an honourable fame, has been passed over by a monarch who is as anxious to recognise eminence and talent and enterprise as she is to maintain with a grace all her own the hospitable character of her royal abode. People who have gone through grave peril in exploring foreign lands, who have penetrated to equatorial jungles or frozen seas, who have done heroic deeds in the cause of humanity or science—Queen Victoria has pleasantly and cheerfully welcomed them all; and those who have had the honour of her summons unite in saying that she puts at their ease, without an effort, even those least familiar with the courts of princes and the *salons* of the great.

"Windsor welcomed a visitor yesterday around whose name and history clusters an exceptional interest. He has done nothing, in the ordinary meaning of the phrase, to win fame. He has produced no work of genius, performed no feat of statesmanship, discovered no new lands. He has not devastated countries with conquest, or colonised them with venturous enterprise. He has done nothing but suffer. He was a slave in the United States when slavery was at the high tide of its cruelty and oppression. He has felt the lash of man-trafficking monsters in human form. He has seen husbands and wives ruthlessly separated for purposes too base to be recalled without a hot tinge of indignation. The Rev. Josiah Henson is a person of rare and special interest, inasmuch as he was the original Uncle Tom of Mrs. Stowe's remarkable novel of slave-life in the Southern States. Who that is over thirty years of age does not remember the deep impression made on the public when that heart-lacerating story made its appearance on this side of the Atlantic? How many thousands of honest British eyes, albeit not used to the melting mood, were wet with the record of poor, patient, noble Tom's sufferings? Who has not laughed over the humour of

Topsy's denseness, and wept over the inexpressible pathos of little Eva's death-bed? Who has not flushed with a righteous anger at the merciless cruelties of Simon Legree, and been thrilled with sympathy for Eliza in her wild flight over the broken ice? No story was ever written that had a more iniquitous wrong to redress; no story was ever written that so deeply stirred the hearts and consciences of the English and American people. 'Uncle Tom's Cabin' was the death-blow to slavery as an American institution.

"No one can help feeling an interest in such a man as Mr. Henson. He was the original, as we have said, of Uncle Tom, and although the incidents of his life were necessarily altered for the purposes of the fiction, the character is said to have been a truthful portrayal of his own. We see in him a man who, by one of the strange and inexplicable freaks of chance, was born under the heel, so to speak, of dominant and cruel task-masters. For years his lot was one of servitude and misery. Sufferance was the badge of all his tribe. When he gained his freedom it was to take no selfish advantage of it, but to toil for the great cause of freedom by which his black brethren might enjoy the inestimable privilege he had gained. There is something almost romantic in the meeting, in Royalty's own home, of the Queen of England with this humble and now aged Uncle Tom, whose only distinction arises from his sufferings, and the patient, sweet philosophy and great-hearted piety with which he bore the harshness of stern oppressors. We can picture the negro patriarch, now in his eighty-eighth year, passing up the corridor and into the Oak Room, where her Majesty, surrounded by lords and ladies in waiting, and officers of state, took him kindly by the hand and spoke generous words of sympathy for the sufferings he had undergone. The scene would be well worth immortalising on the canvas of some great historic painter. Nothing could be more picturesque than the pageantry and grandeur of the surroundings of which this venerable negro was the central figure. Very graciously, the Queen presented Mr. Henson with her portrait and autograph; and he thanked her Majesty for the great honour conferred on himself, and on behalf of his coloured brethren in Canada, and other portions of the Queen's dominions, for her august protection when they were poor fugitive slaves, and for the unspeakable blessings they had at all times enjoyed under her rule. Then, at her Majesty's special request, Mr.

Henson and Mr. Lobb, the Editor of his Autobiography, inscribed their autographs in her private album; and a ceremony, full of interest and grace, was brought to an end.

"Turning from this Windsor reception, we cannot forbear contrasting the present condition of the United States with that which the story of Uncle Tom's life and sufferings recalls. America passed through sharp tribulation to wash out the infamy of slavery. The furnace was fierce, but the purifying was sure. The dross of the old Southern corruption, with its hideous traffic in human creatures, and severance of natural ties, and untold crimes and cruelties, was consumed, and the pure cause of freedom endured. A nation that could thus pluck out the cancerous sore by the roots is capable of a yet mightier future. Notwithstanding all the chicanery and corruption which eat into American public life, there is the vitalising and healing property of a healthy moral force. The sweeping away of the slave system of the South was one of the noblest works ever achieved by any people; and the fire and sword through which the reformers had to pass were the hallowing trials of their noble mission. The venerable Uncle Tom has lived to see the equality of races where, a little while since, men of his own colour were but the chattels of their owners. He, the runaway slave, has lived to be entertained by Queen Victoria in her own royal castle. The whirligig of time does indeed bring about its revenges, and not the least of them is the gracious and interesting ceremony performed at Windsor yesterday."

> A Negro Preacher, bowed with age, is he:
> No sounding titles do his worth attest,
> Yet, in a land where all who tread are free,
> He, slave who was, is now its Sov'reign's guest!
> What deep emotion must possess his breast,
> The humble actor in so strange a scene!
> Once all unknown, unfriended, and opprest,
> He who a legal "chattel" erst had been,
> In friendly converse stands with England's gracious Queen!
>
> What wonder if, amid that courtly throng,
> His startled thoughts fly back through years of pain,
> When, held in cruel bonds by foulest wrong,
> Condemned to labour for a tyrant's gain,
> He felt the lash, and wore the captive's chain?

Hunted by hounds, when fain he would be free;
Accursed, as though he bore the brand of Cain;
Like some wild beast, from men compelled to flee,
In desperate essay to snatch sweet Liberty!
Brave "Uncle Tom"! May happy days be thine—
Days placid, peaceful, uneventful, still!
May tender friendships sweeten thy decline!
As flow'rets fringe the homeward-flowing rill,
May love thy fleeting years with comfort fill—
The Master whom thou lovest doth accord
True freedom unto all who do His will;
And, in the service of their common Lord,
Both Queen and slave at last shall reap a rich reward.

# CHAPTER XXXIII

## MY VISIT TO MY OLD HOME IN MARYLAND

Return to America—Visit to Washington—Call on President Hayes—Revisit My Old Maryland Home, the First Time for Fifty Years—My Old Mistress Recognises Me—My Mother's Grave

After our visit to the Queen, we returned immediately to Scotland, where I filled my list of engagements, accepting as many invitations as my strength would possibly admit, and meeting the kindest receptions on all sides. We sailed for home from Liverpool, April 27, 1877, on board the Cunard steamer "China," bearing with us the best wishes of our friends, money enough to raise all the mortgages from our home and make us comfortable, and many dear souvenirs of our friends, chief among which are the Queen's gift; a handsome gold watch and chain, which was presented me by Mr. and Mrs. Horniman, of London; and a valuable German music-box, which the same kind friends gave my wife, who was also remembered by an elegant watch, chain, and locket of rich yellow gold, from our Edinburgh friends.

Arriving in Boston, we went directly to Canada, where we remained at our own farm, and with our children and friends, until the following winter, when a strange inexpressible longing came over me to see again the home of my boyhood. My wife was also anxious to visit her sister, who is married and living in Baltimore, which was my wife's old home too. So, on the 24th of December, 1877, we started for the South, expecting to take our Christmas dinner with our sister and her husband; but we were delayed on the road, and did not arrive in Baltimore till the 26th. We were received with open arms, as may be supposed, for it was long since these sisters had met. Remaining here till the 3rd of March, we then proceeded to

Washington, where I visited many of the old haunts which were so familiar to me in the long-ago days when I used to bring hither my master's produce.

Of course we went to the White House. I called on his Excellency President Hayes, in his office, while Mrs. Hayes very kindly showed my wife through the house. The President was pleased to be very gracious, and when I rose to take leave, after a pleasant little chat about my trip across the water, he gave me a very cordial invitation to call again, should I ever pay another visit to the capital.

And then we went to my old home. Fifty years, lacking only a few months, had passed since I last saw the old place. Fifty long years! since the day when I left the master's house to return to my family in Kentucky, walking with a swinging step and a jubilant heart, because my great object in life was gained (as I thought in my credulity), my freedom papers being safely stowed away in my bag.

I did not expect to find the old master who had played me such a cruel trick, still alive. I did not know that I should even find the young mistress whose grasping nature had caused me so much trouble in those early years. But I did almost unconsciously expect to see the old place somewhat as I had left it. Notwithstanding all I had heard of the great alterations which had taken place, since coming South, I still pictured to myself the great fertile plantation, with its throngs of busy labourers sowing the seed, tilling the ground, and reaping the valuable harvests as of yore. I saw the "great house," well furnished and sheltering a happy, luxurious, and idle family; I saw the outdoor kitchen, where the coloured cook and her young maids prepared and carried the dinners into the house; I saw the barns and storehouses bursting with plenty; the great cellars filled with casks of cider, apple-brandy, and fruit; and plainer than all I saw the little village of huts called the niggers' quarters, which used to be so full of life, and alas! so full of sorrow.

But the scales have fallen even from the eyes of my imagination, and I realise at last that a change, great and fearful, has indeed come over the land of the modern Pharaohs, who were visited with the Almighty's wrath because they refused to let His people depart out of their bondage.

The old place is situated in Montgomery County, Maryland, about twelve miles from Washington, and four from Rockville. Long before we reached the house where my old master used to live, I saw that it was indeed another land from that of my boyhood. The once great plantation is now but a wilderness; the most desolate, demoralised place one can imagine. The fertile fields where once waved acres upon acres of tasselled corn, of blooming rye, and oats and barley; the once ploughed land where grew the endless rows of potatoes, which I have hoed so many weary hours; the rich pastures where great herds of cattles used to graze,—all these splendid lands are overgrown with trees and underbrush. The fences are all gone; the fruitful orchards worn out and dead; and when we drove at last up the grass-grown road to the house, I saw it standing there all alone, without a single barn or stable or shed to bear it company; and it was in such a dilapidated condition that the windows rattled and the very door sprang ajar as we drove up and stopped before it.

A coloured boy came out at the sound of wheels, and gazed at us open-mouthed.

"Does Mrs. Riley live here?" I asked.

"Yes, sir."

"Is she at home?"

"Yes, sir."

"Can she be seen?"

"Dunno, sir; she's poorly, and isn't out of bed today."

"Well, I have come a very long distance on purpose to see her."

"I'll ask," said the boy, and vanished. Soon I heard a querulous voice ask within, "Who is he?"

"Dunno! He's a black gemman."

"And he wants to see me? Well, tell him to come in."

We went in, and there was the old mistress, sure enough, but instead of the young, blooming woman of twenty, she was a poor, fretful invalid of seventy. Her bed was in the old sitting-room, which was the first place that I had seen that seemed at all familiar. The room and the old corner cupboard, where master used to keep his brandy, just as they were fifty years ago; but the furniture was scanty and dilapidated, and the floor was utterly bare; in fact, there was not a scrap of carpet in the whole house.

I went up to her and bowed.

"How do you do, madam?"

"I am poorly—poorly. How do you do?"

"I am very well, thank you."

"I—I don't seem to know you." said the poor creature, looking hard at me.

"Is that so? You have seen me many a time."

"I don't seem to," she repeated, and thought a moment; when suddenly springing up in bed, she exclaimed,—

*"Can it be Si?"*

"Yes, Madam."

"Not Si Henson!—surely, surely, it can never be!"

"Yes, madam."

"I cannot believe it," she cried in great excitement. "Let me feel of your arms, then I shall know!"

I flung back my cloak, and she put her trembling hands on my arms that were shattered in her husband's defence so long ago. Like the doubting Thomas, this convinced her. She burst into tears, and cried,

"It is Si! Indeed, it is Si! Oh! Si, your master is dead and gone!"

"No, madam. *My* master is alive."

"I mean Mr. Riley. If only he was here you would be good friends now; I know you would. You were always a good man, Si. I never blamed you for running away. Oh! Si, don't you wish you could see your old master again?"

I tried to say yes, and to shed a tear with her; but I couldn't get up a real honest cry, so I gave it up. Pretty soon she became quiet, and, looking at me more attentively, said,

"Why, Si, you are a gentleman!"

"I always was, madam."

"Yes, but you are rich!" And then immediately, "What have you brought me?"

"Nothing. I came to see if you had anything to give me!"

"Oh, no. We are poor; very poor, Si. We do all our own work, my daughter and granddaughters; and we don't have much to eat even."

"Have you any brandy in the old cupboard?"

"No, nothing," she moaned, and then my wife said,

"Why didn't you keep some of your slaves to do your work?"

"Oh, well, Mr. Riley bought lots of niggers after you went away, Si, but some died, and he sold some, and Linkum set the rest free, so I couldn't keep 'em."

"But couldn't you keep them by paying them?" said my wife again, at which the old woman looked surprised.

"Oh! they wasn't worth paying. I never could pay niggers for work, so I let 'em all go."

Of a sudden she began to question me, asking me for many names of officers under whom Mr. Riley served in the war of 1812. My memory did not once fail me, and to her great delight I gave her the required names and dates, which, at her request, her son-in-law wrote down, and I then learned that she was trying to get a pension to which Mr. Riley was entitled, but to secure which she had not the necessary data until I gave them. She said the Lord must have sent me for this. I do not know whether she succeeded in getting the money, but I hope so, for she needed it.

Then I spoke of the last thing which was on my mind, the desire to visit my mother's grave. She said she knew where it was well, and directed her son-in-law to conduct me there. So we went out, and bent our steps toward a little collection of mounds, slightly raised above the surrounding level, but enough to show that they were the final resting-place of many who had passed away from this life and its sorrows. And there, a little removed from the others, was that of my poor, dear old slave-mother; of her who had first pointed me heavenwards; whose early prayers were my salvation.

I bowed myself to the ground, and hid my face in the grass that grows thickly over that beloved form. I wept, and prayed, and made new resolutions that in the days which may yet be before me, I may so live as to honour the memory of her who bore me; and that in the death which cannot long tarry, I may fall asleep in the Lord, as peacefully and as righteously as did my sainted mother.

## CONCLUSION

In closing this volume, we cannot refrain from expressing our joy and amazement that our friend, Father Henson, is still in the possession of vigorous health. During the past year he was, consequently, enabled to serve his coloured brethren by preaching sermons in various parts of Canada on behalf of Sunday Schools, and in aid of the removal of debts from several chapels. It need scarcely be added that, wherever he goes, he is warmly welcomed, and is listened to reverently as a patriarch who is enabled, from long and large experience of God's goodness and faithfulness, to speak with an authority and force of personal testimony that cannot be gained in any other way. When our readers reflect that he is in his ninety-first year, and that for forty-two years he was a slave, exposed to all the hardships of slavery, and suffering therefrom in more than an ordinary degree, they will see in his prolonged vigour and ability to serve God and man, a fulfilment of the ancient promise, "The righteous shall flourish like the palm-tree: he shall grow like a cedar in Lebanon. Those that be planted in the House of the Lord shall flourish in the courts of our God. They shall still bring forth fruit in old age; they shall be fat and flourishing; to show that the Lord is upright, my rock, and that there is no unrighteousness in Him."

At one period certain ignorant and envious persons did their utmost to cast doubts upon Mr. Henson's identity with "Uncle Tom;" but such slanders were effectually refuted and silenced. Fresh witnesses arise to testify to the accuracy of the statements in this volume. Concerning Lewis Clark, the "George Harris" of *Uncle Tom's Cabin* and the husband of "Eliza," to whom we refer on pp. 114-116, *The American Bookseller* for October, 1880, thus writes:—

"Lewis, the George Harris of 'Uncle Tom's Cabin,' is living at Oberlin, Ohio. His skin and beard are almost white. His mother, he says, was a handsome quadroon, the daughter of her master, and his father was a Scotch weaver who fought in the Revolutionary war. He was born in Kentucky, and is sixty-six years old. He was a slave until he was twenty-seven, when he escaped. One of his daughters is a school teacher. He supplied Mrs. Stowe with many incidents for 'Uncle Tom's Cabin.' The original Uncle Tom, Josiah Henson, is now a clergyman in Canada."

Furthermore, in the introduction to the magnificent edition of *Uncle Tom's Cabin,* published in 1879 by Messrs. Houghton, Osgood, and Co., of Boston, it is expressly stated by Mrs. Stowe herself, that as the narrative appeared in the *Era,* sympathetic words began to come to her from old workers who had long been struggling in the anti-slavery cause. She visited Boston, went to the Anti-Slavery Rooms, and reinforced her *repertoire* of facts by such documents as Theodore Weld's "Slavery as it is," The Lives of Josiah Henson and Lewis Clark, *particulars of whose lives were inwoven with the story in the characters of Uncle Tom and George Harris.*

In view of such testimonies as these, our readers will dismiss from their minds the idea that there is anything fictitious in the narrative we have laid before them. No, it is a true record of the career of a good man who still lives, and who is more than compensated for the sufferings of his early life by the consciousness that Mrs. Stowe's immortal story of them was among the most powerful of the influences which, under the providence of God, broke the shackles of the slaves, and set the bondmen free.

## SUMMARY OF 'UNCLE TOM'S' PUBLIC
## SERVICES

In *August,* 1876, on Sunday, at Victoria Park Tabernacle, to a congregation exceeding 2,000 persons.

*At Wood Green,* on Thursday, in the "Tent" erected for evangelistic services by T. B. Smithies, Esq., editor of the "British Workman." In the unavoidable absence of Baroness Coutts, she kindly deputed Rev. Mr. Sinclair to take her carriage and place it at "Uncle Tom's" service at the close of the proceedings.

*In September,* 1876, again at *Wood Green,* in the Wesleyan chapel, which accommodated over 1,000 persons.

*Little Wild Street Baptist Chapel, Drury Lane.*—Crowded beyond the capacity of the place.

*Epsom.*—This neighbourhood has been rarely moved with an excitement like that which followed "Uncle Tom's" visit here.

*Brixton.*—On Friday, at the Congregational Church, to a large and appreciative audience.

*Mildmay Park.*—On Sunday, in this large and beautiful Conference Hall; although it seats 2,500 persons, the building was crowded in every part, and hundreds failed to gain admission.

*Stoke Newington.*—On Sunday evening, in the Congregational Church, Walford Road.

*Wallington.*—On Wednesday the place of meeting was thronged. Rev. Dr. Whittemore, and Rev. J. Williams, of the vicarage, taking part in the proceedings.

*New North Road* Congregational Church, though capacious, was overcrowded on Thursday; and a second meeting in the large schoolroom was conducted at the same time, "Uncle Tom," after the chapel address, adjourning to supplement the other meeting, to the intense delight of all.

*Milton Road* Congregational Church, in Stoke Newington, was also crowded in every part by a large company.

*Mayfield Terrace* Wesleyan Chapel on Sunday was, though large and commodious, filled to overflowing.

*Mile End.*—On Sunday, the great tent belonging to F. N. Charrington, Esq., was filled, "Uncle Tom" also delivering a lecture on the Monday evening.

*The South Coast.*—During the week "Uncle Tom" addressed large audiences in Portsmouth, Southampton, and in the Town Hall at Ryde, Isle of Wight.

*Her Majesty's Ship "Victory."*—"Uncle Tom" visited this famous vessel, which bore Nelson's flag, and on the deck of which he received his death-wound in the moment of triumph over the combined fleets of France and Spain, off Cape Trafalgar. By command, the whole of the ship's officers and crew were collected to receive an address from "Uncle Tom." To each of the company a copy was presented of the *Christian Age,* containing "Uncle Tom's" portrait.

*Peniel Tabernacle, Haverstock Road.*—This Baptist Chapel was thronged on Sunday to hear a sermon from "Uncle Tom."

*Victoria Park Tabernacle.*—On Sunday evening this capacious iron church, the largest in England, accommodating 2,000 persons, was again crammed in every part.

*South Hackney.*—On Wednesday, by invite of Lady Seymour, at Wilton House "Uncle Tom" delivered an effective address to the members of that lady's classes. All present were deeply affected, and three resolved to give their hearts to God. "Uncle Tom" will never forget this meeting.

*Winchmore Hill Congregational Church.*—An interesting meeting thronged this place of worship, and "Uncle Tom" spoke with good effect.

*In October,* 1876.—On Sunday, at Putney Congregational Church, Oxford Road, "Uncle Tom" delivered telling addresses in the afternoon and evening, under a gracious influence.

*Wesley's Chapel, City Road.*—On Tuesday, by the kind invite of J. W. Gabriel, Esq. (brother of the Alderman, and late Lord Mayor), Rev. J. Henson and Mr. Lobb met a select party of friends to tea, and afterwards repaired to this sanctuary, so sacredly memorable to

Methodists everywhere, for its history and associations. It was properly felt by the brethren, Henson and Lobb, to be the most acceptable incident of their lives, and a powerful reminder of the sainted Wesley's ministry, from the very pulpit, which they occupied for about two hours! The occasion was Radnor Street school anniversary, and Rev. J. Henson announced to preach on its behalf. City Road Chapel was full, and overflowing by hundreds.

*Bromley, Kent.* — The residence of M. H. Hodder, Esq., was visited by "Uncle Tom," and an address given at this, the third anniversary of an evangelical mission, promoted in this locality by Mr. Hodder and his estimable wife, G. Williams, Esq., of the Young Men's Christian Association, taking part in the proceedings.

*Twickenham.* — "Uncle Tom's" meeting was held here in the Old Chapel Royal, and Rev. F. J. C. Moran, B.D., Secretary of the "Colonial and Continental Church Society," which is under the patronage of Her Majesty the Queen, took part in the proceedings, which were successful.

*Haverstock Road.* — Peniel Tabernacle had a second visit from "Uncle Tom," with much success.

*Hinde Street Chapel,* Manchester Square, was the scene of a successful meeting.

*Weigh House Chapel, London Bridge.* — This was the famous centre of influence under Rev. Thomas Binney's ministry, and is succeeded by a worthy successor, Rev. W. Braden. "Uncle Tom" attended a deeply interesting service here.

*Whitfield Tabernacle, Tottenham Court Road.* — An interesting gathering.

*Sloane Street Chapel, Chelsea,* a celebrated Wesleyan chapel, was the scene of a delightful "Uncle Tom" meeting.

*Messrs. Hitchcock and Williams',* St. Paul's Churchyard. — "Uncle Tom" gave an address here to the employees, George Williams, Esq., founder of "The Young Men's Christian Association," presiding. Mr. John Lobb, on introducing "Uncle Tom," said, " Here is the hero of Mrs. Harriet Beecher Stowe's "Uncle Tom's Cabin;" the "Uncle Tom" who rescued *Eva* from a watery grave; the "Uncle Tom" who accompanied *George Harris* to Mrs. H. B. Stowe's residence, whose united history furnished her with such interesting records as appear in "Uncle Tom's Cabin," of world-wide fame; the "Uncle Tom," too, so maimed for life by *Legree*, but whose real name is Bryce Litton, as recorded in Mr. Henson's "Life," and confirmed in pages 34 to 57 of Mrs. Stowe's Key to "Uncle Tom's Cabin."

*Victoria Park Tabernacle.*—Over 2,000 persons were present, when a handsomely composed testimonial, duly framed, was presented to 'UNCLE TOM.'

*Barnsbury Chapel.*—This large and beautiful chapel, recently renovated, was crowded to its full capacity. "Uncle Tom" had also visited here in 1851. An extraordinary scene occurred during the proceedings. "Uncle Tom," commenced a "slave song," which was caught up and harmoniously joined in by a coloured lady, who was ultimately discovered to be a freed slave from South Carolina. The audience was excited; she was exhorted to reach the pulpit, and "Uncle Tom," with the "Carolina lady," joined delightfully in the singing, and finally wept together, and rejoiced in the "liberty" which had made them free! The interesting proceedings were of a most enthusiastic character.

*Horne Hill (near Brixton).*—This commodious chapel, belonging to the United Methodist Free church, was crowded in every part at "Uncle Tom's" meeting, which was of a deeply interesting character.

*Brown's Lane, Spitalfields.*—On Sunday afternoon and evening, crowded services were held by "Uncle Tom," assisted by Mr. John Lobb.

*King's Cross Wesleyan Chapel* (which seats over 1,000 people).—"Uncle Tom" gave much satisfaction to a crowded audience here.

*Queen Street, Ratcliff, E.*—This "time-honoured" meeting-house was densely crowded to hear "Uncle Tom" on Sunday, afternoon and evening. A very gracious influence prevailed.

*New Bridge Street, E.C.*—On Monday "Uncle Tom" spoke at Church of England Young Men's Society, when a *conversazione* was held by a distinguished company.

*Bromley Town Hall.*—A second visit was paid to this neighbourhood by "Uncle Tom," with increased interest. The Hon. A. Kinnaird, M.P., presided. "Uncle Tom," Mr. Lobb, the hon. chairman, and his esteemed family, dined with J. Cowie, Esq., of Sandridge Hall, who next day drove him to Hays, where a stone seat still remains as a "memorial" of years gone by. By the tree at its side, the famous Wilberforce first declared his intention to William Pitt of moving a resolution in the Commons House of Parliament for the abolition of slavery. "Uncle Tom" and Mrs. Henson provided themselves with reminders of this pleasant visit.

*Denmark Hill Baptist Chapel.*—An enthusiastic and overcrowded meeting.

*St. John's Wood (Abbey Road Chapel).*—Pastor W. Stott. This large and beautiful house of prayer was crowded, and besieged by anxious hundreds unable to enter.

*Hanwell, Middlesex.*—This suburban locality greeted "Uncle Tom's" arrival, and an excellent meeting was held.

*Canterbury.*—"Uncle Tom" opened the New Primitive Methodist Chapel here on Saturday, addressing crowded congregations afternoon and evening, and took part with Mr. Lobb, of the *Christian Age,* in the services of the following day.

*Tolmer Square Congregational Church.*—Mr. Henson related the story of his escape from slavery to a large and appreciative audience. Rev. Arthur Hall, the pastor, presided.

*Woodford United Methodist Free Church.*—Mr. Henson addressed a crowded audience here. John Kaye, Esq., of Prospect Hall, kindly entertained him.

*Surrey Chapel, Blackfriars.*—This time-honoured place of worship, made memorable by the ministries of the Revs. Rowland Hill, James Sherman, and Newman Hall, and which is now in the hands of the Primitive Methodists, was crowded in every part to hear Mr. Henson; Mr. Lobb, of the *Christian Age,* presided.

*Hackney Road Wesleyan Chapel.*—A crowded audience assembled here to listen to Mr. Henson's story of his slave-life.

*Chelsea (Sloane Terrace Wesleyan Chapel).*—Mr. Henson paid a second visit and preached, on the occasion of the Sunday-school aniversary, to a large congregation.

*Putney Congregational Church.*—"Uncle Tom" officiated here for the second time Sunday afternoon and evening.

*Lambeth (Upton Baptist Chapel).*—"Uncle Tom" gave the story of his escape to a most enthusiastic audience.

*Shoreditch (Bedford Institute, Commercial Street).*—A crowded audience greeted Mr. Henson here.

*Barnsbury Chapel* (Rev. John Morgan's).—Mr. Henson paid a second visit here.

*Folkestone, Kent.*—Mr. Henson addressed crowded meetings in the Town Hall, on Friday, the Mayor presiding; Mr. Lobb and several ministers taking part in the proceedings.

*Ramsgate.*—St. James's Hall was crowded in every part on Saturday to hear the hero of "Uncle Tom's Cabin;" and on Sunday Mr. Henson and Mr. Lobb officiated in the Primitive Methodist Chapel.

*Whitstable.*—The Congregational Church was crowded with enthusiastic hearers. Mr. Lobb, of the *Christian Age* presided. The pastor, Rev. Mr. Andrew, and other ministers taking part in the proceedings.

*Canterbury.*—The interest previously felt in "Uncle Tom," led to a second visit. The Wesleyan Chapel was crowded, and a delightful meeting held. "Uncle Tom" disbelieved the statement that he had preached in the same chapel twenty-five years before, until the register was shown him with the date, his text, his own autograph, and that of his son Isaac, now in heaven! The revival of his memory gave him much joy. Friends who entertained him were kind, unusually so. Mr. C. Carrick, of this city, a clever writing-artist, presented him with a handsome memoral, elaborately and beautifully executed, with the words: "Blest with a noble, generous heart. To the Rev. J. Henson." Another of the same class to the chairman, Mr. J. Lobb.

*Tunbridge, Kent.*—This newly-built and handsome church of the Congregationalists was thronged by many who had travelled very long distances to see the veteran, emancipated slave. Samuel Morley, Esq., M.P., presided. Before introducing "Uncle Tom," he expressed his great pleasure in meeting his old friend after an interval of twenty-five years. He praised the noble efforts of "Uncle Tom," in the face of great risks, on the "Underground Railway," and his patient perseverance with the work of education for the coloured children. Having passed the night at the hospitable residence of M. L. Caley, Esq., at Ramhurst, the carriage of S. Morley, Esq., was sent to conduct "Uncle Tom" and Mr. Lobb to his estate, in the morning, to breakfast. At noon "Uncle Tom" addressed a good company of the villagers at the special request of Mr. Morley.

*Peniel Tabernacle.*—This was the third visit here of "Uncle Tom." He preached a powerful gospel sermon upon the text, "Come unto Me all ye that labour," etc.

*Grafton Road Iron Chapel.*—"Uncle Tom" had a cordial welcome, and deeply interested a crowded audience.

*St. John's Wood.*—Rev. W. Stott's commodious chapel was on this, the second visit of "Uncle Tom," crowded to overflowing. Hundreds, failing to get into the chapel, which accommodates 2,000 persons, crowded into the excellent schoolroom. "Uncle Tom" divided his services, and Mr. Lobb assisted him by an address in the chapel.

*Welsh Calvinistic Methodist Church, Paddington.*—An enthusiastic meeting was held. Rev. G. Davies, of Nassau Street, Soho, presided. There are seven Welsh chapels belonging to this denomination, and the one in which "Uncle Tom" rehearsed his story is the youngest but one of that number. Mr. J. Lobb, of the *Christian Age,* expressed his own pleasure, with that of "Uncle Tom," in meeting their Welsh brethren, as it had been hitherto impossible for them to visit the Principality, from whence so many invitations had come. After they had heard "Uncle Tom" awhile, he would need to rest a few minutes, and perhaps the congregation would favour himself and "Uncle Tom" with a hymn in their native Welsh. This request was promptly gratified. One of Mr. W. William's Hymns, originally composed by him in English, was selected,—No. 478 in the Welsh Hymn Book, beginning at the second verse—

> "Let the Indian, let the negro,
> Let the rude barbarian see
> That Divine and glorious conquest
> Once obtained on Calvary:
> Let the Gospel
> Word resound from pole to pole!"

These words were kindly rendered into Welsh for us, and are as follows:

> "Doed yr Indiaid, doed barbariaid,
> Doed y Negro du yu Uu,
> Iryfeddu 'r ddwyfol gonowest
> Unwaith gaed ar Galfari!
> Swu y frwydyr
> Dreiddio i eithaf conglau 'r byd."

The fire of devotion and harmony of voice overcame us; and "Uncle Tom" will not forget this "happy opportunity," or, to speak in Welsh, *"hwyl!"*

*Bedford Chapel, Oakley Square, N.W.*—"Uncle Tom" gave the story of his life to about 2,000 people. The Rev. J. Hirst Hollowell presided.

*Tunbridge Congregational Church.*—"Uncle Tom" paid a second visit.

*Maidstone, Kent.*—"Uncle Tom" delivered a lecture here to a crowded audience.

*Whitstable.*—"Uncle Tom" paid a second visit, and preached in the Congregational Church.

*Herne Bay.*—"Uncle Tom" officiated Sunday afternoon and evening in the Congregational Church to crowded congregations.

*Brighton.*—The "Great Dome," so familiar to sight-seers of the famous Pavilion, was secured for two rehearsals of "Uncle Tom's Story." Mr. John Lobb presided.

*Upper Norwood (St. Aubyn's Road Congregational Church).*—The Rev. Josiah Henson delivered an address, giving an account of his forty-two years' slave life. Rev. R. Lewis (pastor) presided.

*Forest Hill, December, 1876.*—A local paper, the *Sydenham Gazette,* describes the meeting in these words: " 'Uncle Tom' carried Forest Hill by storm last Wednesday evening! It was intimated that the Rev. Josiah Henson would address a meeting in St. John's Hall, Forest Hill, at half-past seven. At that hour so many persons had assembled that the hall, which accommodates nearly 600 persons, was at once completely filled, and in other ten minutes the Presbyterian Church adjoining (the Rev. Dr. Boyd's) was also crammed with an eager audience. Many who came late had to retire unaccommodated. F. J. Horniman, Esq., presided, and the proceedings being opened with prayer by the Rev. Dr. Rogers, Mr. Henson gave a graphic account of his experiences in slavery. When he had spoken forty minutes he proceeded to the Church, and the meeting he had left was addressed by Mr. Lobb, of the *Christian Age,* and the Rev. Dr. Rogers. In St. John's Church Mr. Henson resumed the narrative of his early experiences, related the interesting circumstances of his conversion, and concluded by singing a negro melody, the audience joining in the refrain. In a short address Mr. Lobb gave a sketch of Mr. Henson's recent history, explaining the object of his visit to England and commending him to the sympathy of the meeting, and presenting some valuable details as to the origin and the difficulties which had attended "The Wilberforce Institution," at Dawn, in Canada. A collection for Mr. Henson's Fund was then taken. Mr. Josiah Henson was the guest of F. J. Horniman, Esq., who invited him to Forest Hill, and after addressing a large assembly of his friends at Surrey House, returned to town accompanied by Mr. Lobb and our esteemed neighbour, George Sturge, Esq." We gratefully acknowledge the receipt of a very handsome and valuable gold watch and chain from F. J. Horniman, Esq., of Surrey House, Forest Hill, in addition to a cheque for £5 on behalf of "Uncle Tom," and a costly musical box, for the recreation of Mrs. Henson and their numerous grandchildren, from Mrs. Horniman.

*On Saturday,* Rev. Josiah Henson, the "Uncle Tom" of Mrs. Stowe's well-known story, addressed a large audience in Forest Hill Lecture Hall, giving a very interesting account of his escape from slavery in Kentucky into Canada, and graphically related how he carried two of his children on his back for upwards of 600 miles through the woods; he also gave incidents in his slave life reminding his hearers of "Legree," "George Harris," "Eliza," "Little Eva," and other well-remembered characters in Mrs. Stowe's tale. F. J. Horniman, Esq., presided.

*Nottingham.*—Exeter Hall, the scene of the Rev. E. J. Silverton's successful ministrations, is one of the handsomest structures in Nottingham. The interior is an amphitheatre, with four tiers of seats, orchestra, double platform, and an arena of three circles. Upwards of 2,000 chairs form the seating accommodation, which is none too much for Mr. Silverton's audiences. Rev. J. Henson (Mrs. Stowe's "Uncle Tom") preached and lectured here, assisted by Mr. Lobb, of the *Christian Age,* on Sunday and Monday, when the hall was filled some time before the services commenced.

*Stepney,*—Rev. J. Henson, "Uncle Tom," gave the story of his life to a crowded audience at "The Edinburgh Castle" (Dr. Bernardo's). Mr. J. Lobb presided.

*Stockwell.*—Mr. C. H. Spurgeon's Orphanage, where "Uncle Tom" gave each boy (250) a halfpenny as a memento of his visit, during the past week. As the time for his departure draws near, the enthusiasm caused by his stirring narratives grows stronger.

*Forest Hill.*—On Sunday evening St. John's Church was crowded to overflowing, when he preached from the Parable of the Ten Virgins, and very much entertained and impressed his auditory. In the afternoon Mr. Henson addressed a few words to the children at St. John's school, which were peculiarly appropriate. Mr. Henson was the guest of F. J. Horniman, Esq., Surrey House.

*Sydenham.*—On Sunday morning Mr. Henson ("Uncle Tom") preached in the Rev. Gray Maitland's Church in the Grove, which was filled; his text was "Come unto Me, all ye that labour and are heavy laden, and I will give you rest." The old gentleman was very eloquent, moving his hearers to tears by his graphic earnestness.

*St. Mary Cray, Kent (the Temple).*—On Monday, January 1st, 1877, Mr. Henson gave the Story of his Life here to a crowded audience. Mr. Lobb presided. Messrs. Henson and Lobb were conducted over the famous paper mills and warehouse of the late Mr. Joynson, of this place, by one of his esteemed executors.

*Upper Clayton Chapel.*—On Thursday Mr. Henson gave the Story of his Life to a crowded audience.

*Mrs. Henson.*—From G. Williams, Esq. (of Messrs. Hitchcock, Williams, and Co.), St. Paul's, two beautiful silk dresses for Mrs. Henson. These are in addition to ten guineas received from Mr. Williams, to "Uncle Tom's" Fund.

*Salisbury.*—Rev. J. Henson ("Uncle Tom") and Mr. John Lobb, of the *Christian Age,* had the honour of a visit to the seat of the Right Hon. Earl Shaftesbury, near Salisbury. The noble Earl's carriage was placed at their service to and from the Verwood railway-station. It was pleasing to witness "Uncle Tom's" gratification on meeting the noble Earl again, after the interval of so many years, and the Earl's hearty reciprocity.

*High Barnet.*—Enthusiastic crowds thronged to hear "Uncle Tom's" story, which was much appreciated.

*Tulse Hill.*—The Wesleyan Chapel was crowded with a large and delighted audience.

*Manchester Square.*—Hinde Street Chapel (Wesleyan) was favoured with a second visit from "Uncle Tom," with great success.

*Hackney.*—Richmond Road Wesleyan Chapel was crowded to overflowing. Hundreds failed to get admission.

*Upper Norwood.*—Wesleyan Schoolroom was thronged to greet "Uncle Tom," and Mr. Lobb, who presided.

*Leicester.*—The Great Temperance Hall was crammed to overflowing, at each meeting.

*Loughborough.*—Mr. Henson appeared in the Corn Exchange, before a crowded audience, and with much success.

*Bristol.*—Mr. Henson preached in this famous city, so memorable in John Wesley's Journals and the history of early Methodism. Services were conducted by "Uncle Tom" in Rev. W. J. Mayer's Baptist Chapel and in the large Wesleyan Chapel. Great interest was felt also at Mr. Muller's establishment by 500 of the children, who received Mr. Henson with much glee.

*Sheffield (Great Albert Hall).*—The first meeting was held at twelve o'clock, and notwithstanding the hour and the inclemency of the weather, the hall was filled in every part. Persons began to assemble as early as half-past ten, and very shortly after the doors were open the galleries and back seats were filled, and the issue of tickets was stopped. There was then a run on the tickets for the better places, and by twelve o'clock there were sufficient persons present to fill the hall. The crowding at the back was relieved by the throwing open of the orchestra and front seats. Rev. Canon Blakeney presided, and Rev. Josiah Henson was accompanied by Rev. R. Stainton, Mr. Hardy, Mr. Hovey, Mr. Peech, of Nottingham, and other gentlemen. There were a great many clergymen and ministers present. Rev. R. Stainton offered prayer. It is a duty we pleasantly fulfil, of acknowledging the extraordinary interest and liberality of the Sheffield people. Nottingham had done nobly and well, but Sheffield exceeded all. The result to "Uncle Tom's" Fund was £186 4s. 10d.

*Holloway.*—A most interesting meeting took place at the St. James's Schools. The chair was taken by B. Venables, Esq., in the absence of the vicar, Rev. W. B. Carpenter.


### SPURGEON'S GREAT METROPOLITAN TABERNACLE

"Uncle Tom's" Farewell Meeting was held on Tuesday, January 30th, 1877. The Right Hon. Earl Shaftesbury, K.G., etc., presided. Nearly 6,000 persons were present. The *Times* report was, that the Metropolitan Tabernacle was filled, floor and both galleries alike, with a meeting brought together to take a farewell, on his approaching return to Canada, of the Rev. Josiah Henson, whose identity with Mrs. H. B. Stowe's "Uncle Tom," on the strength of her own testimony in the "Key" to her great work, is a scarcely disputed article of faith, especially in the religious and philanthropic world. The Rev. J. A. Spurgeon led the devotion, and Mr. Lobb made a statement of the results of the efforts made during the six or eight months of Mr. Henson's stay here to relieve him of pecuniary difficulties incurred in his zeal for public ends, and to render comfortable the few remaining days of this nonagenarian patriarch. Mr. Henson spoke with great freedom and effect for upwards of an hour; and to the delight of the audience sang the following verses:—

SLAVES' PARTING HYMN.

This hymn was composed by "Uncle Tom," and was sung by many thousands of slaves when severed through being bought, sold, and separated by cruel masters. The composition is printed as it was originally sung, without any attempt to adapt it to modern taste, and irrespective of any grammatical or poetical errors.

> My brethren, fare ye well,
> I do you now tell,
> I'm sorry to leave you,
> I love you so well.
>
> I shortly must go,
> And where I don't know;
> Wherever I'm stationed
> The trumpet I'll blow.
>
> Strange people I'll find;
> I hope they'll prove kind;
> Neither places nor faces
> Shall alter my mind.
>
> Wherever I'll be,
> I'll still pray for thee;
> And you, my dear brethren,
> Do the same for poor me.

Mr. Thomas Church had the pleasure of moving a vote of thanks to the noble Earl, for the gracious kindness shown to "Uncle Tom" for the last quarter of a century, and for his presidency on this occasion. The meeting must not forget, when carrying this motion, that the noble Earl had been a consistent opponent of all slavery, whether white or black; that he was a faithful servant of God, a friend of the people, and one of England's most upright nobles. F. J. Horniman, Esq., of Forest-hill, cordially seconded, and the vote was enthusiastically carried. The noble Earl remarked upon the pleasure he felt at being present with the view of expressing their respect and affection for, and for the purpose of taking leave of, that grand old man,

"Uncle Tom," who he trusted would long live as a monument to God's glory. The Rev. Josiah Henson was an example of what could be done with that down-trodden race, the negro. By the blessing of God he had been emancipated from the corruption, immorality, profligacy, and violence that characterised the slave-holders of America. He had been raised to a position which falsified all the prophecies that had been uttered concerning the negro's unfitness for freedom. Men who had spoken to the disparagement of the negroes, knew not the power of the Gospel; they knew not the Spirit of the Lord, who had made all men of one blood to dwell upon the face of the earth. Lord Shaftesbury knew nothing more magnificent for contemplation, or more deserving their gratitude to God for the truth of His revelation, than the conduct and demeanour of black people at the present time. The vast majority of those who had gained their freedom now lived in great happiness, joy, and unity of faith and love to their brethren of the white population. By the liberation of the negro race they had been raised from the depths of degradation; but yet he wanted them to think there was yet much work to be done. By the grace of God we had relieved the West from slavery, but slavery had prevailed in the East, and it was for them to rise up as one man, to combine every effort, and use every endeavour to entirely abolish slavery, such efforts to be devoted so long as they had lips to speak, hearts to feel, and wrongs to redress.

The audience then sang the following hymn with great fervour:—

PARTING WORDS.

Specially composed for the occasion by Rev. G. Hunt Jackson, author of *"The Sculptor, and other Poems."*

> Thy parting words, dear friend, shall leave
> Within our hearts a lingering tone,
> And Memory's hand for thee shall weave
> A wreath of love when thou art gone.
>
> Go, brother of a coloured race,
> And take with thee our prayers to-night,
> That safely to thy native place
> The Lord may steer thy homeward flight.
>
> Go, preacher of the Word of God,
> And tell to others once again
> How much they owe to Freedom's rod
> That broke for them the oppressor's chain.

And when this truth thou shalt proclaim,
  Forget not most to stir their veins
With thoughts of Him whose saving name
  Alone can free the soul from chains.

Farewell, dear friend! and if no more
  We see thy well-known face on earth,
We'll hail thee on the heavenly shore
  Where all are of one blood and birth.

*Grosvenor Crescent, W.*—On Friday, February 9th, 1877, by kind invitation, Rev. J. Henson and Mr. J. Lobb were cordially welcomed by Lady Fowell Buxton and Samuel Gurney, Esq., with other distinguished friends.

*The Tabernacle, Victoria Park.*—Sunday, February 11th, "Uncle Tom's" Mission having received its first public impetus in this house of prayer, Mr. Henson and Mr. Lobb felt it to be a fitting opportunity for their joining pastor Seddon and his Church in public worship, and bidding them farewell. It was an impressive and an interesting service.

As a fitting close to the notices of Mr. Henson's public career in England, we may mention that through the noble generosity of Christian friends, £2,000 were contributed to his fund. By this, the difficulties which had harassed and oppressed Mr. Henson in his work in Canada have been removed, and some provision made for the comfort of himself and wife in their declining days. In February, 1877, Mr. Henson visited Scotland, and it was resolved to raise another large sum, as a present to himself in the evening of his long life. In Edinburgh and the East, which he first visited, £350 was raised, and it was believed that in Glasgow and the West a large amount would also be readily obtained. At a numerously-attended meeting of influential citizens, held in the Religious Institution Rooms, Glasgow, on Monday, the 19th March, John Burns, Esq., of Castle Wemyss, in the chair, and which was addressed by Mr. Henson, a committee was appointed to carry out the object, and it was announced that Mr. James A. Wenley, of the Bank of Scotland, St. Vincent Place, had agreed to receive subscriptions. The committee was composed of the following gentlemen:—John Burns, James White, Sir Peter Coats, Alex. Allan, Bailie William Collins, and William Smeal. Following on the meeting in the Religious Institution Rooms, Mr. Henson addressed crowded audiences in the City Hall and the Kibble Art Palace, Glasgow, capable, respectively, of accommodating 3,000 and 5,000 persons. He likewise addressed meetings in Greenock, Paisley, and other towns, and preached in different churches, as he had done elsewhere. As the result of these efforts, combined with the proceeds of the efforts in Edinburgh and the East of Scotland, at a farewell meeting held in the City Hall, Glasgow, on the evening of Friday, the 20th April, 1877, a testimonial was presented to Mr. Henson, consisting of a cheque for £750, while, at the same time, a beautiful gold watch and chain were give to Mrs. Henson. After Mr. Henson had returned thanks on behalf of Mrs. Henson,

The Rev. Dr. Alex. Wallace was afterwards called upon, and said—On rising to address you to-night, my feelings are of a very mingled character. I don't know that I can stand here to-night without referring, in the presence of our venerable friend, to something at least of the horrors of the hell of slavery from which he has escaped. When the great Italian poet Dante, who lived in Florence, and who wrote that remarkable poem, "The Inferno" —with which his name is always identified, just as Milton's is with "Paradise Lost"—used to pass through the streets, mothers, in a kind of terror, held up their children to look at the weird-like man, and whispered in their ear—"That is the man that has been in hell." And so you see here to-night, on the platform of the City Hall of Glasgow, a man in his eighty-eighth year who was for nearly half a century in the horrid hell of slavery, *redeemed*—not merely redeemed by the proclamation of Abraham Lincoln, that set four millions of slaves free in the United States, but redeemed by the precious blood of the Lamb. Now, I cannot look on "Uncle Tom" without recalling one very memorable fact in the history of the Anti-Slavery struggle. It is not yet much more than a century since Granville Sharp, a noble friend of the slave, obtained a decision of the English judges in the famous case of the negro Somerset, that as soon as a slave sets his foot upon English ground he becomes free. That was quite an era in the struggle against slavery. No slave power could carry Somerset back from this country into the land of bondage. His feet had touched British soil and he was free. (Applause.) Well, there has been a great and mighty struggle since that in order to set the slave free in our West Indian possessions, and afterwards in America. Our friend has referred to his own life, an account of which I hold in my hand,

and I advise every one of you to get it, edited by Mr. Lobb. . . Now, while we thank God with all our hearts to-night, let us remember that there are still millions of human beings in slavery. In 1866 I was brought once face to face with slavery. I never saw flesh and blood sold till that day. I was at Abydos, on the Hellespont, having, along with five or six hundred other passengers ordered into quarantine, been spending the time at the Lazaretto. One beautiful Sabbath morning, when a crowd was collected in the square, on going forward, to my horror I found a Turkish slave auction going on. Shall the people of this land ever fight for Turkey? (Loud cries of "No.") That is one thing that is cast away for ever. Public sentiment will never allow it. (Applause.) Two fine jet-black Nubian boys were exposed for sale; the auctioneer was expatiating on their good qualities. An American friend who was with me asked me to hold his hand, saying—"I feel my blood tingling at the sight, and will smash him unless you hold my hand." I felt it quivering with indignation. The boys were sold for £75 each to a Turkish pasha. "Thank God!" said my friend, "that horrid system of slavery is over in my country;" and here you have a living proof of it before you this evening. . . The Queen never did a nobler thing than when she invited "Uncle Tom" to come and see her. She has done many a noble, womanly thing, for which history will place her name up high on the page of immortal renown; but I don't know anything she has done more to win her affection, and that will tend more to remove that prejudice against colour, than the call to come up and see her in her own palace. (Applause.) I believe that the meeting of "Uncle Tom" and his wife and the Queen will yet form the subject of a great historical painting. Why not? This is a subject worthy of the pencil of the greatest living painter. I am not a prophet; but whoever lives a few years longer will, I dare say, see the Queen's meeting with "Uncle Tom" a great painting. . . In closing, I cannot but refer to the fact that in this same hall many noble advocates for the slave have stood, most of whom have now passed away. I cannot but recall the names of Dr. Heugh, Dr. Wardlaw, Dr. King, Dr. Robson, and, above all, of Dr. William Anderson, who pled for liberty for the slave. (Applause.) And I would refer, too, to our own Livingstone. The words on his tomb are supposed to be the last words he uttered on his knees for Africa. He was found dead on his knees by his devoted attendants. He had bade them "good night." It was his last "good night." He had said to them, "Don't come back;" but, when they thought "Massa was sleeping long," they ventured in, and the sun of Africa had arisen on the face of their dead master. The prayer is now appropriately placed on his tombstone in Westminster Abbey—"May Heaven's rich blessing come down on every one, American, English, or Turk, who will heal the open sore of the world—slavery." The last prayer of David Livingstone was on behalf of the slave. Now I don't know if ever I addressed a meeting with deeper interest and emotion than to-night, and I am sure you all join with me in the words of the benediction uttered by Moses—"The Lord bless thee and keep thee, the Lord make his face shine upon thee, and be gracious unto thee; the Lord lift up his countenance upon thee and give thee peace." (Loud applause.)

(*From the* Dumfries and Galloway Standard *of Wednesday, April 25, 1877.*)

Mr. Henson had made up his mind to make his recent appearance in Glasgow be his last public appearance in Scotland; but a committee of gentlemen had been formed in Dumfries to endeavour to persuade him to pay a visit, and plied by the pertinacious importunity of Mr. John Johnstone, merchant, he at last consented.

Mr. Henson addressed a monster meeting in the Mechanics' Hall, Dumfries. Every part of the hall was crowded, platform, aisles, and doorways; and numbers of people had come in from Annan, Kirkcudbright, and other places nearer and more remote, the audience including several of the county families. On Mr. Henson entering the hall, he was received with great cheering. Mrs. Henson was also on the platform. The chair was taken by Dr. Gilchrist, of the Crichton Royal Institution; and among those present were—Mr. Maxwell, of Munches, Mr. Starke, of Troqueer Holme, Mr. Starke, yr., and Mrs. Starke, Mrs. Davies, Mrs. S. Adamson, Rev. John Paton, Rev. Marshall N. Goold, Rev. John D. M'Kinnon, Rev. G. Rae, Rev. W. Graham, Rev. R. M'Kenna, Rev. J. Strachan, Rev. J. Duff, Rev. W. Tiplady, Rev. T. Bowman, Rev. L. M'Pherson, Rev. Mr. Simpson (Crichton Institution), Mr. Boyd, Kinder House, Mr. Walter Grierson, Chapelmount, Mr. W. Gregan, St. Christopher's, Mr. J. B. Milligan, Mr. James Rodger, Mr. John Johnstone, merchant, Mr. Johnston, Bank of Scotland, Mr. M'Neillie, of Castlehill, Provost Gillies, Mr. R.

B. Carruthers, Mr. M'Dowall, Mr. J. Ewing, Mr. J. Clarke, Mr. Scott, Mr. W. F. Johnstone, Mr. Allan, ironmonger, &c.

Mr. Henson, who was loudly cheered, in the opening part of his address said: There has been so much said and written about me, so much read about me, and so many things thought about me, that I did not know that I could do better than come and let you see me. (Laughter and applause.) It has been spread abroad that "'Uncle Tom' is coming," and that is what has brought you here. Now allow me to say that my name is not Tom, and never was Tom, and that I do not want to have any other name inserted in the newspapers for me than my own. My name is Josiah Henson, always was, and always will be. I never change my colours. (Loud laughter.) I would not if I could, and I could not if I would. (Renewed laughter.) Well, inquiry in the minds of some has led to a deal of inquiry on the part of others. You have read and heard some persons say that, " 'Uncle Tom' was dead, and how can he be here? It is an imposition that is being practised on us." Some people in this town have said so. Very well, I do not blame you for saying that. I do not think you are to blame. A great many have come to me in this country and asked me if I was not dead. (Laughter.) Says I, "Dead?" Says he, "Yes. I heard you were dead, and read you were." "Well," says I, "I heard so too, but I never believed it yet. (Laughter.) I thought in all probability I would have found it out as soon as anybody else." (Laughter.) Well, now, to remove this difficulty, if it exist in your minds. As a matter of course, it is not a very pleasant thing to me to hear that I am traversing the country and practising an imposition upon the people. No, it is not pleasant; and the only way I have to meet it is to say that when people have this doubt upon their minds it shows me they ain't well read, or have forgotten what they have read, if they have ever read at all. (Laughter.) They have forgotten that Mrs. Stowe's "Uncle Tom's Cabin" is a novel; and it must have seemed a glorious finish to that novel that she should kill her hero—a glorious finish. Now you get the Key to "Uncle Tom's Cabin"—you can buy it for about sixpence, fifteen or sixteen cents—and you commence and read it. I see that gentleman along there setting it down. [Referring to our reporter.] That is all right. (Laughter.) I see you. (Laughter.) Well, you commence at the 34th chapter and read up to the 57th chapter of the "Key to Uncle Tom's Cabin," and I think you will there see me. (Laughter and applause.) You remember that when this novel of Mrs. Stowe came out, it shook the foundations of this world. It shook Americans almost out of their shoes, and out of their shirts. (Laughter.) It left some of them on the sandbar barefooted and scratching their heads, without knowing where to go, or what to do or say. However, they came to the conclusion to say that the whole thing was a fabrication, a falsehood, and a lie; and they accused her of writing it, and they demanded of her a clue or key to the novel she had written, the exposure she had made, and the libel she had fixed on the United States. And so, as she was in duty bound to give something, she, I think in 1853, brought out the "Key," between you and she, and in that she spoke of me, and in that way set the negro free. (Laughter and applause.) I am not a Robert Burns—(laughter)—but that is a fact. (Applause.) You will find in that "Key" of me the position which I held in relation to her work. They said there were never any such things perpetrated on the negroes; never any negroes so afflicted, and that the book was a libel on the people of the United States; and when she took to this "Key," she told them where they would find a man called Josiah Henson. She gave me a great name, and said I was a venerable fellow, in which she was not much mistaken, for I was an old man, to be found in Canada West, labouring there as a minister of the gospel of Jesus Christ, preaching to the fugitive slaves, encouraging the cause of education, and building up the poor afflicted race of negroes. (Applause.) Josiah Henson, then, is my name. I am not responsible for anything written in Mrs. Stowe's novel, but only for what she wrote about me. You can find that wherever I have been I have never changed my predilections of colours—(laughter)—for mine is a good substantial, fast colour—(laughter and cheers)—one of the best in the world, and the ladies all love it, for they like to dress in black. (Laughter.) I have nothing but the truth, the whole truth, and my manhood; and they who don't like that may let me alone. I am not ashamed to show my face, and never did anything that I am ashamed of. Do you suppose that such men as Samuel Crossley, Samuel Morley, George Sturge, the Earl of Shaftesbury, Earl Gray, Baptist Noel, and others who have honoured me with their friendship and given me their pulpits, would be deceived by me, or that I, by falsifying one of the highest principles in this world, would practise an imposition on my friends? Never! never! (Cheers.) Too much of a man for that, even though I am a black man. Mr. Henson then proceeded to tell the story of his life. He concluded by thanking them for their patient hearing, and by singing the slave hymn of parting, the audience taking the chorus, "Glory, glory, hallelujah, freedom reigns to-day!" a hymn, which after Lincoln's proclamation received new words, "John Brown," and a quicker time, for the negroes were then made happy from their heads to their heels—he bounding and beaming as he rendered a stave of the joyous strain, the immense audience cheering him to the echo.

During his sojourn in the West of Scotland, Mr. Henson, as already indicated, visited several of the towns adjacent to Glasgow, where he was the guest of a number of well-known philanthropic gentlemen, who showed him and Mrs. Henson every possible kindness, being forward through him to evince their sympathy with a long-oppressed race, and to recognise in him, though of a different colour, a brother man, endowed with more than ordinary powers both of mind and body, and who, as the prototype of the hero of Mrs. Stowe's tale, and on account of his own thrilling story of his experience, was an object of such deep interest. Mr. Henson stayed—at Paisley, with Sir Peter Coats, of Woodside; at Dumbarton, with James White, Esq., of Overtoun; at Helensburgh, with John Ure, Esq., of Cairndbu; at Greenock, with Provost Lyle; at Wemyss Bay, with John Burns, Esq., of Castle Wemyss; at Rothesay, with Provost Orkney; at Coatbridge, with Thomas Ellis, Esq., of the North British Iron Works; at Lenzie, with the Rev. William Miller, of Union Church; and at Dumfries, with Walter Grierson, Esq., of Chapelmount.

# APPENDIX A

## A SKETCH OF MRS. H. BEECHER STOWE

Although this esteemed lady, of a noble family, enjoys a world-wide fame, there may probably be many to whom the succeeding lines, descriptive of her character and history, will be of interest. Her father was Lyman Beecher, D. D., born in 1771, and, until of mature age, he was brought up to the trade of his father, a blacksmith. After leaving it for a course of study at Yale College, New Haven, he entered upon the work of the ministry. For some time Dr. Lyman Beecher was pastor of a church at Lichfield, and here Harriet Beecher was born, A.D. 1812. Ultimately he removed to Boston; and in 1832 quitted it for Lane, in Cincinnati. Here Lyman Beecher took charge of the seminary, and sought to establish collegiate studies in connection with self-supporting labour. In this enterprise Professor Calvin Stowe took part, and for a time their work prospered. The slavery then existing in the United States led to its overthrow. The year 1830 had witnessed the French revolution. An agitation had sprung up in England against Colonial Slavery. American judicial courts had imprisoned and fined many who had spoken against slavery. All these historic facts called the attention of philanthropists in the United States to the evils and crime of slavery; Dr. Beecher's seminary could not resist the rising discussion of that crowned iniquity! The mob threatened, and Kentucky slaveholders went over to urge it on to violence. To save the property, the trustees interfered, and calmed the mob by the assurance that slavery should not further be discussed in the seminary. Another rebellion came from within, for the students *refused* to obey the order of the trustees, and left the seminary in a body. For years Beecher and Stowe sought in vain to restore the prosperity of that seminary. In 1850 they returned to the Eastern States—Stowe to the Professor's chair of Biblical literature in Andover Theological Seminary, and Lyman Beecher to the work of the ministry in Cincinnati.

Harriet Beecher spent eighteen years in this Lane Seminary; having previously assisted her sister Catharine, in the conduct of a training school for female teachers. Cincinnati is a city situated on the northern bank of the Ohio; and upon the high hill, whose point, crowned with an observatory, overhanging the city on the west, was Lane Seminary. The village nearest to it was called the Walnut Hills and one of the prettiest in the environs. It was here, therefore, that Harriet Beecher lived, and helped her sister in teaching, until her marriage, at the age of twenty-five, with Professor Calvin E. Stowe, of the Seminary, over which her father then was president. But few of Mrs. H. Beecher-Stowe's numerous offspring have survived. Mrs. Stowe says:—

"Charlie, the most beautiful of my children, and the most beloved, lies buried near my Cincinnati residence. It was at his dying bed and at his grave that I learnt what a poor slave-mother may feel when her child is torn from her. In the depths of my sorrow, which seemed to me immeasurable, it was my only prayer to God that such anguish might not be suffered in vain.

"There were circumstances connected with this child's death of such peculiar bitterness—of what might seem almost cruel suffering—that I felt I could never be consoled for it, unless it should appear that the crushing of my own heart might enable me to work out some great good to others.

"His death took place during the cholera-summer, when in a circle of five miles around me, 9,000 were buried—a mortality which I have never heard exceeded anywhere.

"My husband, in feeble health, was obliged to be absent the whole time, and I had sole charge of a family of fifteen persons. He did not return to me, because I would not permit it; for in many instances where parents had returned from a distance to their families, and to the infected atmosphere, the result had been sudden death, and the physicians warned me that if he returned, it would only be to die. My poor Charlie died for want of timely medical aid; for in the universal confusion and despair that prevailed, it was often impossible to obtain assistance till it was too late."

Between 1835 and 1847, Cincinnati became the prominent battleground of freedom and slavery. It will now be clear to the reader how painfully familiar Mrs. H. B. Stowe became with the horrors of slavery. The road which ran through Walnut Hills, only a few feet from Mrs. Stowe's door, was ultimately a favourite route of "The Underground Railway," so called, and so familiar in the pages of "Uncle Tom's Cabin." The "railway" consisted of a noble line of Quakers and other anti-slavery friends, who lived at intervals, say, of fifteen or twenty miles, between the Ohio River and the Northern Lakes. These friends had combined to help fugitive slaves forward in their escape to Canada. A fugitive would be taken at night, on horseback or in a covered waggon, from station to station, as described, until *he* stood on a free soil, and found the British banner floating o'er his head. Or,

> "Thus when *her* form flies wildly by,
> With bloodless cheek and fearless eye,
> Resolved to free her child or die,
>     We still our very breath—
> Till, safely on the farther shore
> She stands, the desperate journey o'er
>     So fraught with life and death."

Referring once more to the "Underground Railway," we may remind our readers that the first station north of Cincinnati was a few miles up Mill Creek, at the house of the pious and lion-hearted Vanzant, otherwise called Van Trompe in "Uncle Tom's Cabin." Such being the roadway, Mrs. Stowe would inevitably be roused, and frequently, by the rapid rattle of the covered waggons, and the noisy galloping of the horses ridden by the constables and slave-catchers, who would be in hot pursuit as they madly passed her door. Vanzant (the "Honest John," as he was called) was always ready to turn out with his team, and the hunters were rarely clever enough to come up with him. He has long since filled a martyr's grave. Mrs. Stowe, therefore, during her long residence on the frontier of the slave states, by several visits to them, would naturally become familiar in observations of them, and furnish herself with ample material for her masterpiece on slavery. We cannot refuse one of Mrs. Stowe's sketches in 1840. "The slave-catchers, backed by the riff-raff of the population, and urged on by certain politicians and merchants, attacked the quarters in which the negroes reside. Some of the houses were battered down by cannon. For several days the city was abandoned to violence and crime. The negro-quarters were pillaged and sacked. Negroes attempting to defend their property were killed, and their bodies thrown into the streets. Women cruelly injured by ruffians, some afterwards dying of their injuries. Houses were burnt, and men, women, and children were betrayed in the confusion, and hurried into slavery. From the brow of the hill on which I lived, I could hear the cries of the victims, the shouts of the mob, the reports of guns and cannon, and could see the flames of the conflagration. To more than one of the trembling fugitives I have given shelter, and wept bitter tears with them. After the fury of the mob was spent, many of the coloured people gathered together the little left them of worldly goods and started for Canada. Hundreds passed in front of my house. Some of them were in little waggons. Some trudging along on foot after their household stuff. Some leading their children by the hand. And there were even mothers who walked on suckling their infants, and weeping for the dead, or kipnapped husbands they had left behind." Before concluding this sketch we would observe that, by the verdict of England's people, " 'Uncle Tom's Cabin' takes its place as a standard work amongst the beauties of English literature." As Earl Carlisle said: "Its genius, pathos, and humour, commend themselves." As the Rev. James Sherman said: "It is as irresistibly attractive to the learned and unlearned as Bunyan's Pilgrim's Progress." It has been translated in France, Holland, Germany, Italy, Sweden, Russia, and Spain. The supreme joy, however, to Mrs. Stowe must have been that Providence has prolonged her valuable life to witness the consummation of her prayers and toils— the *abolition* of slavery!

May the closing years of Mrs. Stowe and Josiah Henson be happy and triumphant! May the fruits of their spiritual life-work swell the "multitude of the redeemed!" The night is short, and the morning will soon dawn!

## APPENDIX B

### THE EXODUS

By Bishop Gilbert Haven

The years of Father Henson cover every phase of the great conflict. Between the time of his birth and the present, the institution of American slavery has seen the period of its highest victories, its struggles for existence, its overthrow, and its attempt to re-enslave, in all save name, those who had been torn from its iniquitous grasp. The last phase of the struggle is not the least. It is, as in all true evolution, the best. It betokens the upspringing of that self-reliance which alone can make a man. It is the first step the infant child of freedom has taken of itself. It will soon grow by these struggles into a stalwart humanity. When our old father was young, as his story painfully tells, there was the most unquestioning acceptance of slavery over all the land. If one or two States had abolished it, so far as they were territorially concerned, still they sympathised with it, they associated with it, they intermarried with it, they practically approved it. The foreign slave trade was in full force, the domestic slave trade was beginning to develop into one of the great industries of the country. Coloured men and, especially, coloured women, even of whitest hue, had no rights in law, or in church. They were at the mercy of their owners, and of the worst white men of the vicinage. They were subject to universal contempt and cruelty, dark, deep, damning.

When emancipation came, they were left where they were, at the mercy of their former owners, who looked on them as so much property, wrested from them by superior force. As long as the government that liberated them afforded any protection, however small, they abode quiet, if not contented. But when the nation withdrew its protection, when it solemnly declared through its executive that it had no power to protect them, when the old dogma of State rights was substantially adopted by those who had fought to overcome that pestiferous doctrine, then these victims of ancestral wrong and hate were compelled to see that their only hope of deliverance lay in their escaping from the toils which the rebel local governments with the consent of the nation, were so steadily and skilfully weaving about them.

Hence the Flight. The Pharaohs reluctantly consented to their liberation. In every house there had to be one dead before they granted this God-demanded gift. But as soon as their days of mourning were ended, before they were ended, they began to regret their concession. The freedman seeing this feeling and action in all the South, seeks to escape this danger by becoming a fugitive. Will this be allowed? Only measurably. Already the steamers are forbidden to take them as passengers. Already they are shot, and hung, and otherwise abused and murdered, for even expressing a desire to flee. Already States are passing laws forbidding agents to solicit emigration. Already Pharaoh is pursuing after them to overtake them and to drag them back to the house of bondage. A Southern paper, sympathising with the movement, says they will walk to the Ohio. How can they walk when they are not permitted to ride? They will be forced to remain, their enemies thus treasuring up to themselves wrath against the day of wrath.

What may not Father Henson yet see? He who has felt the slaveholder's lash, nay, who bears in his body to this day the marks of the Lord Jesus, what sight of divine justice may not yet salute his eyes? God forbid that human passions shall minister to the divine displeasure.

The exodus is an attempt to escape to more genial conditions; not of climate, but of society. It will go forward over all the South, until it is violently suppressed. It will not mitigate the condition of those that remain. Nothing but assertion of manhood will mitigate their condition. Pharaoh could have handled two millions of Israelites better than three. The more coloured people there are there, the surer and the speedier their liberation. It will, however, stimulate those that remain; it will awaken sympathy in the breast of the North, and help to soften the still obdurate heart of the nation. It will thus bring them into unity with ourselves, and hasten the hour of their complete emancipation from prejudice, which is but another name for caste, and all its baneful influences.

It is fortunate for our venerable brother that he has lived to see this day. Once, and for much of their lives, these our brethren could not go from a plantation without a pass; now they go to Kansas and California, to Liberia and New England, without let or hindrance. Ere he has really grown old, we trust they will be enjoying all their rights under their own vine and fig-tree, in their own native region, living and beloved by all, equal and fraternal, the population and the power of all that vast belt that forms the base and groundwork of our continent and nation. May the Lord hasten that glorious consummation, and may our still young Uncle Tom live to witness and enjoy it.